AMSTRAD
CPC464 & CPC664
GAMES
BOOK

AMSTRAD
CPC464 & CPC664
GAMES
BOOK

Kevin Bergin & Andrew Lacey

MELBOURNE HOUSE
PUBLISHERS

First Published in the United Kingdom by Beam Software

This Remastered Edition
Published in 2022 by
Acorn Books
acornbooks.uk

This book is a page-by-page reproduction of the original 1985 edition as published by Beam Software. The entirety of the book is presented with no changes, corrections nor updates to the original text, images and layout; therefore no guarantee is offered as to the accuracy of the information within.

CONTENTS

Preface

The Amstrad CPC 464 represents tremendous value for money, and is an extremely easy machine to use. The novice and expert alike should have many hours of entertainment and pleasant surprises ahead of them.

The version of Basic on the Amstrad (LOCOMOTIVE) is very easy to get to grips with and is extremely powerful. Most of the Amstrad's facilities are available to Basic programmers through 'Locomotive'.

This book carries on Melbourne House's tradition of high quality Literature and Software in support of personal computers.

Arrangement of Programs

All the programs have been classified, explained and set out in an easy to read and enter format, with further programming suggestions/ enhancements.

We hope you enjoy this book and the games within and continue to get the 'best' for and from your Amstrad.

Special Characters

In the programs throughout this book spaces have been used to aid readability. You need not enter these as they will waste RAM. There are some lines with only a colon on, again these were inserted to make the programs more legible and need not be entered.

The odd characters between quotes in the program listings have been designed to represent spaces and thus avoid confusion. So where you see the symbol " ▲ " you should enter a space.

The letter "I" and the number "1" can cause some confusion at times, as well as the letter "O" and the number "0".

Once you are familiar with them they don't cause any problems it is just a matter of recognising the difference between them.

The letter I looks like this: I
The number 1 looks like this: 1
The letter O looks like this: O
The number 0 looks like this: Ø

Frequently occurring (and easily overlooked) typing errors with the Amstrad CPC 64/664/464

1. Do not confuse the letter O with the digit Ø (zero).
2. Do not confuse the capital letter I with the digit 1 (one).
3. A comma and a period are not interchangeable.
4. When a colon (:) is required do not type a semi-colon (;). The reverse rule applies as well.

1

5. A double quote (") is not interchangeable with an apostrophe (').

6. When a program shows one or more spaces, do not forget to include them (press the space bar). The computer registers a space as a fulfledged character.

7. Brackets are important, particularly in BASIC versions of mathematical formulae. A bracket too many, or a bracket short, usually causes a syntax error. Exclusion of two outer brackets may cause a 'logic' error; which will enable the program to run but will deliver the wrong results.

8. Do not forget to press the SHIFT key as well, when you have to enter the following characters:

!, ", #, $, %, &, ', (,), =, \, [,], *, +, >, < and ?

9. Brackets are () and not [].

Overall advice:

When you have typed in a program and you can't get it running properly, even after numerous debugging attempts, then put the job at rest for a day or so. It often happens that you will find the bug at once after resuming the job.

CHEXSUM
The unique CHEXSUM program validation
WHY
When a book of programs such as this book is keyed in, everybody invariably makes reading and typing mistakes and then spends ages trying to sort out where and what is causing the error (errors).

Even experienced programmers often cannot identify an error just by listing the relevant line and need to do the tedious job of going back to the book, especially with DATA statements.

Realising that this is a major cause of frustration in keying the programs, we decided to do something about it.

There is a short routine in this book which you should key in and save BEFORE you key in other programs.

Using this routine you will be able to find out if you have made any keying errors at all and in which lines, before you even run the program.

In effect this means that with this book you need not waste time looking for keying errors, you simply run the routines and look at the display to identify lines containing errors. It's that easy.

The principle behind the routines is a unique chexsum which is calculated on each individual line of the program as you have keyed it in. Compare this chexsum value with the value for that line in the list at the end of the program listing; if they are the same the line is correct, if not there is an error in that line.

WHEN
The simplest method is to enter the CHEXSUM program in now and save it to tape or disk.

You can type in the chexsum program at any time, even if you have started to type in a program. You cannot, of course LOAD in CHEXSUM from tape or disk because it will erase all you have typed so far.

The obvious solution is to MERGE the programs. The CHEXSUM program should be saved onto a separate cassette to allow easy access.

HOW CAN YOU TELL IF CHEXSUM HAS BEEN ENTERED CORRECTLY?
After having keyed CHEXSUM the logical thing would be to chexsum the program to make sure it is correct. But is it possible to do this? If you follow the instructions you will be able to check CHEXSUM.

1. Type and save CHEXSUM.
2. RUN ChexSum and it will check itself.
3. Check output against the table of values at the end of the program.
4. If the program is incorrect, edit the incorrect lines and resave the program.

Below is the listing of CHEXSUM and instructions on its use.

```
┌─────────────────────────────────────────────────┐
│                                                 │
│         Initialise program and sort input        │
│                                                 │
└─────────────────────────────────────────────────┘
```

```
60000 CLS : LOCATE 11, 1 : PRINT "CHEXSUM PROGRAM"
60010 LOCATE 1, 5 : PRINT "OUTPUT TO PRINTER (P) OR SCREEN (S
      ) ?";
60020 X$ = INKEY$ : IF X$ = "" THEN 60020
60030 IF X$ = "P" OR X$ = "p" THEN STREAM = 8 : PRINT "P"
60040 IF X$ = "S" OR X$ = "s" THEN STREAM = 0 : PRINT "S"
60050 LOCATE 1, 10 : INPUT "STARTING LINE NUMBER"; X$ : IF VA
      L ( X$ ) > 0 THEN LSTART = VAL ( X$ ) ELSE 60050
60060 TOTAL = 0 : LLIMIT = 62990 : MEM = 368 : NEXTMEM = MEM
```

```
┌─────────────────────────────────────────────────┐
│                                                 │
│              Main program loop                   │
│                                                 │
└─────────────────────────────────────────────────┘
```

```
60070 :
60080 NEXTMEM = PEEK( MEM ) + 256 * PEEK( MEM + 1 ) + NEXTMEM
60090 LN = PEEK( MEM + 2) + 256 * PEEK( MEM + 3 ) : IF LN >=
      LLIMIT THEN 62000 ELSE IF LN < LSTART THEN MEM = NEXTMEM
      : GOTO 60080
60100 MEM = MEM + 4 : CHXSUM = 0 : QUOTE = 0
60110 IF PEEK( MEM ) = 32 THEN MEM = MEM + 1 : GOTO 60110
60120 IF PEEK( MEM ) = 1 OR PEEK( MEM ) = 197 THEN MEM = NEXT
      MEM : GOTO 61000
60130 WHILE MEM < NEXTMEM
60140 TOKEN = PEEK( MEM ) : IF TOKEN = 34 THEN QUOTE = QUOTE
      XOR 1
60150 IF QUOTE = 1 OR TOKEN <> 32 THEN 60170
60160 LASTOK = PEEK( MEM - 1 ) : NEXTOK = PEEK( MEM + 1 ) : G
      OSUB 61500 : IF IGNORE = 1 THEN 60180
60170 CHXSUM = CHXSUM + TOKEN
60180 MEM = MEM + 1 : WEND
61000 PRINT #STREAM, USING "#####"; LN; : PRINT #STREAM, " = 
      "; CHXSUM
61010 TOTAL = TOTAL + CHXSUM : GOTO 60080
```

```
┌─────────────────────────────────────────────────┐
│                                                 │
│              Check for REM's etc                 │
│                                                 │
└─────────────────────────────────────────────────┘
```

```
61490 :
61500 IGNORE = 0
61510 IF LASTOK = 44 OR LASTOK = 32 OR LASTOK = 40 OR LASTOK
      = 1  OR ( LASTOK > 237 AND LASTOK < 250 ) THEN IGNORE =
      1 : RETURN
61520 IF NEXTOK = 41 OR NEXTOK = 1  OR ( NEXTOK > 237 AND NEX
      TOK < 250 ) THEN IGNORE = 1 : RETURN
61530 RETURN
```

```
┌─────────────────────────────────────────────────┐
│                                                 │
│                 Output Total                     │
│                                                 │
└─────────────────────────────────────────────────┘
```

```
61990 :
62000 PRINT #STREAM : PRINT #STREAM, "TOTAL = "; TOTAL
```

4

ChexSum Tables

60000 =	1836		60100 =	3256		61010 =	2587
60010 =	3059		60110 =	3432		61490 =	0
60020 =	2044		60120 =	4947		61500 =	1022
60030 =	3313		60130 =	1687		61510 =	9964
60040 =	3292		60140 =	5092		61520 =	7455
60050 =	5425		60150 =	2802		61530 =	201
60060 =	4283		60160 =	6079		61990 =	25870
60070 =	0		60170 =	2585		62000 =	2964
60080 =	4367		60180 =	1578			
60090 =	9211		61000 =	3897		TOTAL =	96383

USING CHEXSUM

The greatest problem encountered when typing in programs from a book is errors made by the user. Most of these are picked up when the computer responds to the RUN command with the 'Syntax Error' message. The user then has only to LIST the line and compare it with the line in the book. Unfortunately, some errors are more subtle and not fatal to program operation. These types of errors will cause the program to run, but incorrectly, and the computer will not be able to detect them as such.

ChexSum is a special program which generates a unique sum for each line in a program and a grand total of all line sums. After each program listing is a table of check sums. You need only compare the numbers in the ChexSum table for each program with those generated by ChexSum. If two numbers differ, check that particular line.

1. Type in your game program, Patterns, say. Save it to tape or disk with the statement; SAVE "PATTERNS".

2. Reload your game program if necessary, using the statement; LOAD "PATTERNS" for the first game in the book. Do not RUN the game at this point.

3. To join ChexSum to the end of your program, enter the statement; MERGE "CHEXSUM".

4. When merged, enter RUN 60000 to activate ChexSum. The program will prompt:
   OUTPUT TO PRINTER (P) OR SCREEN (S)
Enter a P will cause output to go to the printer, and entering S will cause output to go to the screen.

5. ChexSum next prompts:
   STARTING LINE NUMBER
Enter the first line number in the program to be checked and press ENTER.

6. ChexSum will now output the check-sum table for the program. To halt the program press the escape key once, and to restart the output press any key other than escape. When ChexSum has finished you may remove ChexSum from memory with the DELETE instruction. For example:
   DELETE 60000 — 62990

7. Check your grand total with that in the book. If they differ a line has been entered incorrectly. Compare line numbers until you locate the bad ones and then edit them.

8. Repeat steps 4 to 7 until the games program is debugged. In step 5 enter the line number of the first bad line to avoid ChexSum verifying the games program from the first line.

9. When the games program is running satisfactorily, delete the ChexSum program as described above.

10. Finally save the debugged version onto a clean tape or disk, with:

SAVE "PATTERNS"

PATTERNS

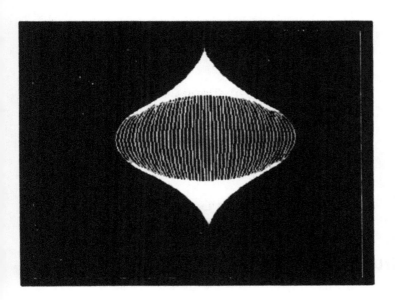

CLASSIFICATION: Interactive Graphics

Create your own fantastic patterns based on rectangles, triangles, ellipses, cardiods, spirals and lemniscates! Just follow the instructions and watch the effects.

For each pattern, a number of questions must be answered. To do this in a number and press <space>, or if you don't want to change the number from the previous pattern, just press <ENTER>.

When the pattern is completed, press <space> to start again.

PROGRAMME SUGGESTIONS

Here are some interesting combinations to get you started:
    Rectangles: 21, −200, 0, 40, 5, −5, 0, 150, 0, 0, 1, −1
    Triangles: 11, −300, −200, 83, 4, 3, 20, 0.2, 2, 0.03
    Ellipses: 24, 0, 0, 25, 0, 0, 200, 90, −8, 4
    Cardioids: 26, −300, 0, 35, 15, 0, 100, −7
    Spirals: 2, 0, 80, 12, −8, −10, 9, 15, 0, 4
    Lemniscates: 15, −100, −50, 10, 20, 15, 20000, −1000
    Simple additions would be sections for drawing lines instead of rectangles or even plotting simple points.

9

PROGRAM
Variables

SX, SY	Start of co-ordinates for first shape
NS	Number of shapes
IX, IY	Increments between shapes in X and Y directions
CL	Pen Colour
Z$	Temporary for Inkey$
AN	Angle in radians
TS	Triangle size
IT	Increment between shapes in TS
IA	Increment in angle
RX(), RY()	Rectangle co-ordinates for two points (corners)
WX, WY	Warp (deformation) of rectangle in each direction.
IW()	Increment in warps X and Y
A, B	Factors in formulae for Ellipses, Cardioids Spirals and Lemniscates
IA, IB	Increments for A and B
MA	Maximum for spiral (radians)
R	For polar co-ordinates

Program Structure

Line Numbers	Function(s)
10 — 30	Initialise colours
50 — 130	Front menu
150 — 220	Input data
240 — 270	Select pattern type
290 — 370	Control for triangles
390 — 500	Control for rectangles
520 — 610	Control for Ellipses
630 — 690	Control for Cardioids
710 — 780	Control for Spirals
800 — 860	Control for Lemniscates
880 — 930	Triangle draw
950 — 1030	Rectangle draw
1050 — 1090	Ellipse draw
1110 — 1160	Cardioid draw
1180 — 1240	Spiral draw
1260 — 1310	Lemniscate draw

```
                        ┌─────────────────────────────────────────┐
                        │                                         │
                        │   Initialise colours                    │
                        │                                         │
                        └─────────────────────────────────────────┘

10      MODE 1
20      BORDER 11 : INK 0,1 : INK 1,24 : INK 2,0
30      PAPER 0 : PEN 1

                        ┌─────────────────────────────────────────┐
                        │                                         │
                        │   Front Menu                            │
                        │                                         │
                        └─────────────────────────────────────────┘

40      :
50      CLS : PRINT SPACE$(15);"PATTERNS"
60      PRINT : PRINT : PRINT ".,Please.Select.One.of.the.follo
        wing"
70      PRINT : PRINT : PRINT ".........TYPE........SELECT.BY.PR
        ESSING"
80      PRINT : PRINT ".....Rectangle";SPACE$(15);"R"
90      PRINT : PRINT : PRINT".....Triangle";SPACE$(16);"T"
100     PRINT : PRINT : PRINT".....Ellipse";SPACE$(17);"E"
110     PRINT : PRINT : PRINT".....Cardioid";SPACE$(16);"C"
120     PRINT : PRINT : PRINT".....Spiral";SPACE$(18);"S"
130     PRINT : PRINT : PRINT".....Lemniscate";SPACE$(14);"L";

                        ┌─────────────────────────────────────────┐
                        │                                         │
                        │   Input Data                            │
                        │                                         │
                        └─────────────────────────────────────────┘

140     :
150     x$=INKEY$ : IF x$="" THEN 150 ELSE IF x$<>"r" AND x$<>"
        R" AND x$<>"t" AND x$<>"T" AND x$<>"e" AND x$<>"E" AND x
        $<>"c" AND x$<>"C" AND x$<>"s" AND x$<> "S" AND x$<>"l"
        AND x$<>"L" THEN 10
160     BORDER 0 : PAPER 2 : CLS : INPUT "Colour";z$ : IF z$<>"
        " THEN cl=VAL(z$) : PRINT
170     INK 1,cl
180     INPUT "Starting.X.co-ord..(-320.to.320)";z$ : IF z$<>""
         THEN sx=VAL(z$) : PRINT
190     INPUT "Starting.Y.co-ord..(-200.to.200)";z$ : IF z$<>""
         THEN sy=VAL(z$) : PRINT
200     INPUT "Number.of.Shapes";z$ : IF z$<>"" THEN ns=VAL(z$)
        : PRINT
210     INPUT "Increment.in.X.(-640.to.640)";z$ : IF z$<>"" THE
        N ix=VAL(z$) : PRINT
220     INPUT "Increment.in.Y.(-400.to.400)";z$ : IF z$<>"" THE
        N iy=VAL(z$) : PRINT

                        ┌─────────────────────────────────────────┐
                        │                                         │
                        │   Select Pattern type                   │
                        │                                         │
                        └─────────────────────────────────────────┘

230     :
240     ORIGIN 320,200
250     MOVE 0,0
260     IF x$="r" OR x$="R" THEN 390 ELSE IF x$="t" OR x$="T" T
        HEN 290 ELSE IF x$="e" OR x$="E" THEN 520
270     IF x$="c" OR x$="C" THEN 630 ELSE IF x$="s" OR x$="S" T
        HEN 710 ELSE 800
```

11

```
280   :
290   INPUT "Start.triangle.Size.(0.to.....)";z$ : IF z$<>"" T
      HEN ts=VAL(z$) : PRINT
300   INPUT "Start.Angle.(0.to.6.3)";z$ : IF z$<>"" THEN an=V
      AL(z$) : PRINT
310   INPUT "Increment.in.Size";z$ : IF z$<>"" THEN it=VAL(z$
      ) : PRINT
320   INPUT "Increment.in.Angle";z$ : IF z$<>"" THEN ia=VAL(z
      $)
330   CLS
340   FOR i=1 TO ns : an=an+ia : sx=sx+ix : sy=sy+iy : ts=ts+
      it
350   GOSUB 880
360   NEXT
370   IF INKEY$= "." THEN 10 ELSE 370
```

```
380   :
390   rx(1)=sx : ry(1)=sy : INPUT "Corner.point.X.(-320.to.32
      0)";z$ : IF z$<>"" THEN rx(2)=VAL(z$) : PRINT
400   INPUT "Corner.point.Y.(-200.to.200)";z$ : IF z$<>"" THE
      N ry(2)=VAL(z$) : PRINT
410   INPUT "Warp.in.X";z$ : IF z$<>"" THEN wx=VAL(z$) : PRIN
      T
420   INPUT "Warp.in.Y";z$ : IF z$<>"" THEN wy=VAL(z$) : PRIN
      T
430   INPUT "Increment.in.X.warp";z$ : IF z$<>"" THEN iw(1)=V
      AL(z$) : PRINT
440   INPUT "Increment.in.Y.warp";z$ : IF z$<>"" THEN iw(2)=V
      AL(z$)
450   CLS
460   FOR i=1 TO ns : rx(1)=rx(1)+ix : ry(1)=ry(1)+iy : rx(2)
      =rx(2)+ix : ry(2)=ry(2)+iy
470   wx=wx+iw(1) : wy=wx+iw(2)
480   GOSUB 950
490   NEXT
500   IF INKEY$="." THEN 10 ELSE 500
```

```
510   :
520   INPUT "Semi-major.axis.(-320.to.320)";z$ : IF z$<>"" TH
      EN a=VAL(z$) : PRINT
530   INPUT "Semi-minor.axis.(-200.to.200)";z$ : IF z$<>"" TH
      EN b=VAL(z$) : PRINT
540   INPUT "Increment.major.axis";z$ : IF z$<>"" THEN ia=VAL
      (z$) : PRINT
550   INPUT "Increment.minor.axis";z$ : IF z$<>"" THEN ib=VAL
      (z$) : PRINT
560   CLS
570   FOR i=1 TO ns : a=a+ia : b=b+ib
580   sx=sx+ix : sy=sy+iy
```

```
590    GOSUB 1050
600    NEXT
610    IF INKEY$="." THEN 10 ELSE 610
```

┌───┐
│   │
│   Control for Cardiods   │
│   │
└───┘

```
620    :
630    INPUT "Cardioid factor (-320 to 320)";z$ : IF z$<>"" TH
       EN a=VAL(z$) : PRINT
640    INPUT "Increment factor";z$ : IF z$<>"" THEN ia=VAL(z$)
       : PRINT
650    CLS
660    FOR i=1 TO ns : a=a+ia : sx=sx+ix : sy=sy+iy
670    GOSUB 1110
680    NEXT
690    IF INKEY$="." THEN 10 ELSE 690
```

┌───┐
│   │
│   Control for Spirals   │
│   │
└───┘

```
700    :
710    INPUT "Spiral factor";z$ : IF z$<>"" THEN a=VAL(z$) : P
       RINT
720    INPUT "Maximum angle";z$ : IF z$<>"" THEN ma=VAL(z$) :
       PRINT
730    INPUT "Increment in factor";z$ : IF z$<>"" THEN ia=VAL(
       z$)
740    CLS
750    FOR i=1 TO ns : a=a+ia : sx=sx+ix : sy=sy+iy
760    GOSUB 1180
770    NEXT
780    IF INKEY$="." THEN 10 ELSE 780
```

┌───┐
│   │
│   Control for Lemniscates   │
│   │
└───┘

```
790    :
800    INPUT "Lemniscate factor (large)";z$ : IF z$<>"" THEN a
       =VAL(z$) : PRINT
810    INPUT "Increment factor";z$ : IF z$<>"" THEN ia=VAL(z$)
820    CLS
830    FOR i=1 TO ns : a=a+ia : sx=sx+ix : sy=sy+iy
840    GOSUB 1260
850    NEXT
860    IF INKEY$="." THEN 10 ELSE 860
```

┌───┐
│   │
│   Triangle Draw   │
│   │
└───┘

```
870    :
880    REM triangle
890    MOVE sx-ts*COS(an),sy-ts*SIN(an)
900    DRAWR 2*ts*COS(an),0
910    DRAWR -ts*COS(an),2*ts*SIN(an)
920    DRAWR -ts*COS(an),-2*ts*SIN(an)
930    RETURN
```

```
940    :
950    REM rectangle
960    t1=rx(1)-rx(2) : t2=ry(1)-ry(2)
970    MOVE rx(1),ry(1)
980    IF t1=0 OR t2=0 THEN DRAW rx(2),ry(2) : RETURN
990    DRAWR wx,wy-t2
1000   DRAW rx(2),ry(2)
1010   DRAWR wx,wy+t2
1020   DRAW rx(1),ry(1)
1030   RETURN
```

```
1040   :
1050   REM ellipse
1060   MOVE sx+a,sy
1070   FOR an = 0 TO 6.3 STEP 0.1
1080   DRAW a*COS(an)+sx, b*SIN(an)+sy
1090   NEXT : RETURN
```

```
1100   :
1110   REM cardioid
1120   MOVE 2*a+sx,sy
1130   FOR an = 0 TO 6.3 STEP 0.1
1140   r=a*(1+COS(an))
1150   DRAW r*COS(an)+sx, r*SIN(an)+sy
1160   NEXT : RETURN
```

```
1170   :
1180   REM spiral
1190   MOVE sx, sy
1200   FOR an=0 TO ma STEP 0.1
1210   r=a*an
1220   DRAW r*COS(an)+sx, r*SIN(an)+sy
1230   NEXT
1240   RETURN
```

```
1250   :
1260   REM lemniscate
1270   FOR an=0 TO 3.2 STEP 0.05
1280   r=(ABS(a*COS(an))) 0.5
1290   PLOT r*COS(an)+sx, r*SIN(an)+sy
1300   PLOT -r*COS(an)+sx, -r*SIN(an)+sy
1310   NEXT : RETURN
```

14

ChexSum Tables

10	=	220	460	=	8534	910	=	3330
20	=	1038	470	=	3443	920	=	3575
30	=	467	480	=	406	930	=	201
40	=	0	490	=	176	940	=	0
50	=	1512	500	=	1652	950	=	0
60	=	3878	510	=	0	960	=	3470
70	=	2795	520	=	5114	970	=	1193
80	=	2226	530	=	5121	980	=	3298
90	=	2294	540	=	4994	990	=	1538
100	=	2176	550	=	5007	1000	=	1169
110	=	2254	560	=	138	1010	=	1537
120	=	2092	570	=	3965	1020	=	1167
130	=	2550	580	=	3206	1030	=	201
140	=	0	590	=	251	1040	=	0
150	=	14059	600	=	176	1050	=	0
160	=	4207	610	=	1507	1060	=	1485
170	=	601	620	=	0	1070	=	2925
180	=	5393	630	=	5135	1080	=	3828
190	=	5421	640	=	4627	1090	=	378
200	=	4552	650	=	138	1100	=	0
210	=	5103	660	=	5866	1110	=	0
220	=	5093	670	=	311	1120	=	1747
230	=	0	680	=	176	1130	=	2925
240	=	576	690	=	1587	1140	=	2007
250	=	278	700	=	0	1150	=	3861
260	=	7008	710	=	4208	1160	=	378
270	=	5025	720	=	4312	1170	=	0
280	=	0	730	=	4682	1180	=	0
290	=	5465	740	=	138	1190	=	1003
300	=	4676	750	=	5866	1200	=	2577
310	=	4665	760	=	381	1210	=	1326
320	=	4562	770	=	176	1220	=	3861
330	=	138	780	=	1422	1230	=	176
340	=	7676	790	=	0	1240	=	201
350	=	336	800	=	5254	1250	=	0
360	=	176	810	=	4435	1260	=	0
370	=	1522	820	=	138	1270	=	3079
380	=	0	830	=	5866	1280	=	2491
390	=	7398	840	=	461	1290	=	3901
400	=	5218	850	=	176	1300	=	4359
410	=	3837	860	=	1502	1310	=	378
420	=	3839	870	=	0			
430	=	4915	880	=	0			
440	=	4725	890	=	4123	TOTAL	=	310147
450	=	138	900	=	1808			

15

3D-DRAW

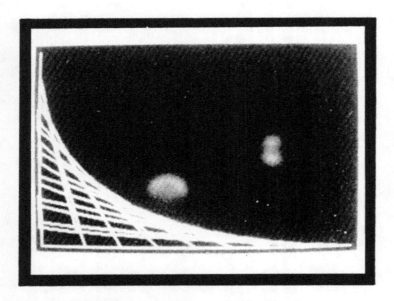

CLASSIFICATION: Interactive Graphics

Use the cursor keys to move the flashing dot around the screen. Position the cursor and press the 'copy' key. Having done this four times the shape is drawn. To return to the menu press the up arrow key.

1. Next Frame — advance to the next frame.
2. Change coordinate — Enter grid reference you wish to change.
3. Redraw last frame — Redraws without altering anything.
4. New frame — Restart.
5. Quit — Exit program.

PROGRAM
Variables

G	Generation of grid step
X(N,N), Y(N,N)	x and y coordinates of grid reference (N,N)
A(G)	Value of grid step
XNV, YNV	New values when changing coordinates
A$,T	Dummy variables

Program Structure

Lines	Function/Activity
30 — 80	Draw routine
100 — 360	Menu
380 — 420	Change Coordinate
440 — 530	Square generation routine
550 — 1040	Initialisation
1060 — 1080	End

```
                        ┌────────────────────────────────┐
                        │                                │
                        │   Draw routine                 │
                        │                                │
                        └────────────────────────────────┘

10      GOSUB 550
                        ┌────────────────────────────────┐
                        │                                │
                        │   Menu                         │
                        │                                │
                        └────────────────────────────────┘

20      :
30      MODE M : FOR T = 1 TO 33 STEP A(G)
40      FOR N = 1 TO 33 - A(G) STEP A(G)
50      PLOT X(N, T), Y(34 - T, N)
60      DRAW X(N + A(G), T), Y(34 - T, N + A(G)), 1
70      PLOT X(T, 34 - N), Y(N, T)
80      DRAW X(T, 34 - (N + A(G))), Y((N + A(G)),T), 1 : NEXT :
        NEXT
                        ┌────────────────────────────────┐
                        │                                │
                        │   Change Coordinates           │
                        │                                │
                        └────────────────────────────────┘

90      :
100     IF INKEY$ = " " THEN GOTO 110 ELSE 100
110     FOR T = 0 TO 26 : INK 1, T : FOR N = 1 TO 50 : NEXT : N
        EXT
120     FOR T = 1 TO 26 : LOCATE 1, 1 : PRINT CHR$(11) : NEXT
130     CLS : MODE 1
140     IF G = 6 THEN 1060
150     PRINT ".FRAME.NUMBER.=." ; G  : PRINT
160     PRINT ".[.1.].NEXT.FRAME."
170     PRINT ".[.2.].CHANGE.CO-ORDINATE"
180     PRINT ".[.3.].REDRAW.THIS.FRAME"
190     PRINT ".[.4.].NEW.FRAME"
200     PRINT ".[.5.].QUIT"
210     PRINT ".[.6.].CHANGE.AMPLITUDE"
220     PRINT ".[.7.].REDRAW.WITH.NEW.AMPLITUDE"
230     IF G = 5 THEN PRINT : PRINT ".LAST.FRAME"
240     A$ = INKEY$
250     LOCATE 1,12 : PRINT "COMMAND.?"
260     PEN RND(1) * 3 + 1
270     IF A$ = "" THEN 240
280     LOCATE 1,12 : PRINT SPACE$(10) : PEN 1
290     IF A$ = "1" THEN GOTO 440
300     IF A$ = "2" THEN GOTO 380
310     IF A$ = "3" THEN GOTO 30
320     IF A$ = "4" THEN RUN
330     IF A$ = "5" THEN 1060
340     IF A$ = "6" THEN LOCATE 2, 10 : : PRINT ".CURRENT.AMPLI
        TUDE.=." ; AMP : INPUT ".AMPLITUDE" ; AMP : LOCATE 2,10
        : PRINT SPACE$(30) : PRINT SPACE$(30) : LOCATE 1,1 : GOT
        O 150
350     IF A$ = "7" THEN REDRAW = 1 : GOTO 440
360     GOTO 240
```

18

```
370   :
380   INPUT "ENTER CO-ORDINATE ";D, E
390   PRINT "CO-ORDINATE"; D;","; E;"IS CURRENTLY"; X(D, E);
      ","; Y(34 - E, D)
400   INPUT "ENTER NEW VALUES "; XNV, YNV
410   X(D, E) = XNV : Y(34 - E, D) = YNV
420   CLS : GOTO 150
```

```
430   :
440   LOCATE 1, 15 : PRINT " Please wait for a bit."
450   FOR T = 1 TO 33 : BORDER RND(1) * 26
460   FOR N = 1 TO 33 - A(G) STEP A(G)
470   X(N + A(G + 1), T) = (( X(N + A(G), T) - X(N, T) ) / 2)
      + X(N, T)
480   Y(N + A(G + 1), T) = (( Y(N + A(G), T) - Y(N, T) ) / 2)
      + Y(N, T) : NEXT : NEXT
490   G = G + 1 : IF REDRAW THEN G = G - 1 : REDRAW = 0
500   FOR T = 1 TO 33 STEP A(G) : BORDER RND(1) * 26
510   FOR N = 1 TO 33 STEP A(G)
520   X(N, T) = X(N, T) + RND((1) * AMP) - AMP / 2
530   Y(N, T) = Y(N, T) + (RND(1) * AMP) - AMP / 2 : NEXT : N
      EXT : BORDER 5 : GOTO 30
```

```
540   :
550   DIM X(33, 33), Y(33, 33), A(6), B(4), C(4)
560   SPEED KEY 20,1
570   G = 1
580   A(1) = 32
590   A(2) = 16
600   A(3) = 8
610   A(4) = 4
620   A(5) = 2
630   A(6) = 1
640   CLS
650   PRINT "MODE ( 0 / 1 / 2) ?" ;
660   A$ = INKEY$ : IF A$ = "" THEN 660
670   IF A$ = "0" THEN M = 0 : GOTO 710
680   IF A$ = "1" THEN M = 1 : GOTO 710
690   IF A$ = "2" THEN M = 2 : GOTO 710
700   GOTO 660
710   PRINT " " ; A$
720   INK 0, 0
730   INK 1, 26
740   BORDER 5
750   INPUT "AMPLITUDE "; AMP : CLS
760   MODE M
770   A = 1 : B = 399
780   FOR T = 1 TO 4
790   FLAG = TEST(A, B)
800   PLOT A, B, 1
```

19

```
810     FOR DELAY = 1 TO 10 : NEXT
820     PLOT A, B, FLAG
830     A = A + (INKEY (8) > -1) - (INKEY (1) > - 1)
840     B = B + (INKEY (2) > -1) - (INKEY (0) > -1)
850     IF A < 1 THEN A = 639
860     IF A > 639 THEN A = 1
870     IF B < 1 THEN B = 399
880     IF B > 399 THEN B = 1
890     IF INKEY (67) = -1 THEN 950 : REM O KEY
900     LOCATE 5,10 : PRINT "X.=." : A - 1
910     LOCATE 5,11 : PRINT "Y.-." : ABS(B - 399)
920     FOR DELAY = 1 TO 3000 : NEXT DELAY
930     LOCATE 5,10 : PRINT SPACE$(13) : PRINT SPACE$(13)
940     GOTO 790
950     IF INKEY (9) > -1 THEN B(1) = A : C(1) = B : PLOT A, B,
        1 : PRINT CHR$(7) : FOR DELAY = 1 TO 500 : NEXT : NEXT
        : FOR T = 2 TO 4 : PLOT B(T - 1), C(T - 1) : DRAW B(T),
        C(T) : NEXT : PLOT B(4), C(4) : DRAW B(1), C(1) : GOTO
        970
960     GOTO 790
970     X(1, 1) = B(1) : Y(33, 1) = C(1) : X(33, 1) = B(2) : Y(
        33, 33) = C(2) : X(33, 33) = B(3) : Y(1, 33) = C(3) : X(
        1, 33) = B(4) : Y(1, 1) = C(4)
980     FOR T = 2 TO 32
990     X(1, T) = X(1, 1) + (RND(1) * AMP) - (AMP / 2) + (((X(1
        , 33) - X(1, 1)) / 33) * T)
1000    X(33, T) = X(33, 1) + (RND(1) * AMP) - (AMP / 2) + (((X
        (33, 33) - X(33, 1)) / 33) * T)
1010    Y(1, T) = Y(1, 1) + (RND(1) * AMP) - (AMP / 2) + (((Y(1
        , 33) - Y(1, 1)) / 33) * T)
1020    Y(33, T) = Y(33, 1) + (RND(1) * AMP) - (AMP / 2) + (((Y
        (33, 33) - Y(33, 1)) / 33) * T)
1030    NEXT
1040    RETURN
```

```
                    End routine
```

```
1050    :
1060    PRINT "bye.for.now"
1070    SPEED KEY 20, 1
1080    END
```

ChexSum Tables

10	=	261	380	=	2020	750	=	1565
20	=	0	390	=	5211	760	=	423
30	=	2244	400	=	2361	770	=	1077
40	=	2558	410	=	3277	780	=	987
50	=	2261	420	=	511	790	=	1579
60	=	3862	430	=	0	800	=	736
70	=	2293	440	=	2580	810	=	1464
80	=	4570	450	=	1907	820	=	1144
90	=	0	460	=	2558	830	=	3123
100	=	1893	470	=	6090	840	=	3086
110	=	2923	480	=	6480	850	=	1554
120	=	2072	490	=	3780	860	=	1551
130	=	359	500	=	2700	870	=	1571
140	=	1033	510	=	1814	880	=	1536
150	=	1859	520	=	4060	890	=	2252
160	=	1462	530	=	4851	900	=	1393
170	=	1928	540	=	0	910	=	1871
180	=	1878	550	=	2216	920	=	2190
190	=	1316	560	=	537	930	=	1571
200	=	1011	570	=	466	940	=	247
210	=	1820	580	=	598	950	=	12909
220	=	2466	590	=	583	960	=	247
230	=	2180	600	=	565	970	=	7779
240	=	757	610	=	562	980	=	1027
250	=	1195	620	=	561	990	=	5842
260	=	1161	630	=	561	1000	=	6014
270	=	1265	640	=	138	1010	=	5846
280	=	1149	650	=	1284	1020	=	6018
290	=	1451	660	=	1933	1030	=	176
300	=	1392	670	=	1937	1040	=	201
310	=	1298	680	=	1939	1050	=	0
320	=	1249	690	=	1941	1060	=	1342
330	=	1118	700	=	372	1070	=	537
340	=	7216	710	=	642	1080	=	152
350	=	2306	720	=	266			
360	=	462	730	=	304	TOTAL	=	211064
370	=	0	740	=	181			

3D MAZE

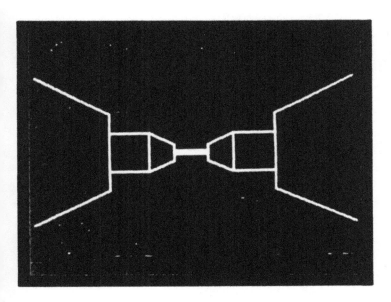

CLASSIFICATION: Interactive Graphics

When the program is first initialised you must define a maze and follow the prompts. To move, east, west, north or south use the cursor keys. To move forward use the 'copy' key, also use the copy key to define the maze and the cursor keys to move around. To quit press 'Q'.

PROGAM
Variables

MOVES	Number of moves
M(N,N)	Maze array containing walls
X,Y	Your coordinates in maze
ADIR, YDIR	X and Y direction in which you are looking can be either −1, Ø, or +1
A,B	Position of curor when defining maze
T,N,A$	Dummy variables

Program Structure

Lines		Function/Activity
30	— 160	Main loop
507	— 610	Draw 3D view
1077	— 3050	Escaped from maze
5000	— 5200	Initialisation
5205	— 5407	Define maze
10000	— 10060	Draw 3D maze

```
                    ┌─────────────────────────────────────────┐
                    │                                         │
                    │   Initialise                            │
                    │                                         │
                    └─────────────────────────────────────────┘
20         GOSUB 5000
                    ┌─────────────────────────────────────────┐
                    │                                         │
                    │   Main program loop                     │
                    │                                         │
                    └─────────────────────────────────────────┘
30         :
100        IF INKEY(1) > -1 THEN XDIR = 1 : YDIR = 0 : INK 1, 0 :
           GOSUB 500 : INK 1, 24
110        IF INKEY(8) > -1 THEN XDIR = -1 : YDIR = 0 : INK 1, 0
           : GOSUB 500 : INK 1, 24
120        IF INKEY(0) > -1 THEN XDIR = 0 : YDIR =-1 : INK 1, 0 :
           GOSUB 500 : INK 1, 24
130        IF INKEY(2) > -1 THEN XDIR = 0 : YDIR = 1 : INK 1, 0 :
           GOSUB 500 : INK 1, 24
140        IF INKEY(47) > -1 AND X + XDIR < 32 AND X + XDIR > 1 A
           ND Y + YDIR < 24 AND Y + YDIR > 1 AND M(X + XDIR, Y + YD
           IR) =32 THEN X = X + XDIR : Y = Y + YDIR : INK 1, 0 : GO
           SUB 500 : INK 1, 24 : MOVES = MOVES + 1 : IF X = 16 AND
           Y = 2 THEN GOSUB 1000
150        IF INKEY(67) > -1 THEN GOTO 3000
160        GOTO 100
                    ┌─────────────────────────────────────────┐
                    │                                         │
                    │   Draw 3D view                          │
                    │                                         │
                    └─────────────────────────────────────────┘
500        :
510        CLS
520        IF M(X + XDIR, Y + YDIR) <> 32 THEN MOVE 1, 368 : DRAW
           639, 368 : DRAW 639, 80 : DRAW 1, 80 : DRAW 1, 368 : RE
           TURN
530        IF XDIR <> 0 THEN GOTO 540
533        IF M(X + YDIR, Y + YDIR) <> 32 THEN MOVE 1, 368 : DRAW
           160, 298 : DRAW 160, 149 : DRAW 1, 80 ELSE MOVE 1, 298
           : DRAW 160, 298 : DRAW 160, 149
534        IF M(X + (YDIR * -1), Y + YDIR) <> 32 THEN MOVE 640, 3
           68 : DRAW 480, 298 : DRAW 480, 149 : DRAW 640, 80 ELSE M
           OVE 640, 298 : DRAW 480, 298 : DRAW 480, 149 : DRAW 640,
           149
540        IF YDIR <> 0 THEN GOTO 550
543        IF M(X + XDIR, Y + (XDIR * -1)) <> 32 THEN MOVE 1, 368
           : DRAW 160, 298 : DRAW 160, 149 : DRAW 1, 80 ELSE MOVE
           1, 298 : DRAW 160, 298 : DRAW 160, 149 : DRAW 1, 149
544        IF M(X + XDIR, Y + XDIR) <> 32 THEN MOVE 640, 368 : DR
           AW 480, 298 : DRAW 480, 149 : DRAW 640, 80 ELSE MOVE 640
           , 298 : DRAW 480, 298 : DRAW 480, 149 : DRAW 640, 149
550        IF M(X + XDIR + XDIR, Y + YDIR + YDIR) <> 32 THEN MOVE
           160, 298 : DRAW 480, 298 : MOVE 160, 149 : DRAW 480, 14
           9 : RETURN
552        IF XDIR <> 0 THEN GOTO 560
553        IF M(X + YDIR, Y + YDIR + YDIR) <> 32 THEN MOVE 160, 2
           98 : DRAW 240, 260 : DRAW 240, 186 : DRAW 160, 149 ELSE
           MOVE 160, 260 : DRAWR 80, 0 : DRAWR 0, -74 : DRAWR -80,
           0
554        IF M(X + (YDIR * -1), Y + YDIR + YDIR) <> 32 THEN MOVE
```

25

```
          480, 298 : DRAW 400, 260 : DRAW 400, 186 : DRAW 480, 14
          9 ELSE MOVE 480, 260 : DRAWR -80, 0 : DRAWR 0, -74 : DRA
          WR 80, 0
560       IF YDIR <> 0 THEN GOTO 570
563       IF M(X + XDIR + XDIR, Y + (XDIR * -1)) <> 32 THEN MOVE
          160, 298 : DRAW 240, 260 : DRAW 240, 186 : DRAW 160, 14
          9 ELSE MOVE 160, 260 : DRAWR 80, 0 : DRAWR 0, -74 : DRAW
          R -80, 0
564       IF M(X + XDIR + XDIR, Y + XDIR) <> 32 THEN MOVE 480, 2
          98 : DRAW 400, 260 : DRAW 400, 186 : DRAW 480, 149 ELSE
          MOVE 480, 260 : DRAWR -80, 0 : DRAWR 0, -74 : DRAWR 80,
          0
570       IF M(X + XDIR + XDIR + XDIR, Y + YDIR + YDIR + YDIR) <
          > 32 THEN MOVE 240, 260 : DRAW 400, 260 : MOVE 240, 186
          : DRAW 400, 186 : RETURN
572       IF XDIR <> 0 THEN GOTO 580
573       IF M(X + YDIR, Y + YDIR + YDIR + YDIR) <> 32 THEN MOVE
          240, 260 : DRAW 288, 238 : DRAW 288, 207 : DRAW 240, 18
          6 ELSE MOVE 240, 238 : DRAWR 48, 0 : DRAWR 0, -31 : DRAW
          R -48, 0
574       IF M(X + (YDIR * -1), Y + YDIR + YDIR + YDIR) <> 32 TH
          EN MOVE 400, 260 : DRAW 352, 238 : DRAW 352, 207 : DRAW
          400, 186 ELSE MOVE 400, 238 : DRAWR -48, 0 : DRAWR 0, -3
          1 : DRAWR 48, 0
580       IF YDIR <> 0 THEN GOTO 590
583       IF M(X + XDIR + XDIR + XDIR, Y + (XDIR * -1)) <> 32 TH
          EN MOVE 240, 260 : DRAW 288, 238 : DRAW 288, 207 : DRAW
          240, 186 ELSE MOVE 240, 238 : DRAWR 48, 0 : DRAWR 0, -31
          : DRAWR -48, 0
584       IF M(X + XDIR + XDIR + XDIR, Y + XDIR) <> 32 THEN MOVE
          400, 260 : DRAW 352, 238 : DRAW 352, 207 : DRAW 400, 18
          6 ELSE MOVE 400, 238 : DRAWR -48, 0 : DRAWR 0, -31 : DRA
          WR 48, 0
590       IF M(X + XDIR + XDIR + XDIR + XDIR, Y + YDIR + YDIR + Y
          DIR + YDIR) <> 32 THEN MOVE 288, 238 : DRAW 352, 238 : M
          OVE 288, 207 : DRAW 352, 207 : RETURN
592       IF XDIR <> 0 THEN GOTO 600
593       IF M(X + YDIR, Y + YDIR + YDIR + YDIR + YDIR) <> 32 TH
          EN MOVE 288, 237 : DRAW 320, 227 : DRAW 320, 221 : DRAW
          288, 208 ELSE MOVE 288, 227 : DRAWR 32, 0 : DRAWR 0, -6
          : DRAWR -32, 0
594       IF M(X + (YDIR * -1), Y + YDIR + YDIR + YDIR + YDIR) <
          > 32 THEN MOVE 352, 237 : DRAW 320, 227 : DRAW 320, 221
          : DRAW 352, 208 ELSE MOVE 352, 227 : DRAWR -32, 0 : DRAW
          R 0, -6 : DRAWR 32, 0
600       IF YDIR <> 0 THEN GOTO 610
603       IF M(X + XDIR + XDIR + XDIR + XDIR, Y + (XDIR * -1)) <
          > 32 THEN MOVE 288, 237 : DRAW 320, 227 : DRAW 320, 221
          : DRAW 288, 208 ELSE MOVE 288, 227 : DRAWR 32, 0 : DRAWR
          0, -6 : DRAWR -32, 0
604       IF M(X + XDIR + XDIR + XDIR + XDIR, Y + XDIR) <> 32 TH
          EN MOVE 352, 237 : DRAW 320, 227 : DRAW 320, 221 : DRAW
          352, 208 ELSE MOVE 352, 227 : DRAWR -32, 0 : DRAWR 0, -6
          : DRAWR 32, 0
610       RETURN
1000      FOR T = 1 TO 24
1010      LOCATE 1, 1
1020      PRINT CHR$(11)
1030      INK 1, T
1040      NEXT T
1050      FOR T = 1 TO 10
1060      FOR N = 500 TO 700 STEP 10
1070      SOUND 129, T, 10, 15
1080      NEXT N : NEXT T
```

```
1090    MODE 0
1100    LOCATE 4, 10 : PEN 7 : PRINT "IT.TOOK.YOU"
1110    LOCATE 4, 12 : PEN 4 : PRINT MOVES; ".MOVES."
1120    PEN 1
1130    FOR T = 1 TO 3000 : NEXT T : GOTO 5010
3000    CLS : PRINT ".[C].....................CONTINUE"
3010    PRINT ".[R]......................RESTART"
3020    A$ = INKEY$ : IF A$ = "" THEN GOTO 3020
3030    IF A$ = "C" OR A$ = "c" THEN GOSUB 500 : GOTO 100
3040    IF A$ = "R" OR A$ = "r" THEN RUN
3050    GOTO 3020
```

┌───┐
│   │
│   Player escaped from maze   │
│   │
└───┘

```
5000    :
5005    DIM M (32, 24)
5010    MOVES = 0
5020    X = 16
5030    Y = 23
5035    XDIR = 0
5037    YDIR = -1
5040    MODE 1
5050    INK 0, 0
5060    INK 1, 24
5070    BORDER 0
5080    PRINT "DEFINE.MAZE?.(Y/N)"
5090    A$ = INKEY$ : IF A$ <> "N" AND A$ <> "Y" AND A$ <> "y"
        AND A$ <> "n" THEN GOTO 5090
5110    IF A$ = "N" OR A$ = "n" THEN GOTO 100
5120    CLS
5130    FOR T = 1 TO 24
5140    FOR N = 1 TO 32
5165    M(N, T) = 233
5170    NEXT N
5180    NEXT T
5185    M(16,23) = 32
5187    M(16, 2) = 32
5190    A = 16
5192    FOR T = 2 TO 31 : M(T, 1) = 154 : M(T, 24) = 154 : NEXT
        T
5193    FOR T = 2 TO 23 : M(1, T) = 149 : M(32, T) = 149 : NEXT
        T
5194    M(1, 1) = 194 : M(32, 1) = 195 : M(1, 24) = 193 : M(32,
        24) = 192
5200    B = 23
5205    GOSUB 10000
5210    LOCATE A, B
5220    PRINT "*"
5230    LOCATE A, B
5240    PRINT CHR$(M(A, B))
5250    A = A + (INKEY(8) > -1) - (INKEY(1) > -1)
5260    IF A > 31 THEN A = 31
5270    IF A < 2 THEN A = 2
5280    B = B + (INKEY(0) > -1) - (INKEY(2) > -1)
5290    IF B > 23 THEN B = 23
5300    IF B < 2 THEN B = 2
5310    IF INKEY(9) > -1 THEN IF M(A, B) = 233 THEN M(A, B) = 3
        2 ELSE M(A, B) = 233
5320    IF INKEY(67) > -1 THEN FOR T = 0 TO 24 : INK 1, T : SOU
        ND 2, 1 * 2, 10 ,15 : NEXT T : RETURN
5330    SOUND 1, 1, 1, 15
5400    GOTO 5210
```

27

```
9999  :
10000 FOR T = 1 TO 24
10010 FOR N = 1 TO 32
10020 LOCATE N, T
10030 PRINT CHR$( M(N, T))
10040 NEXT N
10050 NEXT T
10060 RETURN
```

ChexSum Tables

20	=	376	604	=	9508	5140	=	1020
30	=	0	610	=	201	5165	=	1284
100	=	3802	1000	=	1018	5170	=	427
110	=	4054	1010	=	275	5180	=	433
120	=	4046	1020	=	598	5185	=	728
130	=	3803	1030	=	478	5187	=	696
140	=	17857	1040	=	433	5190	=	486
150	=	1845	1050	=	1004	5192	=	3498
160	=	322	1060	=	1732	5193	=	3488
500	=	0	1070	=	822	5194	=	3477
510	=	138	1080	=	861	5200	=	494
520	=	5320	1090	=	219	5205	=	276
530	=	1452	1100	=	1622	5210	=	658
533	=	6762	1110	=	1928	5220	=	333
534	=	8177	1120	=	234	5230	=	658
540	=	1463	1130	=	2012	5240	=	1318
543	=	7347	3000	=	2430	5250	=	3027
544	=	7588	3010	=	2242	5260	=	1493
550	=	6858	3020	=	2190	5270	=	1416
552	=	1472	3030	=	2769	5280	=	3022
553	=	8099	3040	=	2212	5290	=	1479
554	=	8696	3050	=	437	5300	=	1418
560	=	1483	5000	=	0	5310	=	5593
563	=	8683	5005	=	660	5320	=	4539
564	=	8106	5010	=	788	5330	=	453
570	=	8249	5020	=	509	5400	=	332
572	=	1524	5030	=	517	9999	=	0
573	=	8937	5035	=	705	10000	=	1018
574	=	9434	5037	=	952	10010	=	1020
580	=	1503	5040	=	220	10020	=	689
583	=	9520	5050	=	266	10030	=	1349
584	=	8843	5060	=	302	10040	=	427
590	=	9576	5070	=	176	10050	=	433
592	=	1512	5080	=	1441	10060	=	201
593	=	9225	5090	=	5081			
594	=	10100	5110	=	2324			
600	=	1523	5120	=	138	TOTAL	=	305007
603	=	9807	5130	=	1018			

SPACMAN

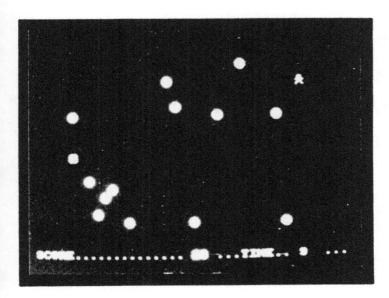

CLASSIFICATION: Time-limit Game

The object of the game is to eat as many of the bits of food the time limit. Watch out for grumps he'll make a nice meal of you!

PROGRAMMING SUGGESTIONS

The game could be made faster but would be too fast to play! There could be more bits of food on the screen or the time limit could be altered.

Use 'A' to move up, 'Z' to move down, 'comma' to move left and 'period' to move right.

PROGRAM
Variables

SCORE	Players score
CREEPX, CREEPY	Monster's co-ordinates
MANX, MANY	Player's co-ordinates
OBJECTS	Number of objects gobbled
TIMER	Seconds remaining
A, B	Random column and row
FLAG	Has the monster hit an object
C1	Counter for alternating colours for ink 2

Program structure

Lines	Function/Activity
10 — 25	Front Screen and Initialise Game
60 — 120	Initialise screen
160 — 300	Main Loop
340 — 380	Player hits object
420 — 460	Game over
470 — 490	Print seconds
3000 — 3010	Alternate Ink 2 Colours

Front screen and initialise game

```
 5      MODE 1 : INK 0, 0 : INK 1, 15 : INK 2, 18 : INK 3, 24 :
        BORDER 0 : PAPER 0 : PEN 1
10      CLS : PEN 3 : PRINT SPACE$(16);"SPACMAN"
12      LOCATE 5,9 : PEN 1 : PRINT "Objects.to.gobble :."; : PE
        N 2 : PRINT ".......";CHR$(150)
14      LOCATE 5,13 : PEN 1 : PRINT "Creepy.monster.to.avoid :.
        "; : PRINT CHR$(225)
16      EVERY 20,2 GOSUB 3000
17      SCORE = 0 : SYMBOL AFTER 150 : SYMBOL 150,60,66,153,189
        ,189,153,66,60
20      LOCATE 10,20 : PEN 1 : PRINT "Hit."; : PEN 3 : PRINT "E
        NTER"; : PEN 1 : PRINT ".to.Begin"
25      IF INKEY(18)<0 THEN 25
```

Initialise screen

```
30      :
60      CLS : PEN 1
70      CREEPX = 32 : CREEPY = 17 : MANX = 20 : MANY = 12 : OBJ
        ECTS = 0
80      LOCATE 1, 25 : PEN 1 : PRINT "SCORE.................
        .TIME........." : PEN 1
90      FOR T = 1 TO 20
100     A = CINT( RND(1) * 30 + 5 ) : B = CINT( RND(1) * 20 + 2
        ) : IF TEST( A * 16 - 8, (25 - B) * 16 + 8 ) OR (A= 20
        AND B = 12) = 2 OR (A = 25 AND B = 17) THEN GOTO 100 ELS
        E LOCATE A, B : PEN 2 : PRINT CHR$(150)
110     NEXT T : PEN 1
120     TIMER = 40 : EVERY 50,1 GOSUB 470
```

Main program loop

```
130     :
160     DI : LOCATE MANX, MANY : PRINT "."
170     IF INKEY(31) > -1 THEN MANX = MANX + 1 : IF MANX > 38 T
        HEN MANX = 2
180     IF INKEY(39) > -1 THEN MANX = MANX - 1 : IF MANX < 2 TH
        EN MANX = 38
190     IF INKEY(71) > -1 THEN MANY = MANY + 1 : IF MANY > 23 T
        HEN MANY = 2
200     IF INKEY(69) > -1 THEN MANY = MANY - 1 : IF MANY < 2 TH
        EN MANY = 23
210     IF TEST(MANX * 16 - 8, (25 - MANY) * 16 + 8) = 2 THEN G
        OSUB 340
220     LOCATE MANX , MANY : PEN 3 : PRINT CHR$(249)
230     LOCATE CREEPX, CREEPY : PRINT "."; : IF FLAG THEN PEN 2
        : PRINT CHR$(8); CHR$(150)
240     CREEPX = CREEPX + ( (MANX < CREEPX) - ( MANX > CREEPX)
        * 0.75 )
250     CREEPY = CREEPY + ( (MANY < CREEPY) - ( MANY > CREEPY)
        * 0.75 )
```

31

```
260    IF TEST(CINT( CREEPX ) * 16 - 8, (25 - CINT( CREEPY ) )
       * 16 + 8) = 2 THEN FLAG = 1 ELSE FLAG = 0
270    LOCATE CREEPX, CREEPY : PEN 1 : PRINT CHR$(225)
280    IF MANX =CREEPX AND MANY = CREEPY THEN GOTO 420
290    EI
300    GOTO 160
```

Player hits object

```
310    :
340    SOUND 1,100,10,5 : OBJECTS = OBJECTS + 1
350    IF OBJECTS = 20 THEN FOR T = 100 TO 4000 STEP 100 : SOU
       ND 2, T, 10 : NEXT T : GOTO 60
360    SCORE = SCORE + OBJECTS
370    LOCATE 20, 25 : PEN 2 : PRINT SCORE : PEN 1
380    RETURN
```

Game over

```
390    :
420    FOR i=200 TO 400 STEP 25 : SOUND 1,i,12,13,2,3 : NEXT
430    FOR T = 1 TO 500 : NEXT T : LOCATE MANX, MANY : PRINT C
       HR$(224)
440    INK 3, 26, 0 : SPEED INK 5, 5 : LOCATE 20, 25 : PEN 3 :
       PRINT SCORE
450    FOR T = 1 TO 2000 : NEXT T
460    RUN
```

Display time in seconds

```
465    :
470    TIMER = TIMER - 1 : LOCATE 33, 25 : PRINT TIMER
480    IF TIMER = 0 THEN GOTO 420
490    RETURN
```

Alternate Ink colours

```
500    :
3000   IF c1=1 THEN c1=0 : INK 2,26 : RETURN
3010   c1=1 : INK 2,18 : RETURN
```

ChexSum Tables

5 =	2061	170 =	4735	370 =	1556
10 =	1672	180 =	4747	380 =	201
12 =	3880	190 =	4764	390 =	0
14 =	4037	200 =	4766	420 =	2686
16 =	742	210 =	3939	430 =	3631
17 =	3284	220 =	2250	440 =	2201
20 =	3509	230 =	4162	450 =	1644
25 =	1191	240 =	5201	460 =	202
30 =	0	250 =	5207	465 =	0
60 =	373	260 =	6144	470 =	2655
70 =	4149	270 =	2486	480 =	1658
80 =	3135	280 =	3763	490 =	201
90 =	1014	290 =	220	500 =	0
100 =	12223	300 =	382	3000 =	2085
110 =	668	310 =	0	3010 =	1043
120 =	1622	340 =	2387		
130 =	0	350 =	4456		
160 =	1688	360 =	2188	TOTAL =	126808

U.F.O.

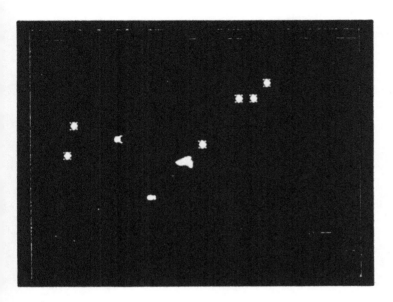

CLASSIFICATION: Shoot-up Game

Chase the retreating fleet of U.F.O.'s in your special astral fighter equipped with rockets. You will eventually leave Earth if you don't crash into the landscape or a U.F.O. and, when you see the massive planet-ship, your time is running out.

Use 'A' to move up, 'Z' to move down, and SPACE to fire.

PROGRAMMING SUGGESTIONS

You could increase the number of U.F.O.'s and add more obstacles. You could also increase the speed of the game this would keep you on your toes.

PROGRAM
Variables

UFOX, UFOY	UFO Co-ordinates
JETX, JETY	Jet's Co-ordinates
ROKX, ROKY	Rocket's Co-ordinates
ADDY	Amount to add to JETY
SCORE	Player's score
JET$	String for Jet
BLANK$	String to blank jet
I, J, K	Temps

Program Structure

Lines	Function/Activity
10 — 130	Initialise
140 — 180	New round
190 — 250	Main loop
260 — 340	Move rocket
350 — 450	Move Jet
460 — 530	Move UFO
540 — 640	Hit UFO
650 — 760	Game over

```
                    ┌─────────────────────────────────────────┐
                    │                                         │
                    │   Initialise Game, UDG's and strings    │
                    │                                         │
                    └─────────────────────────────────────────┘

10      MODE 1 : INK 0, 0 : INK 1, 20 : INK 2, 18 : INK 3, 24
20      SYMBOL 240, 0, 0, 0, 0, 192, 160, 224, 240 : SYMBOL 241
        , 255, 255, 127, 31, 27, 62, 112, 0
30      SYMBOL 242, 0, 0, 0, 0, 0, 0, 0, 56 : SYMBOL 243, 246,
        255, 252, 224, 128, 0, 0, 0
40      SYMBOL 244, 0, 0, 158, 255, 255, 158, 0, 0 : SYMBOL 245
        , 192, 54, 25, 47, 47, 25, 54, 192
50      SYMBOL 246, 4, 32, 129, 8, 64, 8, 2, 32
60      SYMBOL 247, 64, 4, 0, 145, 0, 36, 0, 0 : SYMBOL 248, 16
        , 0, 8, 128, 2, 64, 0, 4
70      SYMBOL 249, 2, 0, 72, 0, 4, 1, 32, 8 : SYMBOL 250, 1, 6
        4, 8, 0, 0, 130, 16, 0 : SYMBOL 251, 153, 40, 84, 170, 1
        70, 84, 40, 153
80      EXPL$( 1 ) = CHR$( 246 )
90      EXPL$( 2 ) = CHR$( 11 ) + CHR$( 247 ) + CHR$( 10 ) + CH
        R$( 249 ) + STRING$( 3, 8 ) + CHR$( 248 ) + CHR$( 10 ) +
        CHR$( 250 )
100     EXPL$( 3 ) = " "
110     EXPL$( 4 ) = CHR$( 11 ) + CHR$( 32 ) + CHR$( 10 ) + CHR
        $( 32 ) + STRING$( 3, 8 ) + CHR$( 32 ) + CHR$( 10 ) + CH
        R$( 32 )
120     JET$ = CHR$( 240 ) + CHR$( 242 ) + CHR$( 10 ) + STRING$
        ( 2, 8 ) + CHR$( 241 ) + CHR$( 243 )
130     BLANK$ = CHR$( 32 ) + CHR$( 32 ) + CHR$( 10 ) + STRING$
        ( 2, 8 ) + CHR$( 32 ) + CHR$( 32 )

                    ┌─────────────────────────────────────────┐
                    │                                         │
                    │          New round of game              │
                    │                                         │
                    └─────────────────────────────────────────┘

135     :
140     UFOX = 10 : UFOY = 12
150     JETX = 1 : JETY = 10 : ADDY = 1
160     PAPER 0 : CLS : BORDER 0
170     PEN 1 : MOVE 0, 0

                    ┌─────────────────────────────────────────┐
                    │                                         │
                    │          Main program loop              │
                    │                                         │
                    └─────────────────────────────────────────┘

500     :
510     GOTO 1000
520     GOTO 2000
530     GOTO 3000
540     IF INKEY( 69 ) > -1 THEN ADDY = -1 ELSE IF INKEY( 71 )
        > -1 THEN ADDY = 1
550     IF INKEY( 47 ) = -1 THEN 510
560     IF JETX > 36 OR ROKX <> 0 THEN 510 ELSE ROCKET = 1 : GO
        TO 510

                    ┌─────────────────────────────────────────┐
                    │                                         │
                    │            Move rocket                  │
                    │                                         │
                    └─────────────────────────────────────────┘

990     :
1000    IF ROCKET = 1 THEN ROCKET = 0 : SCORE = SCORE - 5 : ROK
```

37

```
       X = JETX + 3 : ROKY = JETY : GOTO 520
1005   IF ROKX = 0 THEN 520
1010   LOCATE ROKX, ROKY : PRINT "."
1020   ROKX = ROKX + 2 : IF ROKX > 39 THEN ROKX = 0 : GOTO 520

1030   IF TEST( 16 * ROKX - 16, 415 - 16 * ROKY ) = 2 THEN 400
       0
1035   I = TEST( 16 * ROKX, 415 - 16 * ROKY ) : IF I = 2 THEN
       4000 ELSE IF I = 3 THEN LOCATE ROKX + 1, ROKY : PRINT ".
       "
1040   PEN 3 : LOCATE ROKX, ROKY : PRINT CHR$( 244 )
1050   GOTO 520
```

```
┌─────────────────────────────────────────────┐
│         Move jet                            │
└─────────────────────────────────────────────┘
```

```
1990   :
2000   LOCATE JETX, JETY : PRINT USING "&"; BLANK$
2010   JETX = JETX + 1 : JETY = JETY + ADDY
2020   IF JETX > 39 THEN JETX = 1 : UFOX = 10
2030   IF JETY < 1 THEN JETY = 1 : ADDY = 1 ELSE IF JETY > 22
       THEN 9000
2040   IF TEST( 16 * JETX - 16, 415 - 16 * JETY ) <> 0 THEN 90
       00
2045   IF TEST( 16 * JETX, 415 - 16 * JETY ) <> 0 THEN 9000
2050   IF TEST( 16 * JETX - 16, 399 - 16 * JETY ) <> 0 THEN 90
       00
2055   IF TEST( 16 * JETX, 399 - 16 * JETY ) <> 0 THEN 9000
2060   PEN 1 : LOCATE JETX, JETY : PRINT USING "&"; JET$
2070   GOTO 530
```

```
┌─────────────────────────────────────────────┐
│         Move U.F.O.                         │
└─────────────────────────────────────────────┘
```

```
2990   :
3000   IF UFOX = 0 THEN 540
3010   PEN 3 : LOCATE UFOX, UFOY : IF RND( 1 ) < 0.93 THEN PRI
       NT "." ELSE PRINT CHR$( 251 )
3020   UFOX = UFOX + 1 : IF UFOX > 39 THEN UFOX = 0 : GOTO 540

3030   IF RND( 1 ) < 0.5 THEN UFOY = UFOY + 1 ELSE UFOY = UFOY
       - 1
3040   IF UFOY < 1 THEN UFOY = 1 ELSE IF UFOY > 22 THEN UFOY =
       22
3050   PEN 2 : LOCATE UFOX, UFOY : PRINT CHR$( 245 )
3060   GOTO 540
```

```
┌─────────────────────────────────────────────┐
│         Hit U.F.O.                          │
└─────────────────────────────────────────────┘
```

```
3990   :
4000   IF UFOX < 2 THEN UFOX = 2 ELSE IF UFOX > 38 THEN UFOX =
       38
4010   IF UFOY < 2 THEN UFOY = 2 ELSE IF UFOY > 22 THEN UFOY =
       22
4020   FOR I = 1 TO 4 : LOCATE UFOX, UFOY : PEN 3
4030   INK 3, 2 * I : SOUND 1, 1, 45, 15, 1, 1, 31
4040   PRINT USING "&"; EXPL$( I )
4050   FOR J = 1 TO 350 : NEXT : NEXT
4060   INK 3, 24
4070   SCORE = SCORE + 100 : CLS : PRINT "SCORE. :."; SCORE
```

```
4080    FOR I = 1 TO 1000 : NEXT
4090    ROKX = 0 : GOTO 140
```

```
                        Game over
```

```
8990    :
9000    IF JETX > 38 THEN JETX = 38 ELSE IF JETY < 2 THEN JETY
        = 2
9005    PEN 3 : FOR K = 1 TO 3
9010    FOR I = 1 TO 4 : LOCATE JETX, JETY
9020    SOUND 1, 0, 12, 15, 1, 1, I * K
9030    PRINT USING "&"; EXPL$( I )
9040    FOR J = 1 TO 70 : NEXT
9050    NEXT : NEXT
9060    CLS : LOCATE 10, 2 : PRINT "YOUR.SCORE.WAS :."; SCORE
9070    LOCATE 7, 10 : PRINT "PRESS.A.KEY.FOR.ANOTHER.GAME"
9080    IF INKEY$ = "" THEN 9090 ELSE 9080
9090    IF INKEY$ = "" THEN 9090 ELSE RUN
```

ChexSum Tables

10 =	1389	1005 =	1250	4000 =	4135
20 =	3744	1010 =	1500	4010 =	4107
30 =	3201	1020 =	3640	4020 =	2386
40 =	3540	1030 =	3678	4030 =	1458
50 =	1297	1035 =	6965	4040 =	1428
60 =	2489	1040 =	2277	4050 =	1434
70 =	4311	1050 =	232	4060 =	304
80 =	1389	1990 =	0	4070 =	3195
90 =	6603	2000 =	2339	4080 =	1396
100 =	881	2010 =	3239	4090 =	1081
110 =	5771	2020 =	2698	8990 =	0
120 =	5154	2030 =	4125	9000 =	4109
130 =	4481	2040 =	3561	9005 =	1246
135 =	0	2045 =	3307	9010 =	2135
140 =	1478	2050 =	3577	9020 =	1312
150 =	2128	2055 =	3291	9030 =	1428
160 =	548	2060 =	2441	9040 =	1231
170 =	513	2070 =	242	9050 =	353
500 =	0	2990 =	0	9060 =	2443
510 =	457	3000 =	1268	9070 =	2490
520 =	437	3010 =	4544	9080 =	1685
530 =	449	3020 =	3651	9090 =	1702
540 =	4661	3030 =	4349		
550 =	1694	3040 =	4105		
560 =	4082	3050 =	2273	TOTAL =	177116
990 =	0	3060 =	252		
1000 =	6557	3990 =	0		

ROBOT RAIDERS

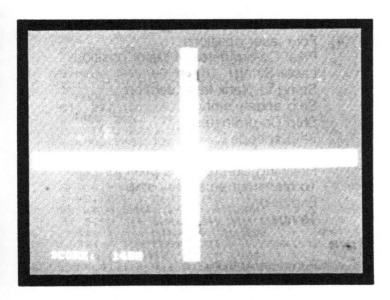

CLASSIFICATION: Shoot-up Game

Swarms of suicidal robot ships are attacking your gun ship. You must use the rotating cannon to blast the raiders before they reach the ship. Some of the robot ships disappear at random, so they are worth more points than others. The score is increased for hits and decreased for misses, so watch that wild shooting.

PROGRAMMING SUGGESTIONS

To increase the difficulty of the game try increasing the speed of the raiders and setting a kill distance for the raiders.

Use 'I' to rotate the laser anti-clockwise, and the spacer bar to fire the laser.

PROGRAM
Variables

CRASH(4)	Required sum of Co-ordinates to give crash
STARTX(4), STARTY(4)	Starting Co-ordinates for each ship
DRN	Direction (1-4) of Laser
EXIST(4)	Existence of each ship
LASERX(4), LASERY(4)	Four laser positions
LSX(4), LSY(4)	Pixel Co-ordinates of Laser positions
LAS$(4)	Laser String
LASBL$(4)	String to blank laser section
SHIP$	Ship enemy string
SHIPX(4), SHIPY(4)	Ship Co-ordinates
SPDX(4), SPDY(4)	Ship speeds
SCORE	Player's Score
FINX, FINY	Finishing Co-ordinates pixel for Laser
BLANK$	To blank out an enemy ship
EXPL$	Explosion
I, J	Temps

Program Structure

Lines	Function/Activity
10 — 319	Initialise
320 — 400	Main loop
100 — 1030	Move ships
1050 — 1080	Fire Laser
2000 — 2140	Hit
3000 — 4020	New Ship
5000 — 5020	Update Score
9000 — 9080	Game over

```
┌────────────────────────────────────────────────┐
│                                                │
│            Initialise game                     │
│                                                │
└────────────────────────────────────────────────┘
```

```
10    MODE 1 : INK 0, 15 : INK 1, 23 : INK 2, 2 : INK 3, 0 :
      DEG
20    SYMBOL 240, 16, 48, 96, 96, 224, 193, 226, 254 : SYMBOL
      241, 231, 199, 195, 224, 96, 96, 48, 16
30    SYMBOL 242, 8, 12, 6, 6, 7, 131, 71, 127 : SYMBOL 243,
      231, 227, 195, 7, 3, 3, 6, 4
40    SYMBOL 244, 1, 1, 1, 3, 15, 12, 27, 251 : SYMBOL 245, 2
      51, 27, 12, 15, 3, 1, 1, 1
50    SYMBOL 246, 128, 128, 128, 192, 240, 48, 216, 223 : SYM
      BOL 247, 223, 216, 48, 240, 192, 128, 128, 128
60    SYMBOL 248, 128, 4, 64, 0, 144, 5, 40, 134 : SYMBOL 249
      , 67, 177, 68, 16, 68, 0, 128, 16
70    SYMBOL 250, 4, 0, 129, 16, 6, 129, 146, 34 : SYMBOL 251
      , 25, 162, 16, 65, 0, 8, 0, 129
80    SHIP$ = CHR$( 240 ) + CHR$( 242 ) + CHR$( 10 ) + STRING
      $( 2, 8 ) + CHR$( 241 ) + CHR$( 243 )
90    EXPL$ = CHR$( 248 ) + CHR$( 250 ) + CHR$( 10 ) + STRING
      $( 2, 8 ) + CHR$( 249 ) + CHR$( 251 )
100   LAS$( 1 ) = STRING$( 2, 206 ) : LAS$( 3 ) = LAS$( 1 )
110   LAS$( 2 ) = CHR$( 206 ) + CHR$( 10 ) + CHR$( 8 ) + CHR$
      ( 206 ) : LAS$( 4 ) = LAS$( 2 )
120   LASBL$( 1 ) = STRING$( 2, 32 ) : LASBL$( 3 ) = LASBL$(
      1 )
130   LASBL$( 2 ) = CHR$( 32 ) + CHR$( 10 ) + CHR$( 8 ) + CHR
      $( 32 ) : LASBL$( 4 ) = LASBL$( 2 )
140   LASERX ( 1 ) = 20 : LASERX ( 2 ) = 19 : LASERX( 3 ) = 2
      0 : LASERX( 4 ) = 22
150   LASERY ( 1 ) = 12 : LASERY ( 2 ) = 13 : LASERY( 3 ) = 1
      5 : LASERY( 4 ) = 13
160   LSX( 1 ) = 320 : LSX( 3 ) = 320 : LSX( 2 ) = 287 : LSX(
      4 ) = 353
170   LSY( 1 ) = 224 : LSY( 2 ) = 191 : LSY( 4 ) = 191 : LSY(
      3 ) = 158
180   DRN = 1 : SPDX( 1 ) = 0 : SPDX( 2 ) = 1 : SPDX( 3 ) = 0
      : SPDX( 4 ) = -1
190   SPDY( 1 ) = 1 : SPDY( 2 ) = 0 : SPDY( 3 ) = -1 : SPDY(
      4 ) = 0
200   PAPER 0 : CLS : BORDER 15
210   BLANK$ = STRING$( 2, 143 ) + CHR$( 10 ) + STRING$( 2, 8
      ) + STRING$( 2, 143 )
220   PEN 1 : FOR I = 1 TO 40 : FOR J = 13 TO 14 : LOCATE I,
      J : PRINT CHR$( 143 ) : NEXT : NEXT
230   FOR I = 20 TO 21 : FOR J = 1 TO 25 : LOCATE I, J : PRIN
      T CHR$( 143 ); : NEXT : NEXT : LOCATE 1, 1
240   PEN 0 : PAPER 1 : LOCATE 19, 12 : PRINT STRING$( 4, 206
      )
250   LOCATE 19, 13 : PRINT CHR$( 206 ); "▴▴"; CHR$( 206 )
260   LOCATE 19, 14 : PRINT CHR$( 206 ); "▴▴"; CHR$( 206 )
270   LOCATE 19, 15 : PRINT STRING$( 4, 206 )
280   PEN 2 : LOCATE 20, 13
290   PRINT CHR$( 244 ) + CHR$( 246 ) + CHR$( 10 ) + STRING$(
      2, 8 ) + CHR$( 245 ) + CHR$( 247 )
300   FOR I = 1 TO 4 : EXIST( I ) = 1 : NEXT
310   DRN = 1 : LOCATE LASERX( DRN ), LASERY ( DRN ) : PRINT
      LASBL$( DRN )
312   EVERY 30, 1 GOSUB 4000
```

```
315     SHIPX( 1 ) = 20 : STARTX( 1 ) = 20 : SHIPX( 2 ) = 1 : S
        TARTX( 2 ) = 1 : SHIPX( 3 ) = 20 : STARTX( 3 ) = 20 : SH
        IPX( 4 ) = 38 : STARTX( 4 ) = 38
317     SHIPY( 1 ) = 1 : STARTY( 1 ) = 1 : SHIPY( 2 ) = 13 : ST
        ARTY( 2 ) = 13 : SHIPY( 3 ) = 23 : STARTY( 3 ) = 23 : SH
        IPY( 4 ) = 13 : STARTY( 4 ) = 13
319     CRASH( 1 ) = 30 : CRASH( 2 ) = 30 : CRASH( 3 ) = 36 : C
        RASH( 4 ) = 36
```

```
┌─────────────────────────────────────────────┐
│              Main program loop                │
└─────────────────────────────────────────────┘
```

```
320     :
325     FOR SP = 1 TO 4
330     IF INKEY( 35 ) > -1 THEN LOCATE LASERX( DRN ), LASERY(
        DRN ) : PEN 0 : PAPER 1 : PRINT LAS$( DRN ) : DRN = ( DR
        N MOD 4 ) + 1 : LOCATE LASERX( DRN ), LASERY( DRN ) : PR
        INT LASBL$( DRN )
340     GOSUB 1000
350     IF INKEY( 47 ) > -1 THEN GOSUB 2000
390     NEXT
400     GOTO 325
```

```
┌─────────────────────────────────────────────┐
│                 Erase ships                   │
└─────────────────────────────────────────────┘
```

```
990     :
1000    IF EXIST ( SP ) = 0 THEN RETURN
1010    PAPER 1 : PEN 1 : LOCATE SHIPX( SP ), SHIPY( SP )
1020    PRINT USING "&"; BLANK$
1030    SHIPX( SP ) = SHIPX( SP ) + SPDX( SP ) : SHIPY( SP ) =
        SHIPY( SP ) + SPDY ( SP )
```

```
┌─────────────────────────────────────────────┐
│                 Move ships                    │
└─────────────────────────────────────────────┘
```

```
1040    :
1050    PEN 2 : LOCATE SHIPX( SP ), SHIPY( SP )
1060    PRINT USING "&"; SHIP$
1070    IF SHIPX( SP ) + SHIPY( SP ) = CRASH( SP ) THEN 9000
1080    RETURN
```

```
┌─────────────────────────────────────────────┐
│                 Fire Laser                    │
└─────────────────────────────────────────────┘
```

```
1990    :
2000    SCORE = SCORE - 25 : GOSUB 5000 : HIT = 0 : IF DRN = 1
        OR DRN = 3 THEN 2050
2010    FINY = LSY( DRN )
2020    IF EXIST( DRN ) = 0 THEN FINX = ( DRN - 2 ) * 304 + LSX
        ( DRN ) : GOTO 2100
2030    HIT = 1 : FINX = 16 * SHIPX( DRN ) - 16
2040    GOTO 2100
2050    FINX = LSX( DRN )
2060    IF EXIST( DRN ) = 0 THEN FINY = -( DRN - 3 ) * 160 + LS
        Y( DRN ) : GOTO 2100
2070    HIT = 1 : FINY = 416 - 16 * SHIPY( DRN )
2100    MOVE LSX( DRN ), LSY( DRN )
2110    DRAW FINX, FINY, 3
```

```
2115    SOUND 1, 100, 5, 15
2120    DRAW LSX( DRN ), LSY( DRN ), 1
2130    IF HIT = 1 THEN GOSUB 3000
2140    RETURN
```

```
2990    :
3000    SCORE = SCORE + 50 : GOSUB 5000 : LOCATE SHIPX( DRN ),
        SHIPY( DRN )
3010    PEN 3 : PRINT USING "&"; EXPL$
3020    SOUND 1, 0, 25, 15, 1, 1, 15
3030    LOCATE SHIPX( DRN ), SHIPY( DRN )
3040    PEN 1 : PRINT USING "&"; BLANK$
3050    EXIST( DRN ) = 0
3060    RETURN
```

```
3990    :
4000    T1 = ( T1 MOD 4 ) + 1 : IF EXIST( T1 ) = 1 THEN RETURN
4010    SHIPX( T1 ) = STARTX( T1 ) : SHIPY( T1 ) = STARTY( T1 )

4020    EXIST( T1 ) = 1 : RETURN
```

```
4990    :
5000    LOCATE 3, 25 : PEN 1 : PAPER 0
5010    PRINT "SCORE :."; SCORE : PAPER 1
5020    RETURN
```

```
8990    :
9000    LOCATE SHIPX( SP ), SHIPY( SP ) : PRINT USING "&"; EXPL
        $ : LOCATE 20, 13 : PRINT USING "&"; EXPL$ : FOR I = 1 T
        O 180 STEP 5
9010    INK 1, INT( RND( 1 ) * 26 )
9020    SOUND 1, ABS( COS( I ) + SIN( I ) * 100 ), 15, 15
9030    NEXT
9040    INK 1, 23 : CLS : PRINT "YOUR.SCORE.WAS :."; SCORE
9050    LOCATE 1, 10 : IF SCORE < 10 THEN PRINT "SAD...." ELSE
        IF SCORE < 100 THEN PRINT "OK...." ELSE IF SCORE < 500 T
        HEN PRINT "GOOD.!!!" ELSE PRINT "A.GRAND.MASTER.!!!!"
9060    LOCATE 6, 20 : PRINT "PRESS.A.KEY.FOR.ANOTHER.GAME"
9070    IF INKEY$ = "" THEN 9080 ELSE 9070
9080    IF INKEY$ = "" THEN 9080 ELSE RUN
```

ChexSum Tables

10	=	1502	315	=	7691	2120	=	1960
20	=	4404	317	=	7641	2130	=	1532
30	=	3063	319	=	3621	2140	=	201
40	=	2688	320	=	0	2990	=	0
50	=	4732	325	=	1066	3000	=	4198
60	=	3145	330	=	10424	3010	=	1370
70	=	3257	340	=	456	3020	=	689
80	=	5235	350	=	1844	3030	=	2220
90	=	5304	390	=	176	3040	=	1415
100	=	2584	400	=	292	3050	=	1241
110	=	4444	990	=	0	3060	=	201
120	=	2836	1000	=	1901	3990	=	0
130	=	4554	1010	=	2559	4000	=	3301
140	=	4010	1020	=	1180	4010	=	4229
150	=	4018	1030	=	6380	4020	=	1349
160	=	3265	1040	=	0	4990	=	0
170	=	3769	1050	=	2326	5000	=	812
180	=	4116	1060	=	1128	5010	=	1607
190	=	3528	1070	=	3820	5020	=	201
200	=	574	1080	=	201	8990	=	0
210	=	3751	1990	=	0	9000	=	6164
220	=	4040	2000	=	4674	9010	=	1318
230	=	4139	2010	=	1529	9020	=	2540
240	=	1770	2020	=	4819	9030	=	176
250	=	2005	2030	=	2874	9040	=	2448
260	=	2006	2040	=	282	9050	=	8428
270	=	1305	2050	=	1527	9060	=	2499
280	=	564	2060	=	5177	9070	=	1665
290	=	4796	2070	=	3022	9080	=	1692
300	=	2241	2100	=	1927			
310	=	4181	2110	=	1186			
312	=	731	2115	=	567	TOTAL	=	236303

SHOOTING GALLERY

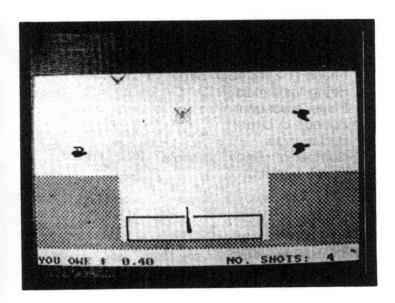

CLASSIFICATION: Target practice game

Step right up and have a go! Only $1.00 for five shots — and you get five shots free!

Scoring:

front ducks   20c

middle ducks   50c

crazy bird $1.00

Use the SPACE bar to shoot at the flying targets.

PROGRAMME SUGGESTIONS

The speed of the birds can be altered in lines 1000 — 1080. Or try putting an extra row of birds with different values to add some variety!

PROGRAM
Variables

HEAD(5)	Columns required for a hit
HIT$	Hit bird string
ADD	Amount to add to Player's account
BLANK$	String to blank birds
BIRD$(5,2)	Strings for each bird
BIRDX(5), BIRDY(5)	Co-ordinates of birds
PHASE(5)	Phase (1-2) of each Bird
MISS$	String for a miss
ACCOUNT	Player's account
SPD(5)	Speeds of birds
BD	Bird number
NS	Number of remaining shots
HIT	Which bird hit?
I, J, T1	Temps

Program Structure

Lines	Function/Activity
10 — 380	Initialise variables
400 — 510	Set up screen
530 — 610	Main loop
1000 — 1080	Move birds
2000 — 2100	Fire Gun
3000 — 3030	Update Account
4000 — 4030	Alter phases
5000 — 5030	More shots
9000 — 9040	Game over

```
                    ┌─────────────────────────────────────────────┐
                    │                                             │
                    │        Initialise variables                 │
                    │                                             │
                    └─────────────────────────────────────────────┘

10      MODE 1 : INK 0, 13 : INK 1, 0 : INK 2, 6 : INK 3, 1
20      SYMBOL AFTER 220 : SYMBOL 220, 128, 64, 96, 56, 28, 13,
        7, 3 : SYMBOL 221, 1, 2, 0, 0, 0, 0, 0, 0
30      SYMBOL 222, 1, 2, 6, 28, 56, 176, 224, 192 : SYMBOL 223
        , 128, 64, 0, 0, 0, 0, 0
40      SYMBOL 224, 0, 0, 0, 0, 0, 1, 7, 15 : SYMBOL 225, 25, 5
        0, 32, 32, 32, 0, 0, 0
50      SYMBOL 226, 0, 0, 0, 0, 0, 128, 224, 240 : SYMBOL 227,
        152, 76, 4, 4, 4, 0, 0, 0
60      SYMBOL 228, 0, 0, 0, 0, 3, 14, 24, 12 : SYMBOL 229, 6,
        115, 255, 63, 7, 0, 0, 0
70      SYMBOL 230, 0, 0, 0, 0, 252, 32, 64, 32 : SYMBOL 231, 2
        48, 255, 255, 254, 252, 248, 0, 0
80      SYMBOL 232, 0, 0, 0, 0, 1, 115, 255, 63 : SYMBOL 233, 3
        , 7, 7, 3, 0, 0, 0, 0
90      SYMBOL 234, 0, 0, 0, 0, 248, 254, 255, 255 : SYMBOL 235
        , 252, 248, 248, 248, 252, 62, 15, 0
100     SYMBOL 236, 0, 0, 0, 0, 63, 4, 2, 4 : SYMBOL 237, 63, 2
        55, 255, 127, 63, 31, 0, 0
110     SYMBOL 238, 0, 0, 0, 0, 192, 112, 24, 48 : SYMBOL 239,
        224, 206, 255, 252, 224, 0, 0, 0
120     SYMBOL 240, 0, 0, 0, 0, 31, 127, 255, 255 : SYMBOL 241,
        63, 31, 31, 31, 63, 124, 240, 0
130     SYMBOL 242, 0, 0, 0, 0, 128, 206, 255, 252 : SYMBOL 243
        , 192, 224, 224, 192, 0, 0, 0, 0
140     SYMBOL 244, 130, 200, 96, 49, 25, 45, 39, 75 : SYMBOL 2
        45, 19, 5, 66, 4, 65, 144, 4, 34
150     SYMBOL 246, 1, 35, 6, 140, 216, 177, 224, 201 : SYMBOL
        247, 196, 144, 66, 32, 4, 18, 128, 1
160     SYMBOL 248, 96, 32, 32, 32, 32, 32, 32, 32 : SYMBOL 249
        , 32, 32, 48, 48, 48, 48, 112, 56 : SYMBOL 250, 48, 56,
        56, 56, 60, 60, 60, 60
170     SYMBOL 251, 255, 255, 255, 223, 207, 195, 129, 80
180     HIT$ = CHR$( 244 ) + CHR$( 246 ) + CHR$( 10 ) + STRING$
        ( 2, 8 ) + CHR$( 245 ) + CHR$( 247 )
190     BLANK$ = CHR$( 32 ) + CHR$( 32 ) + CHR$( 10 ) + STRING$
        ( 2, 8 ) + CHR$( 32 ) + CHR$( 32 )
200     BIRDS$( 5, 1 ) = CHR$( 220 ) + CHR$( 222 ) + CHR$( 10 )
        + STRING$( 2, 8 ) + CHR$( 221 ) + CHR$( 223 )
210     BIRDS$( 5, 2 ) = CHR$( 224 ) + CHR$( 226 ) + CHR$( 10 )
        + STRING$( 2, 8 ) + CHR$( 225 ) + CHR$( 227 )
220     BIRDS$( 4, 1 ) = CHR$( 228 ) + CHR$( 230 ) + CHR$( 10 )
        + STRING$( 2, 8 ) + CHR$( 229 ) + CHR$( 231 )
230     BIRDS$( 4, 2 ) = CHR$( 232 ) + CHR$( 234 ) + CHR$( 10 )
        + STRING$( 2, 8 ) + CHR$( 233 ) + CHR$( 235 )
240     BIRDS$( 3, 1 ) = BIRDS$( 4, 1 )
250     BIRDS$( 3, 2 ) = BIRDS$( 4, 2 )
260     BIRDS$( 2, 1 ) = CHR$( 236 ) + CHR$( 238 ) + CHR$( 10 )
        + STRING$( 2, 8 ) + CHR$( 237 ) + CHR$( 239 )
270     BIRDS$( 2, 2 ) = CHR$( 240 ) + CHR$( 242 ) + CHR$( 10 )
        + STRING$( 2, 8 ) + CHR$( 241 ) + CHR$( 243 )
280     BIRDS$( 1, 1 ) = BIRDS$( 2, 1 )
290     BIRDS$( 1, 2 ) = BIRDS$( 2, 2 )
300     MISS$ = CHR$( 251 ) : HEAD( 1 ) = 19 : HEAD( 2 ) = 19 :
        HEAD( 3 ) = 19 : HEAD( 4 ) = 19 : HEAD( 5 ) = 20
310     FOR I = 1 TO 5 : PHASE( I ) = INT( RND( 1 ) * 2 ) + 1 :
```

49

```
        NEXT
320     BIRDX( 5 ) = 17 : BIRDY( 5 ) = 3
330     BIRDX( 4 ) = 10 : BIRDY( 4 ) = 7
340     BIRDX( 3 ) = 30 : BIRDY( 3 ) = 7
350     BIRDX( 2 ) = 15 : BIRDY( 2 ) = 11
360     BIRDX( 1 ) = 25 : BIRDY( 1 ) = 11
370     SPD( 4 ) = -2 : SPD( 3 ) = -2
380     SPD( 2 ) = 1 : SPD( 1 ) = 1
```

```
┌─────────────────────────────────────────┐
│                                          │
│              Setup screen                │
│                                          │
└─────────────────────────────────────────┘
```

```
390     :
400     PAPER 0 : CLS : BORDER 1
410     PEN 3 : FOR I = 1 TO 40 : FOR J = 1 TO 2 : LOCATE I, J
        : PRINT CHR$( 143 ) : NEXT : NEXT
420     FOR I = 1 TO 11 : FOR J = 15 TO 22 : LOCATE I, J : PRIN
        T CHR$( 206 ) : NEXT : NEXT
430     FOR I = 30 TO 40 : FOR J = 15 TO 22 : LOCATE I, J : PRI
        NT CHR$( 206 ) : NEXT : NEXT
440     FOR I = 1 TO 40 : LOCATE I, 23 : PRINT CHR$( 206 ) : NE
        XT
450     FOR I = 13 TO 28 : LOCATE I, 20 : PRINT CHR$( 208 ) : N
        EXT
460     FOR I = 13 TO 28 : LOCATE I, 22 : PRINT CHR$( 210 ) : N
        EXT
470     LOCATE 12, 20 : PRINT CHR$( 209 ) : LOCATE 12, 21 : PRI
        NT CHR$( 209 ) : LOCATE 12, 22 : PRINT CHR$( 209 )
480     LOCATE 29, 20 : PRINT CHR$( 211 ) : LOCATE 29, 21 : PRI
        NT CHR$( 211 ) : LOCATE 29, 22 : PRINT CHR$( 211 )
490     LOCATE 20, 19 : PEN 1 : PRINT CHR$( 248 ) : LOCATE 20,
        20 : PRINT CHR$( 249 ) : LOCATE 20, 21 : PRINT CHR$( 250
        )
500     EVERY 15, 1 GOSUB 4000
510     NS = 5 : ACCOUNT = 0 : GOSUB 3000
```

```
┌─────────────────────────────────────────┐
│                                          │
│            Main Program loop             │
│                                          │
└─────────────────────────────────────────┘
```

```
520     :
530     FOR BD = 1 TO 5
540     GOSUB 1000
550     IF INKEY( 47 ) > -1 AND HIT = 0 THEN GOSUB 2000 : GOSUB
        3000
560     IF NS = 0 THEN GOTO 5000
590     NEXT : HIT = 0
600     LOCATE 20, 2 : PEN 3 : PRINT CHR$( 143 )
610     GOTO 530
```

```
┌─────────────────────────────────────────┐
│                                          │
│               Move birds                 │
│                                          │
└─────────────────────────────────────────┘
```

```
700     :
1000    LOCATE BIRDX( BD ), BIRDY( BD )
1010    PRINT USING "&"; BLANK$
1020    BIRDX( BD ) = BIRDX( BD ) + SPD( BD )
1025    IF RND( 1 ) < 0.4 THEN BIRDX( BD ) = BIRDX( BD ) + SPD(
        BD )
1030    IF BIRDX( BD ) < 2 THEN BIRDX( BD ) = 37 : ACCOUNT = AC
        COUNT - 0.1 : GOSUB 3000
1040    IF BIRDX( BD ) > 37 THEN BIRDX( BD ) = 2 : ACCOUNT = AC
```

```
        COUNT - 0.1 : GOSUB 3000
1050    IF BD = 5 THEN PEN 2 ELSE PEN 1
1060    LOCATE BIRDX( BD ), BIRDY( BD )
1070    PRINT USING "&"; BIRDS$( BD, PHASE( BD ) )
1080    RETURN
```

```
+--------------------------------------------------+
|                                                  |
|              Fire Gun                            |
|                                                  |
+--------------------------------------------------+
```

```
1990    :
2000    ACCOUNT = ACCOUNT - 0.1 : NS = NS - 1 : SOUND 1, 0, 5,
        15, 1, 1, 31 : HIT = 0 : FOR I = 1 TO 5
2010    IF BIRDX( I ) = HEAD( I ) THEN HIT = I
2020    NEXT
2030    IF HIT = 0 THEN LOCATE 20, 2 : PEN 3 : PRINT CHR$( 251
        ) : RETURN
2040    LOCATE BIRDX( HIT ), BIRDY( HIT )
2050    PEN 2 : PRINT USING "&"; HIT$
2060    FOR J = 1 TO 3 : FOR I = 1 TO 20 STEP 2 : SOUND 1, I, 5
        , 15 : NEXT : NEXT
2070    IF HIT < 3 THEN ADD = 0.2 ELSE IF HIT < 5 THEN ADD = 0.
        5 ELSE ADD = 1
2080    ACCOUNT = ACCOUNT + ADD
2100    RETURN
```

```
+--------------------------------------------------+
|                                                  |
|              Update account                      |
|                                                  |
+--------------------------------------------------+
```

```
2990    :
3000    LOCATE 1, 25 : PRINT SPACE$( 38 ) : PEN 3 : LOCATE 1, 2
        5 : IF ACCOUNT < 0 THEN PRINT "YOU OWE $"; ELSE PRINT "Y
        OU HAVE $";
3010    PRINT USING "###.##"; ABS( ACCOUNT )
3020    LOCATE 25, 25 : PRINT "NO. SHOTS : "; NS
3030    RETURN
```

```
+--------------------------------------------------+
|                                                  |
|              Alter phases                        |
|                                                  |
+--------------------------------------------------+
```

```
3990    :
4000    FOR T1 = 1 TO 5 : IF PHASE( T1 ) = 1 THEN PHASE( T1 ) =
        2 ELSE PHASE( T1 ) = 1
4010    NEXT
4020    IF RND( 1 ) < 0.5 THEN SPD( 5 ) = -1 ELSE SPD( 5 ) = 1
4030    RETURN
```

```
+--------------------------------------------------+
|                                                  |
|              More shots ?                        |
|                                                  |
+--------------------------------------------------+
```

```
4990    :
5000    LOCATE 1, 25 : PRINT SPACE$( 38 ) : PEN 3 : LOCATE 1, 2
        5
5010    PRINT "ANOTHER 5 SHOTS ? (Y/N)"
5020    IF INKEY( 43 ) > -1 THEN 5030 ELSE IF INKEY( 46 ) > -1
        THEN 9000 ELSE 5020
5030    NS = 5 : GOSUB 3000 : GOTO 530
```

```
8990  :
9000  CLS : LOCATE 16, 1 : PRINT "GAME OVER"
9010  LOCATE 1, 10
9020  IF ACCOUNT < -0.01 THEN PRINT "THE BOYS WILL BE SEEING
      YOU SHORTLY" ELSE PRINT "CONGRATS FOR YOUR WINNINGS"
9030  LOCATE 5, 16 : PRINT "ACCOUNT : $"; : PRINT USING "###.
      ##"; ACCOUNT
9040  IF INKEY$ = "" THEN END ELSE 9040
```

ChexSum Tables

10 =	1325	360 =	1794	1990 =	0
20 =	3007	370 =	1942	2000 =	6074
30 =	2856	380 =	1446	2010 =	3077
40 =	2166	390 =	0	2020 =	176
50 =	2797	400 =	549	2030 =	2699
60 =	2479	410 =	3996	2040 =	2184
70 =	3920	420 =	3849	2050 =	1285
80 =	2441	430 =	3918	2060 =	3301
90 =	4384	440 =	2502	2070 =	5373
100 =	2874	450 =	2512	2080 =	2157
110 =	3570	460 =	2548	2100 =	201
120 =	3310	470 =	3409	2990 =	0
130 =	3703	480 =	3434	3000 =	5034
140 =	3089	490 =	3753	3010 =	1874
150 =	3671	500 =	716	3020 =	1756
160 =	4397	510 =	1897	3030 =	201
170 =	2666	520 =	0	3990 =	0
180 =	5172	530 =	1070	4000 =	5072
190 =	4449	540 =	456	4010 =	176
200 =	5410	550 =	3230	4020 =	3225
210 =	5427	560 =	1424	4030 =	233
220 =	5441	590 =	800	4990 =	0
230 =	5458	600 =	1306	5000 =	1503
240 =	1560	610 =	242	5010 =	1760
250 =	1562	700 =	0	5020 =	3704
260 =	5471	1000 =	1994	5030 =	1220
270 =	5488	1010 =	1180	8990 =	0
280 =	1556	1020 =	2959	9000 =	1362
290 =	1558	1025 =	4959	9010 =	295
300 =	5287	1030 =	5877	9020 =	7218
310 =	3488	1040 =	5874	9030 =	2846
320 =	1775	1050 =	1678	9040 =	1602
330 =	1770	1060 =	1994		
340 =	1788	1070 =	2458		
350 =	1786	1080 =	201	TOTAL =	258676

ASTERIOD INVASION

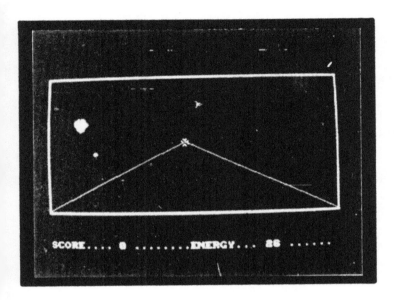

CLASSIFICATION: Time-limit Game

You have thirty seconds to save everything known to man. You do this by blasting the aliens. You have a fully implemented jelly plasma laser, which you can fire after you have lined up the sights on your enemy.

Use 'A' to move up, 'Z' to move down, 'comma' to move left, 'period' to move right and space to fire.

PROGRAMMING SUGGESTIONS

This game can be altered in many ways to make it easier, harder or just more complex. Try a combination of the following: Putting more aliens on the screen, altering the time limit, altering the course and speed of the alien and finally altering the scoring.

PROGRAM
Variables

MET$(4)	Meteor character string
MET(3)	Phase of each meteor
X(3), Y(3)	Meteor columns and rows
SCORE	Player's score
A, B	Cross-hair column, row
Q, W	Pixel equivalents of A and B
Z	Current meteor
ENERGY	Energy
ALX, ALY	Alien's column, row

Program Structure

Lines	Function/Activity
10	Call initialise routine
30 — 190	Main loop
200 — 320	Firing routine
330 — 470	Print meteor block
390 — 480	Game over
490 — 820	Initialise variables
830 — 900	Initialise screen

ASTEROID

```
            ┌─────────────────────────────────────────────────────┐
            │                                                     │
            │   Call initialise routine and Main loop             │
            │                                                     │
            └─────────────────────────────────────────────────────┘

20          GOSUB 500
            ┌─────────────────────────────────────────────────────┐
            │                                                     │
            │   Firing routine                                    │
            │                                                     │
            └─────────────────────────────────────────────────────┘

30          :
40          FOR T = 1 TO 3 : PEN T
50          Z = T : GOSUB 340
60          MET(T) = MET(T) + 1 : IF MET(T) = 5 THEN MET(T) = 1 : X
            (T) = CINT( RND(1) * 30 + 5) : Y(T) = CINT( RND(1) * 10
            + 5) : ENERGY = ENERGY - 1 : LOCATE 30, 24 : PRINT ENERG
            Y : IF ENERGY = 0 THEN GOTO 400
70          NEXT T
80          LOCATE ALX, ALY : PRINT "."
90          ALX = ALX + 1 : IF ALX > 38 THEN ALX = 3 : ALY = CINT(
            RND(1) * 10 + 5)
100         LOCATE ALX, ALY : PRINT CHR$(224)
110         LOCATE A, B : PRINT "."
120         A = A + (INKEY(39) > -1) - (INKEY(31) > -1) : B = B + (
            INKEY(69) > -1) - (INKEY(71) > -1)
130         IF A > 38 THEN A = 3
140         IF A < 3 THEN A = 38
150         IF B > 18 THEN B = 3
160         IF B < 3 THEN B = 18
170         PEN 2 : LOCATE A, B : PRINT CHR$(252)
180         IF INKEY(47) > -1 THEN GOSUB 210
190         GOTO 40
            ┌─────────────────────────────────────────────────────┐
            │                                                     │
            │   Display meteor block                              │
            │                                                     │
            └─────────────────────────────────────────────────────┘

200         :
210         Q = A * 16 - 8 : W = (25 - B) * 16 + 8
220         MOVE 5, 98 : DRAW Q, W, 3
230         MOVE 634, 98 : DRAW Q, W, 3
235         IF INKEY(67) > -1 THEN FOR T = 1 TO 1E+10 : NEXT T
240         FOR N = 1 TO 100 STEP 15 : SOUND 129, N, 10, 15 : NEXT
            N
250         IF A = ALX AND B = ALY THEN SOUND 129, 100, 100, 15, 1,
            1, 1 : ALX = 3 : ALY = CINT( RND(1) * 10 + 5) : SCORE
            = SCORE + 1000 : LOCATE 10, 24 : PRINT SCORE : ENERGY =
            ENERGY + 10 : LOCATE 30, 24 : PRINT ENERGY
260         FOR N = 1 TO 3
270         IF (A = X(N) OR A - 1 = X(N)) AND (B= Y(N) OR B - 1 = Y
            (N)) THEN SCORE = SCORE + CINT( RND(1) * 5000) : ENERGY
            = ENERGY + 20 : LOCATE 10, 24 : PRINT SCORE : LOCATE 30,
             24 : PRINT ENERGY ELSE GOTO 290
280         SOUND 130, 250, 50, 15, 1, 1, 1 : MET(N) = 4 : GOSUB 34
            0
290         NEXT N
300         MOVE 5, 98 : DRAW Q, W, 0
310         MOVE 634, 98 : DRAW Q, W, 0
320         RETURN
```

```
330     :
340     LOCATE X(Z), Y(Z)
350     PRINT LEFT$(MET$(MET(Z)), 2)
360     LOCATE X(Z), Y(Z) + 1
370     PRINT RIGHT$(MET$(MET(Z)), 2)
380     RETURN
```

Initialise variables

```
390     :
400     FOR T = 1 TO 20 : FOR N = 200 TO 0 STEP - 20 : SOUND 12
        9, T, 10, 15 : NEXT N : NEXT T
410     FOR T = 1 TO 26 : LOCATE 1, 1 : PRINT CHR$(11) : NEXT T

420     MODE 0 : PEN 4 : INK 4, 0
430     LOCATE 6, 2 : PRINT "GAME OVER!"
440     FOR T = 1 TO 26 : INK 4, T : SOUND 129, T * 10, 10, 15
        : SOUND 130, T * 5, 10, 15 : SOUND 132, T * 15, 10, 15 :
         NEXT T
450     PEN 7 : LOCATE 1,8 : PRINT "Your Score : ";SCORE
460     LOCATE 1, 14 : PRINT "  PRESS 'R' FOR     ANOTHER GA
        ME."
470     IF INKEY$ = "R" OR INKEY$ = "r" THEN RUN ELSE GOTO 470
480     STOP
```

Initialise screen

```
490     :
500     SYMBOL AFTER 224 : SYMBOL 224,192,96,124,115,124,96,192
        ,0 : SYMBOL 240, 0, 0, 0, 0, 0, 0, 1, 3
510     SYMBOL 241, 0, 0, 0, 0, 0, 0, 192, 224
520     SYMBOL 242, 3, 1, 0, 0, 0, 0, 0, 0
530     SYMBOL 243, 224, 128, 0, 0, 0, 0, 0, 0
540     SYMBOL 244, 0, 0, 0, 0, 1, 3, 14, 31
550     SYMBOL 245, 0, 0, 0, 0, 192, 32, 240, 240
560     SYMBOL 246, 15, 4, 7, 1, 0, 0, 0, 0
570     SYMBOL 247, 224, 192, 128, 128, 0, 0, 0, 0
580     SYMBOL 248, 0, 12, 25, 99, 239, 255, 255, 255
590     SYMBOL 249, 0, 224, 112, 240, 248, 252, 158, 239
600     SYMBOL 250, 255, 127, 55, 23, 27, 13, 6, 3
610     SYMBOL 251, 238, 252, 176, 240, 224, 224, 192
620     SYMBOL 252, 36, 24, 129, 66, 66, 129, 24, 36
630     BORDER 0
640     PAPER 0 : INK 0, 0
650     PEN 1 : INK 1, 18
660     INK 2, 24 : INK 3, 6
670     MODE 1
680     DIM MET$(4)
690     MET$(1) = CHR$(240) + CHR$(241) + CHR$(242) + CHR$(243)

700     MET$(2) = CHR$(244) + CHR$(245) + CHR$(246) + CHR$(247)

710     MET$(3) = CHR$(248) + CHR$(249) + CHR$(250) + CHR$(251)
```

```
720    MET$(4) = "▲▲▲▲"
730    DIM MET(3)
740    MET(1) = 1 : MET(2) = 2 : MET(3) = 3
750    DIM X(3), Y(3)
760    FOR T = 1 TO 3
770    X(T) = CINT( RND(1) * 30 + 5)
780    Y(T) = CINT( RND(1) * 10 + 5)
790    NEXT T
800    SCORE = 0
810    A = 20 : B = 10
820    Z = 3 : ENERGY = 40 : ALX = 3 : ALY = CINT(RND(1) * 10
       + 5)
830    LOCATE 1, 1 : PRINT STRING$(40, CHR$(210))
840    LOCATE 1, 20 : PRINT STRING$(40, CHR$(208))
850    FOR T = 2 TO 19
860    LOCATE 1, T : PRINT CHR$(211)
870    LOCATE 40, T : PRINT CHR$(209)
880    NEXT T
890    LOCATE 1, 24 : PRINT "SCORE....▲0▲........ENERGY...▲40▲
       ......"
900    RETURN
```

ChexSum Tables

20 =	466	320 =	201	630 =	176
30 =	0	330 =	0	640 =	499
40 =	1431	340 =	1328	650 =	531
50 =	1002	350 =	1861	660 =	579
60 =	12973	360 =	1587	670 =	220
70 =	433	370 =	1865	680 =	639
80 =	1310	380 =	201	690 =	3850
90 =	4943	390 =	0	700 =	3867
100 =	1798	400 =	4439	710 =	3884
110 =	982	410 =	2329	720 =	895
120 =	6293	420 =	728	730 =	648
130 =	1461	430 =	1236	740 =	2171
140 =	1464	440 =	5241	750 =	878
150 =	1443	450 =	2456	760 =	986
160 =	1446	460 =	2652	770 =	2098
170 =	1766	470 =	3085	780 =	2079
180 =	1839	480 =	206	790 =	433
190 =	262	490 =	0	800 =	774
200 =	0	500 =	3590	810 =	972
210 =	2825	510 =	1407	820 =	3933
220 =	1128	520 =	974	830 =	1641
230 =	1259	530 =	1345	840 =	1669
235 =	3296	540 =	1043	850 =	1014
240 =	2667	550 =	1721	860 =	1284
250 =	11721	560 =	1012	870 =	1332
260 =	980	570 =	1691	880 =	433
270 =	13148	580 =	2193	890 =	2681
280 =	2326	590 =	2527	900 =	201
290 =	427	600 =	1553		
300 =	1157	610 =	2544		
310 =	1256	620 =	1578	TOTAL =	176462

SPACE WARS

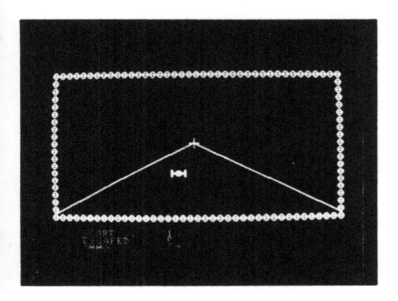

CLASSIFICATION: Shoot-up Game

Slaughter the aliens as they appear within your field of vision, steady on the cross-hair before you fire. Your ammo is limited as are the number of aliens.

Use 'A' to move up, 'Z' to move down, 'comma' to move left, 'period' to move right, and 'space' to fire.

PROGRAMMING SUGGESTIONS

To make the game harder place some obstacles on the screen and alter the alien's movements.

PROGRAM
Variables

ALIENX, ALIENY	Alien's Co-ordinates
SCORE	Player's score
AMMO	Number of shots remaining
ESCAPED	Number of times an alien escaped
ALIEN$	Characters for printing alien
OLDX, OLDY	Save alien's old coordinates
XDIR, YDIR	Adjustments to alien's coordinates

Program Structure

Lines	Function/Activity
60 — 140	Initialisation
160 — 320	Main loop
360 — 460	Firing routine
470 — 540	Alien hit
580 — 640	Alien escaped
680 — 780	Game over
820	Break routine
860 — 980	Instructions

```
┌─────────────────────────────────────────────────────┐
│                                                       │
│            Initialise game                            │
│                                                       │
└─────────────────────────────────────────────────────┘
```

```
60      GOSUB 860
70      SPEED KEY 1 , 1 : ON BREAK GOSUB 820
80      INK 0 , 0 : INK 1 , 24 : INK 2, 20 : INK 3, 6 : PAPER 0
        : BORDER 0 : MODE 1
85      SYMBOL AFTER 238 : SYMBOL 238, 0, 16, 0, 0, 0, 132, 0,
        0 : SYMBOL 239, 32, 0, 0, 0, 8, 0, 0, 0 : SYMBOL 240, 16
        , 0, 0, 130, 0, 0, 16, 0
87      SYMBOL 241, 0, 0, 4, 128, 0, 0, 0, 0 : SYMBOL 242, 136,
        0, 0, 4, 64, 0, 0, 128 : SYMBOL 243, 129, 0, 8, 0, 129,
        0, 0, 64
90      SYMBOL 244 , 192 , 195 , 199 , 255 , 255 , 199 , 195 ,
        192 : SYMBOL 245 , 3 , 195 , 227 , 255 , 255 , 227 , 195
        , 3
95      SYMBOL 246, 33, 68, 37, 40, 157, 34, 34, 17 : SYMBOL 24
        7, 161, 178, 65, 41, 159, 138, 113, 81 : SYMBOL 248, 2,
        128, 144, 0, 130, 16, 64, 144 : SYMBOL 249, 49, 0, 144,
        1, 1, 68, 2, 136 : SYMBOL 250, 194, 36, 1, 145, 0, 132,
        128, 66
97      SYMBOL 251, 1, 69, 17, 64, 152, 1, 129, 100
100     ALIENX = 30 : ALIENY = 10 : SCORE = 0 : ESCAPED = 0 : A
        MMO = 100
110     PEN 1 : LOCATE 1 , 1 : PRINT STRING$ (40 , CHR$ (181) )
        : LOCATE 1 , 20 : PRINT STRING$ (40 , CHR$ (181) ) : FO
        R T = 2 TO 19 : LOCATE 1 , T : PRINT CHR$ (181) : LOCATE
        40 , T : PRINT CHR$ (181) : NEXT T
120     PEN 3 : LOCATE 5 , 22 : PRINT "SCORE....." : LOCATE 5 ,
        23 : PRINT "ESCAPED..." : LOCATE 5 , 24 : PRINT "AMMO..
        ....."
130     ALIEN$ = CHR$ (244) + CHR$ (245)
135     E$(1)=CHR$(246)+CHR$(247) : E$(2)=CHR$(250)+CHR$(11)+CH
        R$(8)+CHR$(248)+CHR$(249)+CHR$(8)+CHR$(10)+CHR$(251)
140     E$(3)=CHR$(8)+CHR$(11)+CHR$(238)+CHR$(239)+CHR$(240)+CH
        R$(10)+STRING$(3,8)+CHR$(241)+CHR$(242)+CHR$(243) : E$(4
        )="▲▲▲"+CHR$(10)+STRING$(3,8)+"▲▲▲"
```

```
┌─────────────────────────────────────────────────────┐
│                                                       │
│            Main program loop                          │
│                                                       │
└─────────────────────────────────────────────────────┘
```

```
160     :
170     LOCATE ALIENX , ALIENY
180     PEN 2 : PRINT ALIEN$
190     MOVE 320, 238 : DRAW 320, 258, 1 : MOVE 321, 238 : DRAW
        321, 258, 1 : MOVE 310, 248 : DRAW 330, 248, 1
200     OLDX = ALIENX : OLDY = ALIENY
210     XDIR = (INKEY (31) > -1) - (INKEY (39) > -1)
220     ALIENX = ALIENX + XDIR
230     YDIR = (INKEY (71) > -1) - (INKEY (69) > -1)
240     ALIENY = ALIENY + YDIR
250     ALIENX = ALIENX + ( ( (ALIENX < 21) - (ALIENX > 20) ) /
        4)
260     ALIENY = ALIENY + ( ( (ALIENY < 12) - (ALIENY >10) ) /
        4)
270     ALIENX = ALIENX + (CINT (RND (1) ) / 2) : ALIENY = ALIE
        NY + (CINT (RND (1) ) / 2)
280     IF ALIENX < 2 OR ALIENX > 37 OR ALIENY < 2 OR ALIENY >
```

```
           19 THEN GOSUB 580
300        IF INKEY (47) > -1 THEN GOSUB 360
310        LOCATE OLDX , OLDY : PRINT "▲▲"
320        GOTO 170
```

```
330        :
360        PLOT 8, 96 : DRAW 320, 248,2 : PLOT 632, 96 : DRAW 320,
           248, 2
370        SOUND 1, 0, 30, 15, 1, 1, 1
380        AMMO = AMMO - 1
390        LOCATE 16, 24
400        PEN 3 : PRINT AMMO ; "▲▲"
410        IF AMMO = 0 THEN GOTO 680
420        PEN 0
430        PLOT 8, 96 : DRAW 320, 248, 0
440        PLOT 632, 96 : DRAW 320, 248, 0
460        IF CINT (OLDX) = 20 AND CINT (OLDY) = 10 THEN GOTO 470
           ELSE RETURN
```

```
465        :
470        MOVE 320, 238 : DRAW 320, 258, 0 : MOVE 321, 238 : DRAW
           321, 258, 0 : MOVE 310, 248 : DRAW 330, 248, 0 : ENV 2,
           7, -1, 10, 8, -1, 40
473        SOUND 1, 200, 200, 15, 2, 2, 2
475        FOR T1=1 TO 3 : LOCATE 20, 10 : PEN 2 : INK 2, 26 : PRI
           NT E$(T1) : FOR T2=1 TO 300 : NEXT : LOCATE 19, 9 : PRIN
           T E$(4) : NEXT
477        INK 2, 20
490        SCORE = SCORE + 1
500        LOCATE 16, 22
510        PEN 3 : PRINT SCORE
520        ALIENY = CINT (RND (1) * 10) +5
530        ALIENY = CINT (RND (1) * 10) +5
540        RETURN
```

```
550        :
580        ESCAPED = ESCAPED + 1
590        SOUND 2, 100, 25, 1, 1, 1
600        ALIENX = CINT (RND (1) * 20) +10
610        ALIENY = CINT (RND (1) * 10) +5
620        LOCATE 16 , 23
630        PEN 3 : PRINT ESCAPED
640        IF ESCAPED < 10 THEN RETURN
```

```
650        :
680        MODE 0
690        LOCATE 5 , 11
700        PRINT "GAME OVER!"
```

62

```
710    PRINT "SCORE...." ; SCORE
720    FOR T = 1 TO 10
730    FOR N =1000 TO 0 STEP -100
740    SOUND 1, N, 3, 15, 0, 0, 0
750    NEXT N
760    NEXT T
770    FOR T = 26 TO 0 STEP -1 : INK 1, T : FOR N = 1 TO 50 :
       NEXT N : NEXT T : CLS : INK 1, 24
780    A$ = INKEY$ : IF A$ = "" THEN GOTO 780 ELSE RUN
```

┌─────────────────────────────────────┐
│   │
│   Break routine   │
│   │
└─────────────────────────────────────┘

```
790    :
820    SPEED KEY 35 , 1 : STOP
```

┌─────────────────────────────────────┐
│   │
│   Instructions   │
│   │
└─────────────────────────────────────┘

```
830    :
860    MODE 0
870    LOCATE 1, 5
880    PRINT "▲'A'▲.......▲UP"
890    PRINT "▲'Z'▲.......▲DOWN"
900    PRINT "▲','▲.......▲LEFT"
910    PRINT "▲'.'▲.......▲RIGHT"
920    PRINT "▲SPACE.....▲FIRE"
930    INK 3, 8, 22
940    PEN 3
950    PRINT
960    PRINT
970    PRINT "▲▲▲▲▲Space▲Wars"
980    A$ = INKEY$ : IF A$ = "" THEN GOTO 980 ELSE PEN 1 : MOD
       E 2 : RETURN
```

ChexSum Tables

60	=	316	360	=	2239	690	=	332
70	=	1054	370	=	669	700	=	954
80	=	1840	380	=	1377	710	=	1499
85	=	4014	390	=	335	720	=	1004
87	=	3783	400	=	1154	730	=	1855
90	=	5622	410	=	1576	740	=	865
95	=	8355	420	=	233	750	=	427
97	=	1578	430	=	1054	760	=	433
100	=	4225	440	=	1180	770	=	4363
110	=	7787	460	=	3835	780	=	2376
120	=	3970	465	=	0	790	=	0
130	=	2256	470	=	4409	820	=	791
135	=	8170	473	=	1085	830	=	0
140	=	10527	475	=	4963	860	=	219
160	=	0	477	=	331	870	=	279
170	=	1458	490	=	1540	880	=	971
180	=	951	500	=	333	890	=	1143
190	=	3282	510	=	981	900	=	1084
200	=	2565	520	=	2198	910	=	1169
210	=	2970	530	=	2198	920	=	1243
220	=	2115	540	=	201	930	=	368
230	=	3041	550	=	0	940	=	236
240	=	2118	580	=	1814	950	=	191
250	=	4247	590	=	692	960	=	191
260	=	4232	600	=	2223	970	=	1388
270	=	5665	610	=	2198	980	=	3032
280	=	5189	620	=	398			
300	=	1766	630	=	1102	TOTAL	=	173592
310	=	1538	640	=	1611			
320	=	392	650	=	0			
330	=	0	680	=	219			

TANK AMBUSH

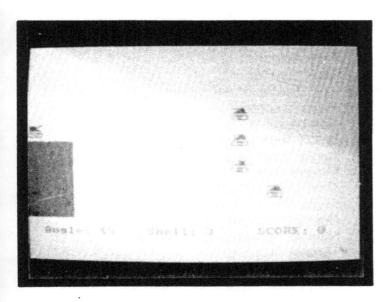

CLASSIFICATION: Simulation Game

An ambush has been planned for a squadron of enemy tanks. Your tank is positioned on a cliff and you fire at the enemy on the right using keys '0' to '9' give angle of projection of your bomb and shell (muzzle velocity 0-9). Then press the space bar to fire, or fire without keying in any numbers to send up a flare.

The game ends when an enmy tank reaches the bottom of the cliff and you score 50 points for each hit.

Use the keys '0' to '9' to make an angle between 00 and 89 degrees, and a 'shell' (muzzle velocity) between 0 and 9. Fire by pressing the space bar.

PROGRAMMING SUGGESTIONS

Some more tanks could be added to make the game harder and more exciting or the tank speed could be altered using the TSPEED variable.

65

PROGRAM
Variables

EXPL$(6,3)	Strings for six explosion phases, each with 3 lines
LT $	Last tank moved
TSPEED(4)	Tank speeds
TANK$	String for printing tank
TCOL	Tank colour
TK	Tank number
TANKX(4), TANKY(4)	Coordinates of each tank
SCORE	Player's score
HIT	Number of tanks hit by bomb
FIRE	Is this shot a flare or a bomb?
ANGLE	Angle of projection
SHELL	Muzzle velocity
T	Time parameter for bomb's trajectory
XIV, YIV	Initial velocity in each direction
BOMBX, BOMBY	Bomb's coordinates
NROUNDS	Number of waves of tanks destroyed
I, J	Temps
CU	Character under Bomb
MSG$(9)	Array of message strings
MN	Message number
EXIST(4)	Does each tank exist?

Program Structure

Lines	Function/Activity
10 — 179	Initialise game
190 — 300	New Round
320 — 480	Editor
500 — 520	Main loop
1000 — 1130	Move bomb
2000 — 2060	Explosion
3000 — 3530	Move/print tanks
4000 — 4040	Hit tank
5000 — 5020	Print message
9000 — 9040	Game over

```
┌─────────────────────────────────────────────────────────┐
│                                                         │
│              Initialise game                            │
│                                                         │
└─────────────────────────────────────────────────────────┘
```

```
10      DEG : MODE 1 : INK 0, 0 : INK 1, 15 : INK 2, 18 : INK 3
        , 24
20      SYMBOL AFTER 232 : SYMBOL 232, 0, 0, 255, 1, 7, 31, 127
        , 0 : SYMBOL 233, 127, 199, 146, 199, 127, 0, 0, 0
30      SYMBOL 234, 0, 64, 248, 248, 248, 252, 254, 0 : SYMBOL
        235, 254, 227, 73, 227, 254, 0, 0, 0
40      SYMBOL 240, 18, 129, 36, 26, 76, 16, 129, 8 : SYMBOL 24
        1, 128, 0, 69, 32, 2, 0, 68, 32 : SYMBOL 242, 64, 0, 16,
        128, 9, 0, 18, 64
50      SYMBOL 243, 0, 0, 64, 8, 2, 32, 4, 33 : SYMBOL 244, 0,
        128, 4, 0, 32, 2, 64, 9 : SYMBOL 245, 144, 2, 16, 0, 66,
        0, 0, 17
60      SYMBOL 246, 64, 4, 0, 144, 1, 16, 4, 64 : SYMBOL 247, 2
        , 33, 0, 18, 8, 128, 0, 16 : SYMBOL 248, 4, 0, 144, 2, 6
        4, 0, 8, 1
70      SYMBOL 249, 0, 0, 63, 63, 63, 63, 127, 0 : SYMBOL 250,
        127, 200, 135, 200, 127, 0, 0, 0 : SYMBOL 251, 1, 7, 156
        , 240, 192, 248, 254, 0 : SYMBOL 252, 254, 19, 225, 19,
        254, 0, 0, 0
80      SYMBOL 253, 0, 0, 24, 60, 60, 24, 0, 0
90      EXPL$(1,1) = "" : EXPL$(1,2) = "." + CHR$(240) + "." :
        EXPL$(1,3) = ""
100     EXPL$(2,1) = "." + CHR$(241) + "." : EXPL$(2,2) = CHR$(
        242) + CHR$(9) + CHR$(244) : EXPL$(2,3) = "." + CHR$(243
        )+"."
110     EXPL$(3,1) = CHR$(245)+CHR$(9)+CHR$(247) : EXPL$(3,2) =
        "" : EXPL$(3,3) = CHR$(246)+CHR$(9)+CHR$(248)
120     EXPL$(4,1) = "" : EXPL$(4,2) = CHR$(9) + "." : EXPL$(4,
        3) = ""
130     EXPL$(5,1) = CHR$(9) + "." : EXPL$(5,2) = "." + CHR$(9)
        + "." : EXPL$(5,3) = CHR$(9) + "."
140     EXPL$(6,1) = "." + CHR$(9) + "." : EXPL$(6,2) = "" : EX
        PL$(6,3) = EXPL$(6,1)
150     TANK$ = CHR$(232)+CHR$(234)+CHR$(10)+STRING$(2,8)+CHR$(
        233)+CHR$(235)
170     MSG$(1) = "Ready.to.fire" : MSG$(2) = "Press.a.key.with
        .a.number.on.it"
175     MSG$(3) = "Waiting.for.second.digit" : MSG$(4) = "Name.
        your.shell.(0.-.9)" : MSG$(5) = "Prepare.to.FIRE.!"
177     MSG$(6) = "PRESS.THE.SPACE.BAR,.SILLY.!" : MSG$(7) = ".
        ..F...I...R...E...!!!"
179     MSG$(8) = "...F...L...A...R...E" : MSG$(9) = "ENEMY.HAS
        .OVERRUN.YOUR.POSITION.!!"
```

```
┌─────────────────────────────────────────────────────────┐
│                                                         │
│              New round of game                          │
│                                                         │
└─────────────────────────────────────────────────────────┘
```

```
180     :
190     FOR I=1 TO 4 : TSPEED(I) = -INT(RND(1)*2) - 1 : TANKX(I
        ) = 34 : EXIST(I) = 1 : NEXT
200     TANKY(1) = INT(RND(1)*5) + 6 : TANKY(2) = TANKY(1) + 3
210     TANKY(3) = TANKY(2) + 3 : TANKY(4) = TANKY(3) + 3
220     NROUNDS = NROUNDS + 1
230     PAPER 0 : BORDER 0 : CLS
240     PEN 1 : LOCATE 1, 10 : PRINT CHR$(249)+CHR$(251)+CHR$(1
```

```
         0)+STRING$(2,8)+CHR$(250)+CHR$(252)
250      FOR I=1 TO 6 : FOR J=12 TO 20 : LOCATE I, J : PRINT CHR
         $(143) : NEXT : NEXT
260      MOVE 0, 78 : DRAWR 640, 0
270      MOVE 0, 226 : DRAWR 30, 0 : DRAWR 10, -3
280      PEN 2 : LOCATE 3, 22 : PRINT "Angle : " : LOCATE 16, 22
          : PRINT "Shell : "
290      LOCATE 29, 22 : PRINT "SCORE : "
300      LOCATE 35, 22 : PEN 2 : PRINT SCORE
```

```
┌─────────────────────────────────────────────┐
│                   Editor                     │
└─────────────────────────────────────────────┘
```

```
310      :
320      MN = 1 : GOSUB 5000
330      D1$ = INKEY$ : IF D1$ = "" THEN GOSUB 3000 : GOTO 330
340      IF D1$ = "." THEN FIRE = 0 : MN = 8 : GOSUB 5000 :  GOT
         O 500
350      IF D1$ < "0" OR D1$ > "8" THEN MN = 2 : GOSUB 5000 : GO
         TO 330
360      MN = 3 : GOSUB 5000
365      PEN 2 : LOCATE 9, 22 : PRINT VAL(D1$)
370      D2$ = INKEY$ : IF D2$ = "" THEN GOSUB 3000 : GOTO 370
380      IF D2$ < "0" OR D2$ > "9" THEN MN = 2 : GOSUB 5000 : GO
         TO 370
390      ANGLE = 10 * VAL(D1$) + VAL(D2$)
400      PEN 2 : LOCATE 11, 22 : PRINT USING "#"; VAL(D2$)
410      MN = 4 : GOSUB 5000
420      D1$ = INKEY$ : IF D1$ = "" THEN GOSUB 3000 : GOTO 420
430      IF D1$ < "0" OR D1$ > "9" THEN MN = 2 : GOSUB 5000 : GO
         TO 420
440      PEN 2 : LOCATE 22, 22 : PRINT VAL(D1$);
450      SHELL = VAL(D1$) : MN = 5 : GOSUB 5000
460      D1$ = INKEY$ : IF D1$ = "" THEN GOSUB 3000 : GOTO 460
470      IF D1$ <> "." THEN MN = 6 : GOSUB 5000 : GOTO 460
480      MN = 7 : GOSUB 5000 : FIRE = 1
```

```
┌─────────────────────────────────────────────┐
│               Main program loop              │
└─────────────────────────────────────────────┘
```

```
490      :
500      SOUND 1, 0, 10, 11, 1, 1, 15
505      GOSUB 1000
510      GOSUB 3000
520      IF BOMBX = 0 THEN 320 ELSE 505
```

```
┌─────────────────────────────────────────────┐
│                  Move bomb                   │
└─────────────────────────────────────────────┘
```

```
990      :
1000     IF (BOMBX <> 0) THEN 1010 ELSE BOMBX = 3 : BOMBY = 8 :
         T = 0 : LOCATE 3, 8 : PEN 3 : PRINT CHR$(253) : CU = 32
1005     IF FIRE = 0 THEN ANGLE = 45 : SHELL = 4
1007     XIV = SHELL * COS(ANGLE) / 3 : YIV = SHELL * SIN(ANGLE)
         / 3
1010     PEN 1 : IF (BOMBX < 39) AND (BOMBY > 0 AND BOMBY < 23)
         THEN LOCATE BOMBX, BOMBY : PRINT CHR$(CU)
1020     T = T + 2
1030     IF (T = 20) AND (FIRE = 0) THEN 2000
1040     BOMBX = INT(3 + T * XIV)
```

68

```
1050   BOMBY = INT(8 - Γ * YIV + 0.049 * 1 * Γ)
1060   IF BOMBY < 1 THEN RETURN
1065   IF BOMBY > 19 THEN BOMBY = 19 : IF BOMBX > 34 THEN BOMB
       X = 34 : GOTO 2000 ELSE GOTO 2000
1070   IF BOMBX > 34 THEN BOMBX = 34 : IF BOMBY < 2 OR BOMBY >
        22 THEN BOMBX = 0 : RETURN ELSE GOSUB 2000 : RETURN
1080   IF TEST(BOMBX * 16 - 8, 400 - BOMBY * 16) = 1 THEN CU =
        143 ELSE CU = 32
1090   HIT = 0 : FOR TK=1 TO 4 : IF EXIST(TK) = 0 THEN 1110 EL
       SE T1 = BOMBX - TANKX(TK) : T2 = BOMBY - TANKY(TK)
1100   IF (T1 = 0 OR T1 = 1) AND (T2 = 0 OR T2 = 1) THEN HIT =
        TK
1110   NEXT
1120   IF HIT = 0 THEN LOCATE BOMBX, BOMBY : PEN 3 : PRINT CHR
       $(253) : RETURN
1130   GOTO 4000
```

┌─────────────────────────────────────┐
│   │
│   Explosion   │
│   │
└─────────────────────────────────────┘

```
1140   :
2000   PEN 3 : FOR I=1 TO 6
2010   LOCATE BOMBX-1, BOMBY-1
2020   PRINT EXPL$(I,1)
2022   LOCATE BOMBX-1, BOMBY
2024   PRINT EXPL$(I,2)
2026   LOCATE BOMBX-1, BOMBY+1
2028   PRINT EXPL$(I,3)
2030   SOUND 1, 0, 15, 15, 1, 1, 31
2035   IF HIT <> 0 THEN 2050
2040   IF INT(I/2) <> I/2 THEN INK 0, 24 : TCOL = 1 : GOSUB 35
       00 ELSE INK 0, 0 : TCOL = 0 : GOSUB 3500
2050   NEXT
2055   IF BOMBX < 8 THEN FOR I=1 TO 6 : FOR J=12 TO 20 : PEN 1
        : LOCATE I, J : PRINT CHR$(143) : NEXT : NEXT
2060   BOMBX = 0 : LOCATE 9, 22 : PRINT "▲▲▲" : LOCATE 22, 22
       : PRINT "▲▲" : RETURN
```

┌─────────────────────────────────────┐
│   │
│   Move and display tanks   │
│   │
└─────────────────────────────────────┘

```
2990   :
3000   IF RND(1) > NROUNDS/100 THEN RETURN
3010   LT = LT + 1 : IF LT = 5 THEN LT = 1
3020   IF EXIST(LT) = 0 THEN 3010
3030   TANKX(LT) = TANKX(LT) + TSPEED(LT)
3040   IF TANKX(LT) <= 6 THEN TCOL = 3 : GOSUB 3500 : GOTO 900
       0
3050   RETURN
3500   FOR TK=1 TO 4
3510   IF EXIST(TK) = 0 THEN 3530 ELSE LOCATE TANKX(TK), TANKY
       (TK) : PEN TCOL
3520   PRINT TANK$
3530   NEXT : RETURN
```

┌─────────────────────────────────────┐
│   │
│   Hit tanks   │
│   │
└─────────────────────────────────────┘

```
3990   :
4000   EXIST(HIT) = 0 : SCORE = SCORE + 50 : LOCATE 35, 22 : P
       EN 2 : PRINT SCORE
```

```
4010    K = BOMBX : GOSUB 2000 : BOMBX = K : GOSUB 2000 : BOMBX
        = K : GOSUB 2000
4020    HIT = 0 : BOMBX = K : GOSUB 2000
4030    IF EXIST(1) = 0 THEN IF EXIST(2) = 0 THEN IF EXIST(3) =
        0 THEN IF EXIST(4) = 0 THEN 190
4040    RETURN
```

```
┌─────────────────────────────────────────────────────────┐
│                                                         │
│         Display message                                 │
│                                                         │
└─────────────────────────────────────────────────────────┘
```

```
4990    :
5000    LOCATE 4, 24 : PEN 3 : PRINT SPACE$(34)
5010    LOCATE 4, 24 : PRINT MSG$(MN)
5020    RETURN
```

```
┌─────────────────────────────────────────────────────────┐
│                                                         │
│         Game over                                       │
│                                                         │
└─────────────────────────────────────────────────────────┘
```

```
8990    :
9000    MN = 9 : GOSUB 5000 : FOR I=1 TO 1000 STEP 10 : SOUND 1
        , I, 8, 15 : NEXT
9010    FOR I=1 TO 22 : PRINT : NEXT
9020    PRINT "▲▲▲▲▲▲PRESS▲A▲KEY▲FOR▲ANOTHER▲TRY"
9030    IF INKEY$<>"" THEN 9030
9040    IF INKEY$="" THEN 9040 ELSE RUN
```

ChexSum Tables

10	=	1530	370	=	2613	2022	=	1540
20	=	3886	380	=	3292	2024	=	1022
30	=	4396	390	=	2491	2026	=	1799
40	=	4164	400	=	1865	2028	=	1023
50	=	3655	410	=	930	2030	=	695
60	=	3762	420	=	2661	2035	=	1158
70	=	7174	430	=	3340	2040	=	5004
80	=	1193	440	=	1503	2050	=	208
90	=	3947	450	=	2301	2055	=	5272
100	=	7174	460	=	2701	2060	=	2372
110	=	6735	470	=	2442	2990	=	0
120	=	3370	480	=	1623	3000	=	2417
130	=	4993	490	=	0	3010	=	2707
140	=	4256	500	=	670	3020	=	1900
150	=	5197	505	=	456	3030	=	3285
170	=	5553	510	=	416	3040	=	3076
175	=	7761	520	=	1821	3050	=	201
177	=	4248	990	=	0	3500	=	1062
179	=	4741	1000	=	5790	3510	=	4830
180	=	0	1005	=	2764	3520	=	656
190	=	6190	1007	=	5008	3530	=	378
200	=	3922	1010	=	6052	3990	=	0
210	=	3521	1020	=	949	4000	=	4177
220	=	1886	1030	=	2410	4010	=	4229
230	=	548	1040	=	2224	4020	=	2033
240	=	5347	1050	=	3970	4030	=	5742
250	=	3768	1060	=	1467	4040	=	201
260	=	763	1065	=	5338	4990	=	0
270	=	1333	1070	=	6398	5000	=	1190
280	=	2570	1080	=	5015	5010	=	1275
290	=	1076	1090	=	8033	5020	=	201
300	=	1333	1100	=	4621	8990	=	0
310	=	0	1110	=	176	9000	=	3321
320	=	927	1120	=	3675	9010	=	1374
330	=	2571	1130	=	397	9020	=	2353
340	=	3170	1140	=	0	9030	=	1259
350	=	3249	2000	=	1215	9040	=	1652
360	=	929	2010	=	1800			
365	=	1388	2020	=	1021	TOTAL	=	301283

COSMIC CRITTERS

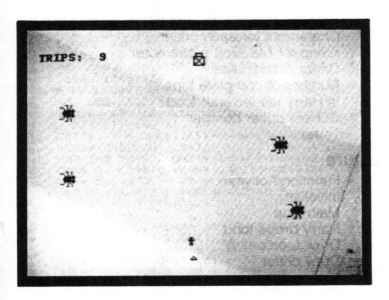

CLASSIFICATION: Evasion game

Use the keys shown below to help Harry the Hungry, Hairy Mountain Man leave his camp at the bottom of the screen, manoeuvre through the dangerous cosmic critters and to the stolen food at the top of the screen.

Harry must then return to his camp and repeat this process as many times as possible!

To move use: 'A' up, 'Z' down, 'comma' left, and 'period' right.

PROGRAMMING SUGGESTIONS

The game be altered to make the closest critter move towards Harry more often or the speed of the critters could be altered, as could Harry's speed.

PROGRAM
Variables

DIR(5)	Directions for each critter
CC	Closest critter (1-5)
HCOL, HROW	Harry's column and row
HSPX, HSPY	Harry's speed in each direction
CRIT$(5)	Characters for each critter
BLANK$	String for blanking a character
CRITX(5), CRITY(5)	Critter coordinates
NT	Number of complete trips
LOADED	Is Harry loaded with food?
CT	Current critter number
I	Temp

Program Structure

Lines	Function/Activity
30 — 130	Initialise
160 — 300	Main loop
500 — 530	Harry drops food
1000 — 1090	Draw food/camp
2000 — 2020	Draw critter
3000 — 3080	Move critter
4000 — 4040	Read keyboard
9000 — 9070	Game over

```
                    ┌────────────────────────────────────────┐
                    │                                        │
                    │        Initialise game                 │
                    │                                        │
                    └────────────────────────────────────────┘

30    MODE 1 : INK 0,13 : INK 1,0 : INK 2,3 : INK 3,19 : PAPE
      R 0 : BORDER 13 : CLS
40    SYMBOL 240, 3, 0, 240, 8, 4, 7, 15, 31 : SYMBOL 241, 31
      , 15, 15, 4, 8, 240, 0, 3 : SYMBOL 242, 136, 136, 136, 1
      44, 166, 255, 255, 246 : SYMBOL 243, 246, 255, 255, 166,
       144, 136, 136, 136
50    SYMBOL 244, 68, 34, 17, 17, 17, 63, 127, 255 : SYMBOL 2
      45, 255, 127, 63, 17, 17, 17, 34, 68 : SYMBOL 246, 64, 3
      2, 16, 17, 17, 250, 252, 252 : SYMBOL 247, 252, 252, 250
      , 17, 17, 16, 32, 64
60    CRIT$(1) = CHR$(244)+CHR$(246)+CHR$(10)+CHR$(8)+CHR$(8)
      +CHR$(245)+CHR$(247)
70    FOR I=2 TO 5 : CRIT$(I) = CHR$(240)+CHR$(242)+CHR$(10)+
      CHR$(8)+CHR$(8)+CHR$(241)+CHR$(243) : NEXT I
80    CC = 5 : HCOL = 20 : HROW = 24 : HSPX = 0 : HSPY = -1 :
       CRCOL(1) = 3 : FOR I = 2 TO 5 : CRCOL(I) = 2 : NEXT
90    DIR(1) = -3 : DIR(2) = 2 : DIR(3) = -2 : DIR(4) = 1 : D
      IR(5) = -1
100   BLANK$ = " ▲"+CHR$(10)+CHR$(8)+CHR$(8)+" ▲"
110   CRITX(1) = 34 : CRITY(1) = 3 : CRITX(2) = 2 : CRITY(2)
      = 7 : CRITX(3) = 32 : CRITY(3) = 11 : CRITX(4) = 3 : CRI
      TY(4) = 15 : CRITX(5) = 33 : CRITY(5) = 19
120   NT = -1 : GOSUB 500 : LOADED = 1 : GOSUB 1000 : LOADED
      = 0
125   EVERY 30, 1 GOSUB 4000
130   FOR CT=1 TO 5 : GOSUB 2000 : NEXT

                    ┌────────────────────────────────────────┐
                    │                                        │
                    │        Main program loop               │
                    │                                        │
                    └────────────────────────────────────────┘

140   :
160   FOR CT = 1 TO 5
170   GOSUB 3000
180   NEXT
190   LOCATE HCOL, HROW : PRINT " ▲"
200   HCOL = HCOL + HSPX : HROW = HROW + HSPY : CC = INT(ABS(
      (HROW - 2)/4)) + 1
205   CC = CC + (CC = 6)
210   IF HCOL < 1 THEN HCOL = 35
220   IF HCOL > 35 THEN HCOL = 1
230   IF HROW < 2 THEN HROW = 2
240   IF HROW > 24 THEN HROW = 24
250   PEN 1 : LOCATE HCOL, HROW : PRINT CHR$(248)
260   T1 = CRITY(CC) - HROW : T2 = CRITX(CC) - HCOL
270   IF (T1=-1 OR T1 = 0) AND (T2=-1 OR T2=0) THEN 9000
280   IF (LOADED = 0) AND HCOL = 21 AND HROW = 2 THEN GOSUB 1
      000 : LOADED = 1 : PRINT CHR$(7)
290   IF LOADED AND (HCOL = 20) AND (HROW = 24) THEN GOSUB 50
      0
300   GOTO 160
```

```
400     :
500     GOSUB 1000
510     LOADED = 0 : NT = NT + 1
515     LOCATE 1, 1 : PEN 1 : PRINT "TRIPS :_";NT
520     FOR I=1 TO 1000 STEP 20 : SOUND 1, I, 2, 15, 1, 1, 0 :
        NEXT
530     RETURN
```

```
540     :
1000    IF LOADED THEN T = 1 ELSE T = 0
1010    MOVE 320, 390 : DRAWR 0, -16, T
1020    DRAWR 20, 0, T : DRAWR 0, 16, T
1030    DRAWR -20, 0, T : DRAWR 20, -16, T
1040    MOVER 0, 16 : DRAWR -20, -16, T
1050    MOVER 4, 16 : DRAWR 0, 6, T
1060    DRAWR 12, 0, T : DRAWR 0, -4, T
1070    MOVE 308, 4 : DRAWR 12, 0, 1
1080    DRAWR -6, 6, 1 : DRAWR -6, -6, 1
1090    RETURN
```

```
1100    :
2000    LOCATE CRITX(CT), CRITY(CT)
2010    PEN CRCOL(CT) : PRINT CRIT$(CT)
2020    RETURN
```

```
2030    :
3000    LOCATE CRITX(CT), CRITY(CT) : PRINT BLANK$ : CRITX(CT)
        = CRITX(CT) + DIR(CT)
3010    IF CRITX(CT) <= 1 THEN CRITX(CT) = 1 : DIR(CT) = -DIR(C
        T)
3020    IF CRITX(CT) >= 35 THEN CRITX(CT) = 34 : DIR(CT) = -DIR
        (CT)
3030    GOSUB 2000
3040    IF CC <> CT THEN RETURN
3050    IF RND(1) < 0.4- NT/10 THEN RETURN
3060    IF CRITX(CT) > HCOL THEN DIR(CT) = -ABS(DIR(CT)) : RETU
        RN
3070    DIR(CT) = ABS(DIR(CT))
3080    RETURN
```

```
3090    :
4000    IF INKEY(39) >= 0 THEN HSPX = -1 : HSPY = 0 : RETURN
4010    IF INKEY(31) >= 0 THEN HSPX = 1 : HSPY = 0 : RETURN
```

```
4020   IF INKEY(69) >= 0 THEN HSPY = -1 : HSPX = 0 : RETURN
4030   IF INKEY(71) >= 0 THEN HSPY = 1 : HSPX = 0 : RETURN
4040   RETURN
```

```
┌─────────────────────────────────────────────────────┐
│                                                       │
│        Game over                                      │
│                                                       │
└─────────────────────────────────────────────────────┘
```

```
4050   :
9000   LOCATE 5, 24 : PEN 1 : PRINT "POOR.HARRY.!!"
9010   ENT 1, 45, 21,11, 10, -1, 1, 10, 1, 1, 5, -1, 1 : FOR C
       T=1 TO 5 : GOSUB 2000 : NEXT
9020   DEG : FOR I=0 TO 180 STEP 6 : INK 2, RND(1)*26 : INK 3,
       RND(1)*26
9030   SOUND 1, 1000*SIN(I), 15, 15, 0, 1
9040   NEXT
9050   LOCATE 5, 24 : PEN 1 : PRINT "PRESS.A.KEY.FOR.ANOTHER.G
       AME"
9060   IF INKEY$<>"" THEN 9060
9070   IF INKEY$="" THEN 9070 ELSE RUN
```

ChexSum Tables

30 =	1924	280 =	5317			3010 =	4779
40 =	7706	290 =	3782			3020 =	4993
50 =	7725	300 =	382			3030 =	436
60 =	5770	400 =	0			3040 =	1502
70 =	7355	500 =	456			3050 =	3031
80 =	6770	510 =	1924			3060 =	4569
90 =	4323	515 =	1656			3070 =	2049
100 =	3066	520 =	2565			3080 =	201
110 =	10251	530 =	201			3090 =	0
120 =	3367	540 =	0			4000 =	3040
125 =	731	1000 =	2199			4010 =	2787
130 =	1669	1010 =	1297			4020 =	3070
140 =	0	1020 =	1103			4030 =	2827
160 =	1055	1030 =	1592			4040 =	201
170 =	416	1040 =	1345			4050 =	0
180 =	176	1050 =	839			9000 =	1680
190 =	1465	1060 =	1317			9010 =	3219
200 =	6214	1070 =	683			9020 =	3567
205 =	1648	1080 =	1320			9030 =	1658
210 =	1917	1090 =	201			9040 =	176
220 =	1914	1100 =	0			9050 =	2737
230 =	1926	2000 =	2062			9060 =	1289
240 =	1989	2010 =	2138			9070 =	1682
250 =	2212	2020 =	201				
260 =	4197	2030 =	0				
270 =	4307	3000 =	5814			TOTAL =	177980

AMSTRADOIDS

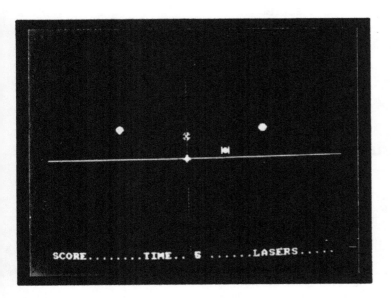

SCORE........TIME... 6 ......LASERS.....

CLASSIFICATION: Time-limit game

You have a limited amount laser power to wipe stop the assorted nasties overunning your base. You also have another problem a limited amount of time. To shoot the enemy you wait until they are in your line of fire. Using a combination of the keys given below, you can conserve your laser power and shoot as many aliens as possible.

Use 'space' to fire in all directions. Use 'Z' to fire horizontally and 'backslash' to fire vertically.

PROGRAMMING SUGGESTIONS

The time and number of shots could be altered to make the game easier or harder. There could be some random harmless obstacles placed on the screen as decoys to infuriate the player. A final suggestion would be to change the colours of the display as the time increases and have a warning noise to indicate impending doom.

PROGRAM
Variables

C, T	Temps
LASERS	Number of shots remaining
SCORE	Player's score
S$	Space
AX(4), AY(4)	Alien coordinates
AXV(4), AYV(4)	Speeds
AC(4)	Alien characters
NOW	Time at gate start
ELAPSED	Time elapsed
WEAPON	Firing all drns, vert. or horiz. (1, 2, 3 respectively)

Program Structure

Lines	Function/Activity
10	Start game
30	Calculate time elapsed
50	Call initialise
70 — 210	Main loop
230 — 390	Firing/align hit routine
410 — 660	Introduction
680 — 820	Game over
840 — 850	Alternate alien's shape

```
┌────────────────────────────────────────────┐
│                                            │
│          Start Game                        │
│                                            │
└────────────────────────────────────────────┘
```

```
10      GOTO 50
```

```
┌────────────────────────────────────────────┐
│                                            │
│          Calculate time elapsed            │
│                                            │
└────────────────────────────────────────────┘
```

```
20      :
30      DI : LOCATE 20,25 : ELAPSED =INT(( TIME - NOW)/100) : P
        RINT ELAPSED ; : EI :   RETURN
```

```
┌────────────────────────────────────────────┐
│                                            │
│          Call Initialise routine           │
│                                            │
└────────────────────────────────────────────┘
```

```
40      :
50      GOSUB 410
```

```
┌────────────────────────────────────────────┐
│                                            │
│          Main program loop                 │
│                                            │
└────────────────────────────────────────────┘
```

```
60      :
70      DI : FOR T = 1 TO 4 : LOCATE AX(T), AY(T) : PRINT "▲"
80      IF ELAPSED >210 THEN FOR a = 200 TO 500 : SOUND 1,a,1 :
        NEXT : PEN 3 : LOCATE 1,8 : PRINT "Your time ran out !!
        " : GOTO 730
90      AX(T) = AX(T) + AXV(T) : AY(T) = AY(T) + AYV(T)
100     IF AX(T) > 39 THEN AX(T) = 2
110     IF AX(T) < 2 THEN AX(T) = 38
120     IF AY(T) > 23 THEN AY(T) = 2
130     IF AY(T) < 2 THEN AY(T) = 23
140     LOCATE AX(T), AY(T) : PRINT CHR$( AC(T))
150     IF AX(T) = 20 AND AY(T) = 12 THEN GOTO 680
160     NEXT : EI
170     IF RND(1) > 0.7 THEN SOUND 1,RND(1) * 300 + 300,10
180     IF INKEY(47) > -1 THEN LASERS = LASERS - 2 : WEAPON = 1
        : GOSUB 230 : GOTO 70
190     IF INKEY(22) > -1 THEN LASERS = LASERS - 1 : WEAPON = 2
        : GOSUB 230 : GOTO 70
200     IF INKEY(71) > -1 THEN LASERS = LASERS - 1 : WEAPON = 3
        : GOSUB 230
210     GOTO 70
```

```
┌────────────────────────────────────────────┐
│                                            │
│          Firing and alien hit routine      │
│                                            │
└────────────────────────────────────────────┘
```

```
220     :
230     DI : SOUND 1, 1000, 15, 15, 0, 0, 0
240     IF WEAPON = 1 OR WEAPON = 3 THEN MOVE 304, 216 : DRAWR
        -304, 0, 3 : MOVE 320, 216 : DRAWR 320, 0, 3
250     IF WEAPON = 1 OR WEAPON = 2 THEN MOVE 312, 224 : DRAWR
        0, 184, 3 : MOVE 312, 208 : DRAWR 0, -200, 3
260     FOR T = 1 TO 4
270     IF WEAPON = 1 THEN IF AX(T) = 20 AND AY(T) = 12 THEN SC
        ORE = SCORE + 1000
```

81

```
280    IF WEAPON = 1 THEN IF AX(T) = 20 OR AY(T) = 12 THEN SCO
       RE = SCORE + 250 : GOTO 320
290    IF WEAPON = 2 THEN IF AX(T) = 20 THEN SCORE = SCORE + 2
       50 : GOTO 320
300    IF WEAPON = 3 THEN IF AY(T) = 12 THEN SCORE = SCORE + 2
       50 : GOTO 320
310    GOTO 330
320    LOCATE AX(T), AY(T) : PRINT CHR$(238); : AX(T) = CINT(
       RND(1) * 36) + 2 : AY(T) = CINT( RND(1) * 18) + 2 : SOUN
       D 1, 200, 15, 15, 0, 0, 0 : SOUND 1, 250, 15, 15, 1, 1,
       1
330    PRINT CHR$(8); S$ ;
340    NEXT
350    MOVE 304, 216 : DRAWR -304, 0, 0 : MOVE 320, 216 : DRAW
       R 320, 0, 0
360    MOVE 312, 224 : DRAWR 0, 184, 0 : MOVE 312, 208 : DRAWR
       0, -200, 0
370    LOCATE 7, 25 : PRINT SCORE ;
380    LOCATE 34, 25 : PRINT LASERS; : IF LASERS <= 0 THEN GOT
       O 680
390    EI : RETURN
```

Introduction and Initialise

```
400    :
410    MODE 0 : PEN 2 : LOCATE 5, 6 : PRINT "AMSTRADOIDS"
420    FOR T = 1 TO 100 : SOUND 2, T * 30, 5, 13, 1, 1, 1 : PE
       N 3 : LOCATE 10, 12
430    PRINT CHR$ (238) : PEN 1 :  LOCATE 10, 12 : PRINT "▲" :
       NEXT T
440    SOUND 1, 500, 100, 15, 1, 1, 1 : FOR T = 0 TO 64 STEP 6
       : C = ROUND( RND(1) * 14) + 1 : GOSUB 470 : NEXT T
450    C = 0 : FOR T = 0 TO 64 STEP 6 : GOSUB 470 : NEXT T
460    GOTO 480
470    PLOT 312 + T, 216, C : PLOT 312 + T, 216 + T, C : PLOT
       312 + T, 216 - T, C : PLOT 312, 216 + T, C : PLOT 312, 2
       16 - T, C : PLOT 312 - T, 216 - T, C : PLOT 312 - T, 216,
       C : PLOT 312 - T, 216 + T, C : RETURN
480    A$ = INKEY$
490    LOCATE 1,15 : PEN INT(RND(1) * 4 + 1)
500    PRINT "Hit▪a▪key▪to▪start▪▪mission"
510    IF A$ = "" THEN 480
520    SCORE = 0 : LASERS = 50
530    S$ = "▪"
540    MODE 1 : INK 0, 0 : INK 1, 18 : INK 2, 24 : INK 3, 6 :
       PAPER 0 : PEN 1 : BORDER 0
550    LOCATE 1, 25 : PRINT "SCORE........TIME...........LASER
       S....."
560    DIM AX(4), AY(4), AXV(4), AYV(4) : FOR T = 1 TO 4
570    AX(T) = CINT( RND(1) * 36) + 2 : AY(T) = CINT( RND(1) *
       18) + 2
580    AXV(T) = CINT( RND(1) * 3) - 2 : AYV(T) = CINT( RND(1)
       * 3) - 2
590    IF AXV(T) = 0 OR AYV(T) = 0 THEN GOTO 570
600    NEXT
610    DIM AC(4) : AC(1) = 181 : AC(2) = 224 : AC(3) = 231 : A
       C(4) = 202
620    SYMBOL AFTER 181 : SYMBOL 224, 24, 126, 213, 171, 255,
       66, 60, 24 : SYMBOL 181, 36, 66, 165, 24, 24, 165, 66, 3
       6 : SYMBOL 231, 129, 153, 165, 219, 255, 165, 153, 129
630    SYMBOL 240, 24, 24, 60, 255, 255, 60, 24, 24 : LOCATE 2
       0, 12 : PEN 1 : PRINT CHR$(240) : PEN 2
```

82

```
640    NOW = TIME
650    EVERY 10, 1   GOSUB 30 : EVERY 40, 2 GOSUB 840
660    RETURN
```

```
┌────────────────────────────────────────────────────┐
│                                                      │
│          Game over                                   │
│                                                      │
└────────────────────────────────────────────────────┘
```

```
670    :
680    V = REMAIN (1) : V = REMAIN (2) : LOCATE 20, 12 : PRINT
       CHR$ (238) : SOUND 0, 200, 100, 15, 1, 1, 1 : SOUND 1,
       250, 100, 15, 1, 1, 1 : SOUND 2, 300, 100, 15, 1, 1 ,1
690    FOR T = 1 TO 100 : PEN 3 : LOCATE 20, 12 : PRINT CHR$ (
       238) : PEN 1 :  LOCATE 20, 12 : PRINT "▲" : NEXT T
700    C = 3 : INK 3, 24, 6 : SPEED INK 10, 15 : FOR N = 1 TO
       2 : FOR T = 0 TO 64 STEP 6
710    PLOT 312 + T, 216, C : PLOT 312 + T, 216 + T, C : PLOT
       312 + T, 216 - T, C : PLOT 312, 216 + T, C : PLOT 312, 2
       16 - T, C : PLOT 312 - T, 216 - T, C : PLOT 312 - T, 216,
       C : PLOT 312 - T, 216 + T, C
720    NEXT T : C = 0 : NEXT N : INK 3, 6
730    LOCATE 1,10 : PEN 1 : PRINT "another▲mission?▲(y=yes,n=
       no)"
740    A$ = INKEY$
750    LOCATE 14,1 : PEN INT(RND(1) * 4 + 1) : PRINT "AMSTRADO
       IDS"
760    IF A$ = "" THEN 740
770    IF A$ = "Y" OR A$ = "y" THEN RUN
780    IF A$ = "N" OR A$ = "n" THEN 800
790    GOTO 740
800    LOCATE 1,8 : PRINT SPACE$(20)
810    LOCATE 1,10 : PEN 1 : PRINT "bye▲for▲now" : SPACE$(20)
820    END
```

```
┌────────────────────────────────────────────────────┐
│                                                      │
│          Alternate Alien's shape                     │
│                                                      │
└────────────────────────────────────────────────────┘
```

```
830    :
840    IF C1=1 THEN C1=0 : SYMBOL 202, 0, 60, 126, 143, 255, 2
       41, 126, 60 : RETURN
850    C1=1 : SYMBOL 202, 0, 60, 126, 241, 255, 143, 126, 60 :
       RETURN
```

ChexSum Tables

10	=	272	310	=	297	610	=	3931
20	=	0	320	=	8459	620	=	6581
30	=	4596	330	=	980	630	=	3409
40	=	0	340	=	208	640	=	949
50	=	376	350	=	2124	650	=	1204
60	=	0	360	=	2424	660	=	201
70	=	2978	370	=	1152	670	=	0
80	=	6825	380	=	3201	680	=	5705
90	=	4742	390	=	422	690	=	3838
100	=	2249	400	=	0	700	=	3736
110	=	2251	410	=	1859	710	=	12361
120	=	2235	420	=	2794	720	=	1599
130	=	2238	430	=	2168	730	=	3508
140	=	2588	440	=	5109	740	=	737
150	=	2959	450	=	2704	750	=	2929
160	=	397	460	=	447	760	=	1255
170	=	2939	470	=	12563	770	=	2226
180	=	4705	480	=	789	780	=	2067
190	=	4680	490	=	1811	790	=	452
200	=	4437	500	=	2757	800	=	909
210	=	292	510	=	1250	810	=	2399
220	=	0	520	=	1720	820	=	152
230	=	1118	530	=	553	830	=	0
240	=	4646	540	=	2041	840	=	3734
250	=	4945	550	=	2847	850	=	2732
260	=	987	560	=	3045			
270	=	5698	570	=	4316			
280	=	6002	580	=	4420	TOTAL	=	227013
290	=	4810	590	=	2969			
300	=	4804	600	=	176			

84

MIDGET MONSTER TRAMP

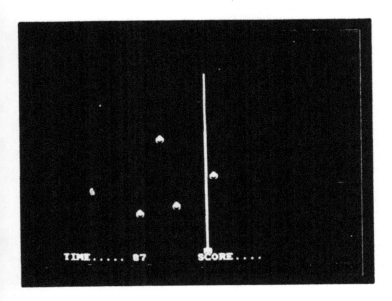

CLASSIFICATION: Time-limit game

This is a simple but effective version of space invaders. The aliens advance upon you in a random fashion and you must shoot as many as possible within the time limit.

Use 'Space' to fire, 'comma' to move left, and 'period' to move right.

PROGRAMMING SUGGESTIONS

The game could be updated to give the player more men, and make the aliens travel slower, but thicker on the ground.

PROGRAM
Variables

TIMER	Time remaining in seconds
SCORE	Player's score
SHIP	Ship's column
XSHIP(4), YSHIP(4)	Coordinates of alien ships (col, row)
SHIP$	Characters to print when ship is moved
FLAG	One second has passed

Program Structure

Lines	Function/Activity
10 — 70	Call initialise screen, initialise variables
80 — 240	Main loop
250 — 310	Firing routine·
320 — 340	Interrupt routine
350 — 360	Break routine
370 — 410	Game over
420 — 580	Front screen

```
                    +------------------------------------+
                    | Initialise screen and variables    |
                    +------------------------------------+

20      GOSUB 430
30      MODE 1 : BORDER 0 : INK 0, 0 : INK 1, 18 : INK 2, 24 :
        INK 3, 6, 24 : SPEED INK 3, 1 : PAPER 0 : PEN 1 : SPEED
        KEY 1, 1 : ON BREAK GOSUB 360 : EVERY 50 GOSUB 330
40      TIMER = 100 : SCORE = 0 : SHIP = 20 : DIM XSHIP (4), YS
        HIP (4) : FOR T = 1 TO 4 : XSHIP (T) = CINT (RND (1) * 3
        6) + 2 : YSHIP (T) = CINT (RND (1) * 10) + 1 : NEXT T
50      SHIP$ = "▲" + CHR$ (240) + "▲"
60      FLAG = 0 : SYMBOL 240, 24, 24, 189, 189, 255, 187, 153,
          129 : SYMBOL 241, 24, 60, 90, 219, 255, 153, 129, 66
70      LOCATE 1, 25 : PRINT "TIME.....▲▲▲▲▲▲▲▲▲▲SCORE...."

                    +------------------------------------+
                    | Main program loop                  |
                    +------------------------------------+

80      :
90      LOCATE SHIP, 24
100     PEN 2
110     PRINT SHIP$
120     PEN 1
130     FOR T = 1 TO 4
140     LOCATE XSHIP (T), YSHIP (T) : PRINT "▲"
150     YSHIP (T) = YSHIP (T) + 1 : IF YSHIP (T) > 23 THEN YSHI
        P (T) = 1
160     XSHIP (T) = XSHIP (T) + CINT (RND (1) * 3) - 2 : IF XSH
        IP (T) > 39 OR XSHIP (T) < 2 THEN XSHIP (T) = CINT (RND
        (1) * 36) + 2 : YSHIP (T) = 1
170     LOCATE XSHIP (T), YSHIP (T) : PRINT CHR$ (241)
180     NEXT T
190     IF INKEY (47) > -1 THEN GOSUB 260
200     SHIP = SHIP + (INKEY (39) > -1) - (INKEY (31) > -1)
210     IF SHIP < 2 THEN SHIP =2
220     IF SHIP > 37 THEN SHIP =37
230     IF FLAG = 1 THEN TIMER = TIMER - 1 : LOCATE 10, 25 : PR
        INT TIMER : FLAG = 0 : IF TIMER = 0 THEN GOTO 380
240     GOTO 90

                    +------------------------------------+
                    | Firing                             |
                    +------------------------------------+

250     :
260     PEN 3 : FOR T = 23 TO 1 STEP -1 : LOCATE SHIP + 1, T :
        PRINT CHR$ (149) : NEXT T
270     ENV 1, 7, -1, 10, 8, -1, 40 : SOUND 2, 0, 25, 13, 1, 1,
        1
280     FOR T = 23 TO 1 STEP -1 : LOCATE SHIP + 1, T : PRINT "▲
        " : NEXT T : PEN 1
290     FOR T = 1 TO 4 : IF XSHIP (T) = SHIP + 1 THEN SOUND 1,
        250, 50, 15, 1, 1, 1 : SCORE = SCORE + 25 : LOCATE 30, 2
        5 : PRINT SCORE : XSHIP (T) = CINT (RND (1) * 36 ) + 2 :
         YSHIP (T) = 1
300     NEXT T
310     RETURN
```

87

```
320    :
330    FLAG = 1
340    RETURN
```

```
350    :
360    SPEED KEY 30,1 : STOP
```

```
370    :
380    MODE 0 : LOCATE 6, 7 : PRINT "TIME.UP!" : PRINT : PRINT
       "YOU.SHOT." : SCORE / 25 : PRINT ".,.MIDGET.MONSTERS" :
       PRINT
390    PRINT ".AND.YOU.SCORED" : PRINT SCORE ; ".POINTS"
400    FOR T = 1000 TO 0 STEP - 10 : SOUND 1, T, 5, 15, 0, 0,
       0 : NEXT T
410    A$ = INKEY$ : IF A$ = "" THEN GOTO 410 ELSE RUN
```

```
420    :
430    MODE 0
440    INK 14, 11 : INK 15, 23 : INK 3, 6
450    FOR T = 0 TO 640 STEP 64
460    FOR N = 0 TO 15
470    MOVE N * 4 + T, 0 : DRAWR 0, 400, N
480    NEXT N : NEXT T
490    LOCATE 8, 5 : PRINT "MIDGET"
500    LOCATE 8, 7 : PRINT "MONSTER"
510    LOCATE 8, 9 : PRINT "TRAMP"
520    LOCATE 8, 13 : PRINT"*******"
530    A$ = INKEY$ : IF A$ = "" THEN GOTO 530 ELSE FOR T = 1 T
       O 26 : LOCATE 1, 1 : PRINT CHR$ (11) : NEXT T
540    LOCATE 3, 1 : PRINT "'.'.,...LEFT" ; CHR$ (11) : CHR$
       (11) : LOCATE 3, 1 : PRINT "'.'.,...RIGHT" ; CHR$ (11)
       ; CHR$ (11) : LOCATE 3, 1 : PRINT "SPACE....FIRE"
550    FOR T = 1 TO 10 : LOCATE 1, 1 : PRINT CHR$ (11) : NEXT
       T
560    FOR T = 1 TO 100 : SOUND 1, T, 2, 10, 1, 1 , 1 : NEXT T
570    FOR T = 1 TO 15 : LOCATE 1, 1 : PRINT CHR$ (11) : NEXT
       T
580    RETURN
```

ChexSum Tables

20	=	396		220	=	1991		420	=	0
30	=	4249		230	=	6097		430	=	219
40	=	10368		240	=	312		440	=	916
50	=	2002		250	=	0		450	=	1507
60	=	4937		260	=	4158		460	=	1002
70	=	2019		270	=	1792		470	=	1890
80	=	0		280	=	3711		480	=	861
90	=	743		290	=	10561		490	=	1020
100	=	235		300	=	433		500	=	1132
110	=	662		310	=	201		510	=	970
120	=	234		320	=	0		520	=	859
130	=	987		330	=	677		530	=	4540
140	=	2320		340	=	201		540	=	6080
150	=	5035		350	=	0		550	=	2345
160	=	10335		360	=	754		560	=	2397
170	=	2857		370	=	0		570	=	2350
180	=	433		380	=	5080		580	=	201
190	=	1666		390	=	2744				
200	=	3660		400	=	3047				
210	=	1902		410	=	2516		TOTAL	=	127604

89

WEIRD INVADERS

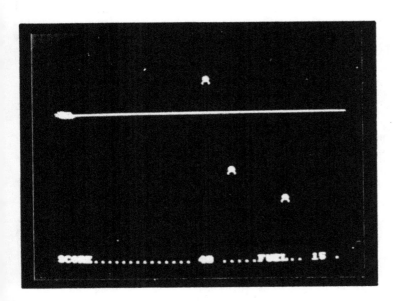

CLASSIFICATION: Shoot-up game

Guide your ship through this strange galaxy avoiding and shooting the monsters. You are doomed to run out of fuel and die, so you may as well shoot your way out.

Use 'A' to move up, 'Z' to move down, and 'space' to fire.

PROGRAM
Variables

HEIGHT	Row of ship
SCORE	Player's score
ALIENX(4), ALIENY(4)	Coordinates of aliens (col, row)
FUEL	Amount of fuel left
Y	Vertical coordinates of ship
T	Temp

Program Structure

Lines	Function/Activity
50 — 120	Initialise
160 — 270	Main loop
310 — 380	Firing routine
420 — 460	Game over

```
50      SYMBOL 240, 0, 9, 4, 81, 2, 40, 3, 0 : SYMBOL 241, 0, 2
        24, 127, 248, 120, 255, 127, 255 : SYMBOL 242, 0, 0, 224
        , 16, 8, 255, 255, 252 : SYMBOL 243, 60, 90, 126, 102, 6
        0, 66, 129, 129
60      HEIGHT = 12
70      SCORE = 0
80      DIM ALIENX(4), ALIENY(4) : FOR T = 1 TO 4 : ALIENX(T) =
        CINT( RND(1) * 20 + 18 ) : ALIENY(T) = CINT( RND(1) * 2
        0 +1) : NEXT T
90      MODE 1 : BORDER 0 : PAPER 0 : PEN 2 : INK 0, 0 : INK 1,
        18 : INK 2, 24 : INK 3, 7, 24 : SPEED INK 10, 5 : ENV 1
        , 7, -1, 10, 8, -1, 40
100     LOCATE 1, 25 : PRINT "SCORE.....................FUEL.
        ......"
110      FUEL = 50
120     LOCATE 1, HEIGHT : PEN 3 : PRINT CHR$(240); : PEN 1 : P
        RINT CHR$(241); CHR$(242) : PEN 2
```

```
130     :
160     FOR T = 1 TO 4
170     LOCATE ALIENX(T), ALIENY(T) : PRINT "."
180     ALIENX(T) = ALIENX(T) - 1 : IF ALIENX(T) < 3 THEN IF AL
        IENY(T) = HEIGHT THEN GOTO 420 ELSE ALIENX(T) = 39 : ALI
        ENY(T) = CINT( RND(1) * 20 + 1)
190     LOCATE ALIENX(T), ALIENY(T) : PRINT CHR$(243)
200     NEXT T
210     IF INKEY(69) > -1 THEN LOCATE 1, HEIGHT : PRINT "..." :
         HEIGHT = HEIGHT - 1 : LOCATE 1, HEIGHT : PEN 3 : PRINT
        CHR$(240); : PEN 1 : PRINT CHR$(241); CHR$(242) : PEN 2
220     IF HEIGHT < 2 THEN LOCATE 1, 1 : PRINT "..." : HEIGHT =
        23 : LOCATE 1, 23 : PEN 3 : PRINT CHR$(240); : PEN 1 :
        PRINT CHR$(241); CHR$(242) : PEN 2
230     IF INKEY(71) > -1 THEN LOCATE 1, HEIGHT : PRINT "..." :
         HEIGHT = HEIGHT + 1 : LOCATE 1, HEIGHT : PEN 3 : PRINT
        CHR$(240); : PEN 1 : PRINT CHR$(241); CHR$(242) : PEN 2
240     IF HEIGHT > 23 THEN LOCATE 1, 24 : PRINT "..." : HEIGHT
        = 2 : LOCATE 1, 2 : PEN 3 : PRINT CHR$(240); : PEN 1 :
        PRINT CHR$(241); CHR$(242) : PEN 2
250     IF INKEY(47) > -1 THEN GOSUB 310
260     FUEL = FUEL - 1 : LOCATE 35, 25 : PRINT FUEL : IF FUEL
        <= 1 THEN GOTO 420
270     GOTO 160
```

```
280     :
310     Y = ( 25 - HEIGHT ) * 16 + 4
320     MOVE 48, Y : DRAW 640, Y, 3
330     SOUND 129, 100, 50, 15, 1, 1, 1
```

```
340    FOR T = 1 TO 4
350    IF HEIGHT = ALIENY(T) THEN SCORE = SCORE + T * 10 : LOC
       ATE 20, 25 : PRINT SCORE : FUEL = FUEL + 5 : LOCATE ALIE
       NX(T), ALIENY(T) : PRINT "▲" : SOUND 2, 1000, 50, 15, 1,
       1, 1 : ALIENX(T) = CINT( RND(1) * 20 + 18 ) : ALIENY(T)
       = CINT( RND(1) * 20 + 1 )
360    NEXT T
370    MOVE 48, Y : DRAW 640, Y, 0
380    FUEL = FUEL - 1 : RETURN
```

```
┌─────────────────────────────────────────────────────┐
│                                                       │
│        Game over                                      │
│                                                       │
└─────────────────────────────────────────────────────┘
```

```
390    :
420    SOUND 2, 200, 100, 1, 1, 1
430    LOCATE 1, HEIGHT : PRINT "▲▲"
440    LOCATE 20, 25 : PEN 3 : PRINT SCORE
450    FOR T = 1 TO 3000 : NEXT T
460    RUN
```

ChexSum Tables

50	=	7390	200	=	433	350	=	14934
60	=	890	210	=	8320	360	=	433
70	=	774	220	=	6294	370	=	1222
80	=	7945	230	=	8289	380	=	1583
90	=	3763	240	=	6293	390	=	0
100	=	2662	250	=	1684	420	=	867
110	=	755	260	=	3981	430	=	1198
120	=	3963	270	=	382	440	=	1322
130	=	0	280	=	0	450	=	1624
160	=	987	310	=	2008	460	=	202
170	=	2362	320	=	1225			
180	=	10365	330	=	939			
190	=	2869	340	=	1019	TOTAL	=	108977

93

LEAPFROG

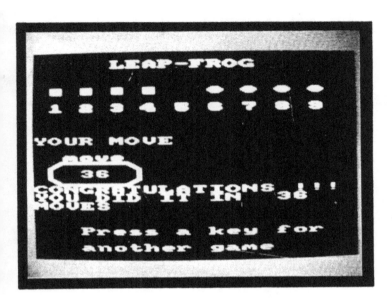

CLASSIFICATION: Puzzle

Using the keys given below solve this age old puzzle. Exchange the frogs in the shortest time possible. You can jump into an empty space over one of the men. The game is completed when all the squares and circles have moved across to the opposite position!

Press the number (0-9) on the keyboard representing the number you wish to move. Press 0 to finish the game if you are stuck.

PROGRAM
Variables

XSAVE, YSAVE	Save col, row values in interrupt routine
EMPTY	Position No. that is empty
COUNT	Number of moves
ASPACE	Character value for a space
ADIAMOND	Character value for a diamond
ASQUARE	Character value for a square
A(9)	Characters at each position
T	Temp
FROM	Position from which a shape is to be moved

Program Structure

Lines	Function/Activity
60 — 130	Initialise
140 — 270	Draw characters
280 — 470	Main loop
510 — 560	Player wins
600 — 690	Draw screen/initialise
730 — 740	Print player's move
780 — 800	Game over

```

                              ┌─────────────────────────────────────────┐
                              │                                         │
                              │   Initialise game                       │
                              │                                         │
                              └─────────────────────────────────────────┘

60       GOSUB 600
70       DIM A (9)
80       FOR T = 1 TO 4
90       A (T) = ADIAMOND
100      A (T + 5) = ASQUARE
110      NEXT T
120      A (5) = ASPACE
130      GOTO 280

                              ┌─────────────────────────────────────────┐
                              │                                         │
                              │   Draw characters                       │
                              │                                         │
                              └─────────────────────────────────────────┘

135      :
140      PRINT CHR$(7)
150      DI
160      FOR t = 1 TO 9
170      LOCATE T * 2, 5
180      PEN 12
190      PRINT CHR$ (A (T))
200      LOCATE T * 2 - 1, 7
210      PEN 7
220      PRINT T
230      NEXT T
240      EI
250      LOCATE 3,15 : PEN 4 : PRINT COUNT
260      EVERY 10 GOSUB 730
270      RETURN

                              ┌─────────────────────────────────────────┐
                              │                                         │
                              │   Main program loop                     │
                              │                                         │
                              └─────────────────────────────────────────┘

275      :
280      GOSUB 140
290      LOCATE 1, 10
300      PEN 10
340      A$ = INKEY$ : IF A$ = "" THEN 340
350      IF A$ = "0" THEN 780
360      IF ASC(A$) < 49 OR ASC(A$) > 57 THEN SOUND 1,400,50,7,0
         ,0,1 : GOTO 340
370      FROM = VAL(A$)
380      IF ABS(FROM - EMPTY) > 2 OR FROM = EMPTY THEN SOUND 1,3
         00,50,7,0,0,1 : GOTO 340
390      A(EMPTY) = A(FROM)
400      A(FROM) = ASPACE : EMPTY = FROM
410      COUNT = COUNT + 1
450      FOR t = 1 TO 4
460      IF a(t) = ASQUARE AND a(t + 5) = ADIAMOND AND a(5) = AS
         PACE THEN NEXT : GOTO 510
470      GOTO 280
```

```
480     :
510     GOSUB 140 : LOCATE 1, 17 : PEN 2
520     PRINT "CONGRATULATIONS.!!!"
530     PRINT "YOU.DID.IT.IN.";
540     PEN 1 : PRINT COUNT ;
550     PEN 2 : PRINT "MOVES"
560     GOTO 790
```

```
570     :
600     MODE 0 : PEN 3 : BORDER 12
610     LOCATE 6,2 : PRINT "LEAP-FROG"
620     EMPTY = 5 : COUNT = 1
630     ASPACE = 32 : ADIAMOND = 231 : ASQUARE = 233
640     LOCATE 3,13
650     PRINT "move"
660     PRINT "." CHR$(204) STRING$(4,CHR$(208)) CHR$(205)
670     PRINT "." CHR$(211) SPACE$(4) CHR$(209)
680     PRINT "." CHR$(205) STRING$(4,CHR$(210)) CHR$(204)
690     RETURN
```

```
700     :
730     DI : XSAVE = POS(#0) : YSAVE = VPOS(#0) : LOCATE 1,11 :
        PEN INT(RND(1) * 4 + 1) : PRINT "YOUR.MOVE" : EI
740     LOCATE XSAVE, YSAVE : RETURN
```

```
750     :
780     DI : LOCATE 1,18 : PEN 1 : PRINT "bye.for.now"
790     LOCATE 4, 22 : PRINT "Press.a.key.for." : LOCATE 4, 24
        : PRINT "another.game"
800     IF INKEY$ = "" THEN 800 ELSE RUN
```

ChexSum Tables

60	=	311	270	=	201	560	=	247
70	=	521	275	=	0	570	=	0
80	=	987	280	=	361	600	=	656
90	=	1497	290	=	295	610	=	1210
100	=	1717	300	=	254	620	=	1587
110	=	433	340	=	1868	630	=	3245
120	=	1147	350	=	1088	640	=	300
130	=	247	360	=	3642	650	=	730
135	=	0	370	=	1249	660	=	2649
140	=	583	380	=	4893	670	=	1943
150	=	219	390	=	1802	680	=	2651
160	=	1024	400	=	2774	690	=	201
170	=	751	410	=	1566	700	=	0
180	=	256	450	=	1019	730	=	5780
190	=	1138	460	=	6199	740	=	1512
200	=	1013	470	=	247	750	=	0
210	=	240	480	=	0	780	=	2101
220	=	448	510	=	900	790	=	3808
230	=	433	520	=	1571	800	=	1572
240	=	220	530	=	1248			
250	=	1298	540	=	1083			
260	=	697	550	=	921	TOTAL	=	78553

EXIT

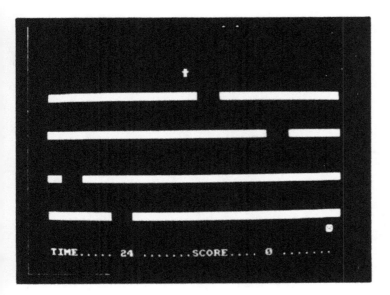

CLASSIFICATION: Obstacle game

Try to find your way through the sliding maze in time to find home, beware of the elusive gap it can cut your journey short.

Use 'A' to move up, 'Z' to move down, 'comma' to move left, 'period' to move right.

PROGRAM
Variables

SCORE	Player's score
NR	Number of rounds
TIMER	Number of seconds remaining
WALL(4)	Column of each wall's hole
VWALL(4)	Row of each wall
DIR(4)	Movement of holes; direction and speed
LIMIT(4)	Points at which hole has reached side of screen
START(4)	Points at which to reset hole
XMAN, YMAN	Man's coordinates (col, row)
CREEP	Monster's column
HOLE$	Characters for a hole
T	Temp

Program Structure

Lines	Function/Activity
7Ø	Call initialise
5Ø — 26Ø	Main loop
3ØØ — 36Ø	Man crashes
4ØØ — 44Ø	Man reaches bottom
48Ø — 51Ø	Interrupt routine
55Ø — 69Ø	Initialise
1ØØØ — 1Ø1Ø	Alternate Monster's Character definition

```
                    ┌──────────────────────────────────┐
                    │                                  │
                    │   Call Initialise                │
                    │                                  │
                    └──────────────────────────────────┘

10      GOSUB 550
                    ┌──────────────────────────────────┐
                    │                                  │
                    │   Main program loop              │
                    │                                  │
                    └──────────────────────────────────┘

20      :
50      DI : LOCATE XMAN, YMAN : PRINT CHR$(248)
60      PEN 3
70      FOR T = 1 TO 4
80      WALL(T) = WALL(T) + DIR(T)
90      IF WALL(T) = LIMIT(T) THEN LOCATE LIMIT(T), VWALL(T) :
        PRINT CHR$(143); CHR$(143); CHR$(143); CHR$(143) ;CHR$(1
        43) : WALL(T) = START(T)
100     LOCATE WALL(T), VWALL(T)
110     PRINT HOLE$
120     NEXT T
130     IF CREEP < 1 THEN LOCATE 1,22 ELSE IF CREEP > 39 THEN L
        OCATE 39,22 ELSE LOCATE CREEP,22
140     PEN 2 : PRINT "."; CHR$(225); "."
150     CREEP = CREEP + ((XMAN < (CREEP + 1)) - (XMAN > (CREEP
        + 1))) * 0.9
160     PEN 1
170     IF TEST(XMAN * 16 - 8, (25 - YMAN) * 16 + 8) > 1 THEN G
        OTO 300
180     LOCATE XMAN, YMAN : PRINT "."
190     XMAN = XMAN + (INKEY(39) > -1) - (INKEY(31) > -1) : YMA
        N = YMAN + (INKEY(69) > -1) - (INKEY(71) > -1)
200     IF XMAN < 2 THEN XMAN = 38
210     IF XMAN > 38 THEN XMAN = 2
220     IF YMAN < 1 THEN YMAN = 1
230     IF YMAN > 23 THEN GOTO 400
240     IF TEST(XMAN * 16 - 8, (25 - YMAN) * 16 + 8) > 1 THEN G
        OTO 300
250     EI
260     GOTO 50
                    ┌──────────────────────────────────┐
                    │                                  │
                    │   Man crashes                    │
                    │                                  │
                    └──────────────────────────────────┘

270     :
300     SOUND 1, 500, 100, 15, 1, 1, 1
310     FOR T = 1 TO 40 : INK 1, RND(1) * 26 : INK 2, RND(1) *
        26 : INK 3, RND(1) * 26 : SOUND 2, T, 10, 15, 1, 1, 1 :
        NEXT T
320     MODE 0 : INK 1, 24 : LOCATE 1, 10 : PRINT "Time.left :.
        ";TIMER; : LOCATE 3,12 : PRINT "seconds"
330     LOCATE 6, 15 : PEN 7 : PRINT "You.scored" : PRINT "....
        ."; SCORE;"points."
340     FOR T = 1 TO 4000 : NEXT T
350     MODE 0 : LOCATE 5, 8 : PEN 8 : PRINT "PRESS.SPACE" : LO
        CATE 4, 10 : PRINT ".TO.TRY.AGAIN"
360     IF INKEY$ <> "." THEN GOTO 360 ELSE RUN
```

```
370    :
400    MODE 0 : SOUND 1, 1, 50, 15
410    LOCATE 8, 12 : PRINT "BONUS!"
420    FOR T = 2000 TO 0 STEP - 100 : SOUND 2, T, 10 : NEXT T
430    NR=NR+1 : BONUS = NR+TIMER : SCORE = SCORE + BONUS * 10
       00 : LOCATE 9, 14 : PRINT BONUS*1000 : FOR T = 1 TO 2000
       : NEXT T
440    GOSUB 560 : GOTO 50
```

```
450    :
480    PEN 2 : TIMER = TIMER - 1 : LOCATE 10, 25 : PRINT TIMER
       : IF TIMER > 0 THEN PEN 1 : RETURN
490    FOR T = 3000 TO 4000 STEP 100 : SOUND 1, T, 10, 15, 1,
       1, 1 : NEXT T
500    MODE 0 : LOCATE 7, 10 : PRINT "TIME▴UP!"
510    FOR T = 1 TO 2000 : NEXT T : RUN
```

```
520    :
550    SYMBOL AFTER 225 : SCORE = 0 : DIM WALL(4), DIR(4), VWA
       LL(4), LIMIT(4), START(4)
560    MODE 1 : PAPER 0 : INK 0, 0
570    PEN 1 : INK 1, 20
580    BORDER 0 : INK 2, 15 : INK 3, 18
590    XMAN = 20 : YMAN = 1
600    CREEP = 38
610    TIMER = 25-NR : EVERY 50, 1 GOSUB 480 : DI : EVERY 20,
       2 GOSUB 1000
620    LOCATE 1, 25 : PEN 2 : PRINT "TIME................SCORE
       ............."
630    LOCATE 30, 25 : PRINT SCORE
640    WALL(1) = 20 : WALL(2) = 30 : WALL(3) = 1 : WALL(4) = 1
       0 : DIR(1) = 1 : DIR(2) = -0.5 : DIR(3) = 1 : DIR(4) = -
       1
650    VWALL(1) = 4 : VWALL(2) = 9 : VWALL(3) = 15 : VWALL(4)
       = 20
660    HOLE$ = CHR$(143) + "▴▴▴" + CHR$(143)
670    PEN 3 : FOR T = 1 TO 4 : LOCATE 1, VWALL(T) : PRINT STR
       ING$(40, CHR$(143)) : NEXT T
680    LIMIT(1) = 36 : START(1) = 1 : LIMIT(2) = 1 : START(2)
       = 36 : LIMIT(3) = 36 : START(3) = 1 : LIMIT(4) = 1 : STA
       RT(4) = 36
690    PEN 1 : RETURN
```

```
900    :
1000   IF c1=1 THEN c1=0 : SYMBOL 225,24,126,255,189,153,60,23
       1,66 : RETURN
1010   c1=1 : SYMBOL 225,24,126,255,189,189,24,24,60 : RETURN
```

ChexSum Tables

10 = 261	250 = 220	550 = 4678
20 = 0	260 = 272	560 = 720
50 = 2200	270 = 0	570 = 533
60 = 236	300 = 996	580 = 770
70 = 987	310 = 5246	590 = 1438
80 = 2655	320 = 4045	600 = 810
90 = 9183	330 = 3733	610 = 3166
100 = 1833	340 = 1604	620 = 2901
110 = 650	350 = 3290	630 = 1095
120 = 433	360 = 1869	640 = 6779
130 = 4389	370 = 0	650 = 3599
140 = 1430	400 = 733	660 = 2332
150 = 5873	410 = 1020	670 = 4055
160 = 234	420 = 2876	680 = 7255
170 = 3898	430 = 8724	690 = 436
180 = 1468	440 = 544	900 = 0
190 = 7265	450 = 0	1000 = 3925
200 = 1949	480 = 4607	1010 = 2678
210 = 1946	490 = 3090	
220 = 1902	500 = 1346	TOTAL = 147517
230 = 1593	510 = 1847	
240 = 3898	520 = 0	

MEGAWORM

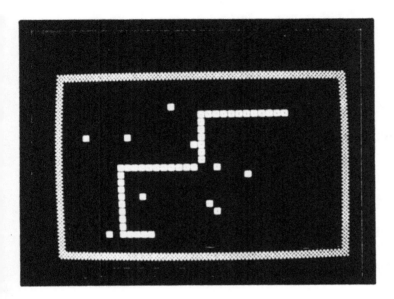

CLASSIFICATION: Educational

You start off as a small snake, the object as in real life is to survive and grow. Unlike reality, all you have to do in the game is catch the obstacles before they disappear, to collect points and grow in length (and stature!). The catch (there is always one) is the border, your survival is cut short if you hit it. This obviously gets harder as you grow (sound familiar?).

To move use: 'A' up, 'Z' down, 'comma' left, 'period' right.

PROGRAMMING SUGGESTIONS

Decrease the time the objects stay on the screen and increase the speed of the worm and the length of the segments.

PROGRAM
Variables

X(250), Y(250)	Coordinates of each segment of worm
LENGTH	Length of worm plus one
SCORE	Player's score
HEAD	Index for accessing worm's head coordinates
XHEAD, YHEAD	Coordinates of worm's head
OBJX, OBJY	The object's coordinates
XDIR, YDIR	Amounts to add to coordinates when moving
COUNT	For timing movement of object
T	Temp

Program Structure

Lines	Function/Activity
60 — 180	Initialise
220 — 360	Main loop
400 — 600	Front screen
640 — 690	Game over
730 — 770	Victory to player

```
┌─────────────────────────────────────────────────┐
│                                                   │
│              Initialise game                      │
│                                                   │
└─────────────────────────────────────────────────┘
```

```
60      MODE 1 : INK 2 , 24 , 17
70      INK 1 , 15 : INK 0 , 0 : BORDER 0 : PAPER 0 : PEN 1
80      DIM X (250) : DIM Y (250)
90      LENGTH = 4 : SCORE = 0
100     GOSUB 400
110     MODE 0
120     FOR T = 0 TO 26 : INK 1 , T : LOCATE 6 , 10 : PRINT "ME
        GAWORM" : NEXT T
130     FOR T = 0 TO 1000 STEP 2 : SOUND 1 , T , 1 , 7 , 0 , 0
        , 1 : INK 1 , (T / 50) : NEXT T
140     MODE 1
150     HEAD = 1 : XHEAD = 20 : YHEAD = 10
160     PEN 3 : FOR T = 1 TO 40 : LOCATE T , 1 : PRINT CHR$ (20
        6) : LOCATE T , 25 : PRINT CHR$ (206); : NEXT T
170     FOR T = 2 TO 24 : LOCATE 1 , T : PRINT CHR$ (206); + SP
        ACE$(38) + CHR$ (206) : NEXT T
180     OBJX = 5 : OBJY = 6 : XDIR = 1 : YDIR = 0 : FOR T = 1 T
        O 4 : X (T) = 20 : Y (T) = 10 : NEXT T : COUNT = 1
```

```
┌─────────────────────────────────────────────────┐
│                                                   │
│              Main program loop                    │
│                                                   │
└─────────────────────────────────────────────────┘
```

```
190     :
220     X (HEAD) = XHEAD + XDIR : Y (HEAD) = YHEAD + YDIR : PEN
         1 : LOCATE X (HEAD) , Y (HEAD) : PRINT CHR$ (232) : XHE
        AD = XHEAD + XDIR : YHEAD = YHEAD + YDIR
230     HEAD = HEAD + 1 : IF HEAD > LENGTH THEN HEAD = 1
240     LOCATE X (HEAD) , Y (HEAD) : PRINT " "
250     A$ = INKEY$
260     IF A$ = "." THEN XDIR = 1 : YDIR = 0
270     IF A$ = "," THEN XDIR = -1 : YDIR = 0
280     IF A$ = "Z" OR A$ = "z" THEN YDIR = 1 : XDIR = 0
290     IF A$ = "A" OR A$ = "a" THEN YDIR = -1 : XDIR = 0
300     COUNT = COUNT -1 : SPEED INK COUNT + 1 , COUNT + 1 : IF
         COUNT = 0 THEN LOCATE OBJX , OBJY : PRINT " " ELSE 330
310     OBJX = RND (1) * 37 + 2 : OBJY = RND (1) * 22 + 2 : IF
        TEST (OBJX * 16 -4 , (26 - OBJY) * 16 -4) > 0 THEN GOTO
        310 ELSE LOCATE OBJX , OBJY : PEN 2 : PRINT CHR$ (233) :
        ENV 1 , 7 , -1 , 9 , 8 , -1 , 40 : SOUND 1 , 300 , 10 ,
        15 , 1 , 1 , 1 : PEN 3
320     COUNT = 50
330     IF XHEAD = CINT (OBJX) AND YHEAD = CINT(OBJY) THEN COUN
        T =1 : SCORE = SCORE + 20 : LENGTH = LENGTH + 4 : IF LEN
        GTH > 250 THEN GOTO 730 ELSE SOUND 1 , 478 , 20 , 15 : F
        OR T = LENGTH - 4 TO LENGTH : X (T) = 2 : Y (T) = 2 : NE
        XT T
340     IF XHEAD < 2 OR XHEAD > 39 OR YHEAD < 2 OR YHEAD > 24 T
        HEN GOTO 650
350     IF TEST ( (XHEAD + XDIR) * 16 - 4 , (26 - (YHEAD + YDIR
        ) ) * 16 - 4) > 0 AND XHEAD <> CINT (OBJX) AND YHEAD <>
        CINT (OBJY) THEN GOTO 650
360     GOTO 220
```

109

```
370    :
400    PRINT "    DO YOU WANT INSTRUCTIONS ?"
410    A$ = INKEY$ : IF A$ = "" THEN GOTO 410
420    IF A$ = "Y" OR A$ = "y" THEN GOTO 430 ELSE RETURN
430    CLS : PRINT "            INSTRUCTIONS"
440    LOCATE 1 , 8 : PRINT "   MOVE THE WORM AROUND THE SCREE
       N"
450    INK 1 , RND (1) * 26
460    PRINT "   AND COLLECT THE OBJECTS.  IF"
470    INK 1 , RND (1) * 26
480    PRINT "   YOU CRASH INTO YOURSELF OR THE"
490    INK 1 , RND (1) * 26
500    PRINT "   WALL , THE GAME IS OVER"
510    PRINT "   WHEN YOU COLLECT AN OBJECT"
520    PRINT "   YOU MAY SHED SOME SKIN. "
530    INK 1 , RND (1) * 26
540    PRINT "    'A' = UP      'Z' = DOWN"
550    INK 1 ,18
560    PRINT "   ',' = LEFT    '.' = RIGHT"
570    LOCATE 1 , 22 : PRINT "   PRESS ANY KEY TO CONTINUE"
580    A$ = INKEY$ : IF A$ = "" THEN GOTO 580
590    INK 1 , 11
600    RETURN
```

```
610    :
640    A$ = INKEY$ : IF A$="" THEN GOTO 640
650    ENT 1 , 127 , 2 , 2 : SOUND 1 , 200 , 200 , 1 , 1 , 1
660    FOR T = 1000 TO 500 STEP - 5 : LOCATE 40 , 25 : PRINT "
       ." : SOUND 1 , T , 5 , 15 , 2 , 1 , 1 : NEXT T
670    MODE 0 : LOCATE 6 , 10 : INK 2 ,18 , 11 : PEN 2 : PRINT
       "GAME OVER"
680    FOR T = 1 TO 1000 : NEXT T : SPEED INK 10 , 10 : PRINT
       " You scored " ; SCORE ; "     points"
690    A$ = INKEY$ : IF A$ = "" THEN GOTO 690 ELSE RUN
```

```
700    :
730    PEN 2
740    MODE 0 : LOCATE 3 , 7 : PRINT "CONGRATULATIONS" : LOCAT
       E 1 , 10 : PRINT " YOU HAVE GROWN TO" : PRINT " YOUR FUL
       L LENGTH ! " : FOR T = 500 TO 600 STEP 5 : SOUND 0 , T ,
       25 , 15 , 0 , 0 , 0 : SOUND 1 , T , 25 , 15 , 1 , 1 , 1
750    SOUND 2 , 600 - T + 500 , 25 , 15 , 0 , 1 , 1 : NEXT T
760    PRINT " SCORE = " ; SCORE ; " !"
770    A$ = INKEY$ : IF A$ = "" THEN GOTO 770 ELSE RUN
```

110

ChexSum Tables

60 =	674	300 =	6728	540 =	1617
70 =	1269	310 =	12225	550 =	328
80 =	1594	320 =	848	560 =	1692
90 =	1623	330 =	15428	570 =	2525
100 =	366	340 =	4919	580 =	2045
110 =	219	350 =	9473	590 =	321
120 =	3196	360 =	442	600 =	201
130 =	3899	370 =	0	610 =	0
140 =	220	400 =	2273	640 =	2105
150 =	2236	410 =	2130	650 =	1739
160 =	4487	420 =	2806	660 =	4137
170 =	4367	430 =	1763	670 =	2152
180 =	6735	440 =	2885	680 =	5251
190 =	0	450 =	1034	690 =	2541
220 =	11161	460 =	2212	700 =	0
230 =	3734	470 =	1066	730 =	235
240 =	2116	480 =	2502	740 =	9161
250 =	757	490 =	1066	750 =	2377
260 =	2454	500 =	1874	760 =	1728
270 =	2697	510 =	2174	770 =	2366
280 =	3439	520 =	1954		
290 =	3634	530 =	1066	TOTAL =	180266

MINOTAUR MASTERMIND

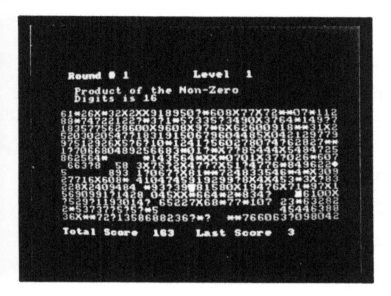

CLASSIFICATION: Educational game

This is a strategic game which will test the brain power of even the most experienced masterminds. The challenge is to guess a secret number between 0 and 1000 by working your way through a maze of numbers and symbols without being gobbled by the minotaur.

Your score is the sum of the digits that you step on — so the lower scores are better. When you reach the exit at the right end of the maze, you get a chance to guess the secret number. The non-numeric symbols have different effects when stepped on:

'X' — supplies a clue

'?' — has random value

'*' — Randomly alters your score

To move: 'P' moves up, ':' moves down, 'O' moves left, '@' moves right, '0' moves up and left, 'minus' moves up and right, 'L' moves down and left, ';' moves down and right, and 'T' is pressed when you are trapped and it is impossible to move.

PROGRAMMING SUGGESTIONS

Minotaur Mastermind could be made into a very complex game by adding more clues (lines 1190 — 1490) and by adding more symbols.

PROGRAM
Variables

LD	Level of difficulty
R, LS, TS	Round No., last score, total score
SN	Secret number
D1, D2, D3	Digits of SN
C, Q	For flashing effect
CU	Character under minotaur
CP	Character under player
PR, PC	Player's row and column
NC	Number of clues
T(10)	Truth array: clues used
G1, G2, G3	Digits of player's
MR, MC	Minotaur's row and column

Program Structure

Lines	Function/Activity
10 — 100	Initialise
120 — 210	New round
230 — 400	Editor/main loop
420 — 740	Recognise allowed moves
760 — 860	Check move
880 — 1060	Move minotaur
1080 — 1180	Player on '?'
1190 — 1490	Player on 'X'
1510 — 1550	Player on '*'
1570 — 1650	Game over
1670 — 1680	Blank message area
1700 — 1710	Update score
1730 — 1820	Guess secret number

```
                    ┌─────────────────────────────────────┐
                    │                                     │
                    │         Initialise game             │
                    │                                     │
                    └─────────────────────────────────────┘

10      RANDOMIZE TIME
20      MODE 1 : BORDER 0 : INK 0,0 : INK 1,16 : INK 2,20 : INK
        3,24 : PAPER 0 : PEN 2 : CLS
30      PRINT SPACE$(8);"MINOTAUR MASTER-MIND"
40      PRINT : PRINT : PRINT : PRINT "Level of Difficulty (1-9
        )";
50      ld=VAL(INKEY$) : IF ld<1 OR ld>9 THEN 50 ELSE PRINT ld
60      SYMBOL AFTER 136 : SYMBOL 136,165,126,219,126,102,126,8
        2,60 : SYMBOL 144,198,108,56,56,108,198,0 : SYMBOL 1
        52,60,108,6,12,24,0,24,0 : SYMBOL 160,0,102,60,255,60,10
        2,0,0 : SYMBOL 168,16,56,124,254,124,56,16,0
70      FOR i=1 TO 8 : PRINT : NEXT : PRINT SPACE$(9);"Hit any
        Key to Start"
80      IF INKEY$="" THEN 80
90      DIM sc(40,21)
100     ts=0 : nc=0 : FOR i=1 TO 10 : t(i)=0 : NEXT : r=1 : sn=
        INT(RND(1)*1000) : rs=sn : d1=INT(sn/100) : d2=INT((sn-d
        1*100)/10) : d3=INT(sn-d1*100-d2*10)

                    ┌─────────────────────────────────────┐
                    │                                     │
                    │        New round of game            │
                    │                                     │
                    └─────────────────────────────────────┘

110     :
120     CLS : pr=13 : pc=2 : mr=pr : mc=20
130     FOR i=1 TO 40 : FOR j=5 TO 21 : sc(i,j)=32 : NEXT : NEX
        T
140     FOR i=2 TO 39 : FOR j=6 TO 20 : k1=INT(RND(1)*13) : LOC
        ATE i,j : PEN 1 : IF k1<10 THEN PRINT CHR$(k1+48) : sc(i
        ,j)=k1+48 : GOTO 180
150     PEN 3 : IF k1=10 THEN PRINT CHR$(144) : sc(i,j)=144 : G
        OTO 180
160     IF k1=11 THEN PRINT CHR$(152) : sc(i,j)=152 : GOTO 180
170     PRINT CHR$(160) : sc(i,j)=160
180     NEXT : NEXT
190     sc(pc,pr)=48 : LOCATE pc,pr : PEN 1 : PRINT "0" : ls=0
        : cu=sc(mc,mr) : LOCATE mc,mr : PEN 2 : PRINT CHR$(136)
        : sc(39,pr)=168 : LOCATE 39,pr : PRINT CHR$(168) : cp=48

200     LOCATE 1,1 : PRINT " Round #";r;SPACE$(8);"Level ";ld
210     GOSUB 1700

                    ┌─────────────────────────────────────┐
                    │                                     │
                    │    Editor and main program loop     │
                    │                                     │
                    └─────────────────────────────────────┘

220     :
230     c=0 : q=1
240     x$=INKEY$ : c=c+1
250     IF c=7 THEN q=1-q : c=0
260     IF q<>0 THEN 290
270     IF sc(pc,pr)=233 THEN sc(pc,pr)=cp : LOCATE pc,pr : PRI
        NT CHR$(cp) : q=1 : GOTO 290
280     sc(pc,pr)=233 : LOCATE pc,pr : PRINT CHR$(233) : q=1
290     IF x$="" THEN 240
```

115

```
300     GOSUB 1670
310     IF x$="t" OR x$="T" THEN 740
320     IF x$="p" OR x$="P" THEN 420
330     IF x$="o" OR x$="O" THEN 460
340     IF x$="@" OR x$=" [" THEN 500
350     IF x$=";" OR x$="+" THEN 700
360     IF x$="-" OR x$="=" THEN 580
370     IF x$="0" OR x$=" _ " THEN 620
380     IF x$="l" OR x$="L" THEN 660
390     IF x$=" : " OR x$="*" THEN 540
400     GOTO 240
```

```
410     :
420     IF sc(pc,pr-1)=32 THEN 240
430     ls=cp-48
440     sc(pc,pr)=32 : LOCATE pc,pr : PRINT "▲" : pr=pr-1
450     GOTO 760
460     IF sc(pc-1,pr)=32 THEN 240
470     ls=cp-48
480     sc(pc,pr)=32 : LOCATE pc,pr : PRINT "▲" : pc=pc-1
490     GOTO 760
500     IF sc(pc+1,pr)=32 THEN 240
510     ls=cp-48
520     sc(pc,pr)=32 : LOCATE pc,pr : PRINT "▲" : pc=pc+1
530     GOTO 760
540     IF sc(pc,pr+1)=32 THEN 240
550     ls=cp-48
560     sc(pc,pr)=32 : LOCATE pc,pr : PRINT "▲" : pr=pr+1
570     GOTO 760
580     IF sc(pc+1,pr-1)=32 THEN 240
590     ls=cp-48
600     sc(pc,pr)=32 : LOCATE pc,pr : PRINT "▲" : pr=pr-1 : pc
        pc+1
610     GOTO 760
620     IF sc(pc-1,pr-1)=32 THEN 240
630     ls=cp-48
640     sc(pc,pr)=32 : LOCATE pc,pr : PRINT "▲" : pr=pr-1 : pc
        pc-1
650     GOTO 760
660     IF sc(pc-1,pr+1)=32 THEN 240
670     ls=cp-48
680     sc(pc,pr)=32 : LOCATE pc,pr : PRINT "▲" : pc=pc-1 : pr
        pr+1
690     GOTO 760
700     IF sc(pc+1,pr+1)=32 THEN 240
710     ls=cp-48
720     sc(pc,pr)=32 : LOCATE pc,pr : PRINT "▲" : pc=pc+1 : pr
        pr+1
730     GOTO 760
740     GOSUB 880 : IF (mr<>pr) OR (mc<>pc) THEN 740 ELSE 1570
```

Check move

```
750     :
760     cp=sc(pc,pr)
770     IF (ls>9) OR (ls<1) THEN ls=0
780     IF cp=152 THEN GOSUB 1050
790     IF cp=144 THEN GOSUB 1080
```

116

```
800     IF cp=160 THEN GOSUB 1510
810     IF cp=168 THEN 1730
820     k1=cp-48 : IF k1<0 OR k1>9 THEN k1=0
830     IF ls+k1>=10-ld THEN GOSUB 880
840     ts=ts+k1 : GOSUB 1700
850     IF (pr=mr) AND (pc=mc) THEN 1570
860     GOTO 230
```

┌───┐
│   │
│   Move minotaur   │
│   │
└───┘

```
870     :
880     t1=mc : t2=mr
890     IF mc<>pc THEN 920
900     IF mr>pr THEN mr=mr-1 : GOTO 980
910     mr=mr+1 : GOTO 980
920     IF mr<>pr THEN 950
930     IF mc>pc THEN mc=mc-1 : GOTO 980
940     mc=mc+1 : GOTO 980
950     IF mc>pc THEN 970
960     mc=mc+1 : GOTO 980
970     IF mr<pr THEN mr=mr+1 ELSE mr=mr-1
980     sc(t1,t2)=cu : LOCATE t1,t2 : IF cu<58 THEN t3=1 ELSE t
        3=3
990     PEN t3 : PRINT CHR$(cu)
1000    cu=sc(mc,mr)
1010    sc(mc,mr)=136 : LOCATE mc,mr : PEN 2 : PRINT CHR$(136)
1020    SOUND 1,200,15,15
1030    RETURN
```

┌───┐
│   │
│   Player on ?   │
│   │
└───┘

```
1040    :
1050    i=INT(RND(1)*10) : sc(pc,pr)=i+48 : LOCATE pc,pr : PEN
        1 : PRINT CHR$(i+48)
1060    cp=i+48 : RETURN
```

┌───┐
│   │
│   Player on X   │
│   │
└───┘

```
1070    :
1080    sc(pc,pr)=48 : LOCATE pc,pr : PEN 1 : PRINT "0" : FOR i
        =1000 TO 200 STEP -100 : SOUND 1,i,8,15 : NEXT
1090    IF nc >= 9 THEN 1190
1100    k2=INT(RND(1)*9+1) : IF t(k2)=1 THEN 1100
1110    t(k2)=1 : nc=nc+1
1120    ON k2 GOTO 1130,1150,1190,1220,1260,1290,1340,1360,1410

1130    LOCATE 4,3 : PEN 3 : PRINT "Sum.of.Digits.of.Secret" :
        LOCATE 4,4 : PRINT "Number.Equals.";
1140    PRINT d1+d2+d3 : RETURN
1150    LOCATE 4,3 : PEN 3 : PRINT "Secret.Number.is.";
1160    IF sn/2 = INT(sn/2) THEN PRINT "Even" : GOTO 1180
1170    PRINT "Odd"
1180    RETURN
1190    k=INT(RND(1)*200+sn) : j=k-200 : IF j<0 THEN j=0
1200    IF k>1000 THEN k=1000
1210    LOCATE 4,3 : PEN 3 : PRINT "Number.is.Between";j : LOCA
        TE 4,4 : PRINT "and";k : RETURN
```

117

```
1220    LOCATE 4,3 : PEN 3 : PRINT "Number.is.";
1230    IF sn/5 = INT(sn/5) THEN PRINT "Divisible" : GOTO 1250
1240    PRINT "Not.Divisible"
1250    LOCATE 4,4 : PRINT "by.5" : RETURN
1260    l=d1 : IF d2>l THEN l=d2
1270    IF d3>l THEN l=d3
1280    LOCATE 4,3 : PEN 3 : PRINT "Largest.Digit.in.the" : LOC
        ATE 4,4 : PRINT "Secret.Number.is.";l : RETURN
1290    LOCATE 4,3 : PEN 3 : PRINT "First.Digit.in.the.Secret"
        : LOCATE 4,4 : PRINT "Number.is.";
1300    IF d1>5 THEN PRINT "Larger.than.5" : GOTO 1330
1310    IF d1<5 THEN PRINT "Less.than.5" : GOTO 1330
1320    PRINT "Equal.to.5"
1330    RETURN
1340    LOCATE 4,3 : PEN 3 : PRINT "Sum.of.First.and.Third" : L
        OCATE 4,4 : PRINT "Digits.is.";
1350    PRINT d1+d3 : RETURN
1360    LOCATE 4,3 : PEN 3 : PRINT "One.of.the.Digits.in.the" :
        LOCATE 4,4 : PRINT "Secret.Number.is.";
1370    k=INT(RND(1)*3) : IF k=0 AND sn>99 THEN PRINT d1 : GOTO
        1400
1380    IF k=1 AND sn>9 THEN PRINT d2 : GOTO 1400
1390    PRINT d3
1400    RETURN
1410    LOCATE 4,3 : PEN 3 : PRINT "Product.of.the.Non-Zero" :
        LOCATE 4,4 : PRINT "Digits.is.";
1420    IF d1=0 AND d2=0 THEN PRINT d3 : GOTO 1490
1430    IF d1=0 AND d3=0 THEN PRINT d2 : GOTO 1490
1440    IF d1=0 THEN PRINT d2*d3 : GOTO 1490
1450    IF d2=0 AND d3=0 THEN PRINT d1 : GOTO 1490
1460    IF d2=0 THEN PRINT d1*d3 : GOTO 1490
1470    IF d3=0 THEN PRINT d1*d2 : GOTO 1490
1480    PRINT d1*d2*d3
1490    RETURN
```

```
┌─────────────────────────────────────────────┐
│                  Player on *                  │
└─────────────────────────────────────────────┘
```

```
1500    :
1510    sc(pc,pr)=48 : LOCATE pc,pr : PEN 1 : PRINT "0"
1520    IF ts<11 THEN RETURN
1530    i=INT(RND(1)*100) : IF i>50 THEN ts=ts-10 : SOUND 1,300
        0,55,15 : RETURN
1540    IF i<10 THEN ts=ts+50 : SOUND 1,40,15,15 : RETURN
1550    ts=ts+10 : SOUND 1,200,15,15 : RETURN
```

```
┌─────────────────────────────────────────────┐
│                  Game over                    │
└─────────────────────────────────────────────┘
```

```
1560    :
1570    CLS : IF pr=mr AND pc=mc THEN 1610
1580    FOR i=1 TO 17 : PRINT SPACE$(9);"Congratulations!." : N
        EXT : PRINT
1590    PRINT "You.have.beaten.the.minotaur" : PRINT "Your.scor
        e.is.";ts
1600    PRINT "in.";r;".rounds" : GOTO 1630
1610    FOR i=1 TO 17 : PRINT SPACE$(4);"MINOTAUR.WINS..MINOTAU
        R.WINS" : NEXT : PRINT
1620    PRINT "The.secret.number.was.";sn
1630    PRINT : PRINT "Hit.any.key.for.another.game"
1640    IF INKEY$="" THEN 1640
1650    RUN
```

```
1660  :
1670  LOCATE 1,3 : PRINT SPACE$(79)
1680  RETURN
```

```
1690  :
1700  LOCATE 2,22 : PEN 2 : PRINT "Total.Score.";ts;TAB(21);"
      Last.Score.";ls;
1710  RETURN
```

```
1720  :
1730  LOCATE 4,3 : PEN 3 : PRINT "Guess.at.the.Secret.Number"

1740  LOCATE 4,4 : INPUT "and.press.RETURN";k$
1750  i=VAL(k$) : IF i=sn THEN 1570
1760  q1=INT(i/100) : q2=INT((i-q1*100)/10) : q3=i-q1*100-q2*
      10
1770  CLS : PRINT : IF d1=q1 THEN PRINT "First.Digit.Correct"
      : PRINT
1780  IF d2=q2 THEN PRINT "Second.Digit.Correct" : PRINT
1790  IF d3=q3 THEN PRINT "Third.Digit.Correct"
1800  IF d1<>q1 AND d2<>q2 AND d3<>q3 THEN PRINT "No.Digits.C
      orrect"
1810  FOR t=1 TO 2000 : NEXT
1820  r=r+1 : GOTO 120
```

ChexSum Tables

10 =	583		220 =	0		430 =	1273
20 =	2172		230 =	1002		440 =	3986
30 =	2186		240 =	1791		450 =	472
40 =	3014		250 =	2493		460 =	2485
50 =	4135		260 =	1067		470 =	1273
60 =	8704		270 =	6625		480 =	3956
70 =	3912		280 =	3991		490 =	472
80 =	1231		290 =	1320		500 =	2484
90 =	770		300 =	361		510 =	1273
100 =	13736		310 =	2416		520 =	3955
110 =	0		320 =	2311		530 =	472
120 =	2996		330 =	2349		540 =	2484
130 =	3689		340 =	2387		550 =	1273
140 =	9132		350 =	2246		560 =	3985
150 =	3816		360 =	2130		570 =	472
160 =	3596		370 =	2207		580 =	2744
170 =	2145		380 =	2288		590 =	1273
180 =	353		390 =	2084		600 =	5189
190 =	10820		400 =	462		610 =	472
200 =	3042		410 =	0		620 =	2745
210 =	391		420 =	2485		630 =	1273

640 = 5190	1050 = 5862	1460 = 2525
650 = 472	1060 = 1356	1470 = 2525
660 = 2744	1070 = 0	1480 = 1588
670 = 1273	1080 = 6014	1490 = 201
680 = 5189	1090 = 1305	1500 = 0
690 = 472	1100 = 3326	1510 = 3051
700 = 2743	1110 = 2089	1520 = 1342
710 = 1273	1120 = 2504	1530 = 4866
720 = 5188	1130 = 4831	1540 = 3047
730 = 472	1140 = 1786	1550 = 2153
740 = 3737	1150 = 2415	1560 = 0
750 = 0	1160 = 3409	1570 = 2933
760 = 1790	1170 = 570	1580 = 3795
770 = 2832	1180 = 201	1590 = 4989
780 = 1511	1190 = 5036	1600 = 2001
790 = 1533	1200 = 1987	1610 = 4144
800 = 1724	1210 = 4120	1620 = 2759
810 = 1506	1220 = 1769	1630 = 3083
820 = 3675	1230 = 4010	1640 = 1261
830 = 2602	1240 = 1551	1650 = 202
840 = 1916	1250 = 1079	1660 = 0
850 = 2948	1260 = 2828	1670 = 963
860 = 452	1270 = 2051	1680 = 201
870 = 0	1280 = 5291	1690 = 0
880 = 1805	1290 = 4638	1700 = 4360
890 = 1620	1300 = 2757	1710 = 201
900 = 3094	1310 = 2562	1720 = 0
910 = 1664	1320 = 1139	1730 = 3221
920 = 1648	1330 = 201	1740 = 2250
930 = 3066	1340 = 4322	1750 = 2470
940 = 1634	1350 = 1251	1760 = 6408
950 = 1666	1360 = 5121	1770 = 3931
960 = 1634	1370 = 4415	1780 = 3686
970 = 4069	1380 = 2797	1790 = 3399
980 = 5032	1390 = 515	1800 = 5479
990 = 1447	1400 = 201	1810 = 1419
1000 = 1789	1410 = 4433	1820 = 1351
1010 = 3512	1420 = 2846	
1020 = 688	1430 = 2846	
1030 = 201	1440 = 2525	TOTAL = 448869
1040 = 0	1450 = 2846	

FIFTEEN PUZZLE

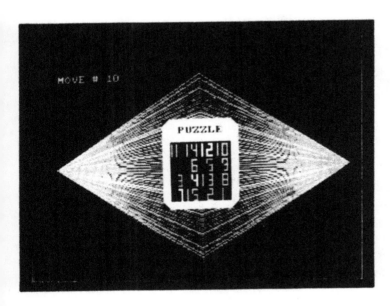

CLASSIFICATION: Educational

Use the cursor movement keys to arrange the numbers into order with the minimum number of moves. Press 'Q' to quit the game.

PROGRAM
Variables

CHAR$(16)	Defines 16 character strings for the numbers
XCOOR(16), YCOOR(16)	Each number's coordinates
POSITION(16)	The number contained in each position
DISPLAY	Flag for displaying move number
FEEDBACK	Flag for audio feedback each move
WIN	Can win if random set-up
R1, R2	Random numbers
SPACE	Blank position
COL(16)	Colours for each number
COUNT	Count of moves
T, A, B, C, D	Temps

121

Program Structure

Lines	Function/Activity
40	Call initialisation
80 — 190	Main loop
230 — 280	Games won
320 — 890	Character/variable initialisation
900 — 1240	Screen/other initialisation
1270 — 1340	Character block print
1380 — 1390	Game over

```
                    ┌─────────────────────────────────────────┐
                    │                                         │
                    │   Call initialisation routine           │
                    │                                         │
                    └─────────────────────────────────────────┘

40      GOSUB 320 : COUNT = 1

                    ┌─────────────────────────────────────────┐
                    │                                         │
                    │   Main loop                             │
                    │                                         │
                    └─────────────────────────────────────────┘

50      :
80      A$ = INKEY$ : IF A$ = "" THEN 80
90      IF A$ = "Q" OR A$ = "q" THEN 1380
100     IF DISPLAY THEN PEN 2 : LOCATE 1,1 : PRINT "MOVE.#" : C
        OUNT
110     IF ASC(A$) = 240 AND SPACE > 4 THEN POSITION(SPACE) = P
        OSITION(SPACE - 4) : POSITION(SPACE - 4) = 16 : SPACE =
        SPACE - 4 : Z = POSITION(SPACE) : X = XCOOR(SPACE) : Y =
        YCOOR(SPACE) : GOSUB 1270 ELSE 130
120     Z = POSITION(SPACE + 4) : X = XCOOR(SPACE + 4) : Y = YC
        OOR(SPACE + 4) : GOSUB 1270
130     IF ASC(A$) = 241 AND SPACE < 13 THEN POSITION(SPACE) =
        POSITION(SPACE + 4) : POSITION(SPACE + 4) = 16 : SPACE =
        SPACE + 4 : Z = POSITION(SPACE) : X = XCOOR(SPACE) : Y
        = YCOOR(SPACE) : GOSUB 1270 ELSE 150
140     Z = POSITION(SPACE - 4) : X = XCOOR(SPACE - 4) : Y = YC
        OOR(SPACE - 4) : GOSUB 1270
150     IF ASC(A$) = 242 AND (SPACE <> 1 AND SPACE <> 5 AND SPA
        CE <> 9 AND SPACE <> 13) THEN POSITION(SPACE) = POSITION
        (SPACE - 1) : SPACE = SPACE - 1 : POSITION(SPACE) = 16 E
        LSE 170
160     Z = POSITION(SPACE + 1) : X = XCOOR(SPACE + 1) : Y = YC
        OOR(SPACE + 1) : GOSUB 1270 : Z = POSITION(SPACE) : X =
        XCOOR(SPACE) : Y = YCOOR(SPACE) : GOSUB 1270
170     IF ASC(A$) = 243 AND (SPACE <> 4 AND SPACE <> 8 AND SPA
        CE <> 12 AND SPACE <> 16) THEN POSITION(SPACE) = POSITIO
        N(SPACE + 1) : SPACE = SPACE + 1 : POSITION(SPACE) = 16
        ELSE 80
180     Z = POSITION(SPACE - 1) : X = XCOOR(SPACE - 1) : Y = YC
        OOR(SPACE - 1) : GOSUB 1270 : Z = POSITION(SPACE) : X =
        XCOOR(SPACE) : Y = YCOOR(SPACE) : GOSUB 1270
190     COUNT = COUNT + 1 : FOR T = 1 TO 16 : IF POSITION(T) =
        T AND WIN = 1 THEN NEXT T : GOTO 230 ELSE 80

                    ┌─────────────────────────────────────────┐
                    │                                         │
                    │   Player wins                           │
                    │                                         │
                    └─────────────────────────────────────────┘

200     :
230     MODE 0 : SOUND 1, 200, 100, 15, 1, 1, 1
240     LOCATE 3, 8 : PEN 7 : PRINT "CONGRATULATIONS!"
250     PEN 10 : LOCATE 14, 10 : PRINT "You.did.it.in"
260     PRINT COUNT; "MOVES."
270     FOR T = 1 TO 3000 : NEXT T
280     RUN

                    ┌─────────────────────────────────────────┐
                    │                                         │
                    │   Character and variable initialisation │
                    │                                         │
                    └─────────────────────────────────────────┘
```

```
290      :
320      MODE 1
330      BORDER 0
340      PAPER 0
350      INK 0, 0
360      INK 1, 18
370      INK 2, 15
380      INK 3, 24
390      SYMBOL 240, 0, 0, 96, 96, 96, 96, 96, 96
400      SYMBOL 241, 0, 0, 3, 3, 3, 3, 3, 3
410      SYMBOL 242, 0, 0, 99, 99, 99, 99, 99, 99
420      SYMBOL 243, 96, 96, 96, 96, 96, 96, 96, 96
430      SYMBOL 244, 99, 99, 99, 99, 99, 99, 99, 99
440      SYMBOL 245, 0, 0, 248, 248, 0, 0, 0, 0
450      SYMBOL 246, 0, 0, 248, 248, 24, 24, 24, 24
460      SYMBOL 247, 0, 0, 24, 24, 24, 24, 24, 24
470      SYMBOL 248, 248, 248, 24, 24, 24, 24, 24, 24
480      SYMBOL 249, 248, 248, 0, 0, 0, 0, 248, 248
490      SYMBOL 250, 24, 24, 24, 24, 24, 24, 248, 248
500      SYMBOL 251, 248, 248, 24, 24, 24, 24, 248, 248
510      DIM CHAR$(16)
520      FOR T = 1 TO 16
530      READ A, B, C, D
540      CHAR$(T) = CHR$(A) + CHR$(B) + CHR$(C) + CHR$(D)
550      NEXT T
560      DATA 241, 32, 209, 32
570      DATA 32, 246, 209, 249
580      DATA 32, 246, 32, 251
590      DATA 241, 247, 32, 248
600      DATA 241, 245, 32, 251
610      DATA 241, 245, 209, 251
620      DATA 32, 246, 32, 149
630      DATA 241, 246, 209, 251
640      DATA 241, 246, 32, 251
650      DATA 242, 246, 244, 250
660      DATA 242, 32, 244, 32
670      DATA 240, 246, 244, 249
680      DATA 240, 246, 243, 251
690      DATA 242, 247, 243, 248
700      DATA 242, 245, 243, 251
710      DATA 32, 32, 32, 32
720      DIM XCOOR(16), YCOOR(16), POSITION(16)
730      FOR T = 1 TO 16 : POSITION(T) = T : NEXT T
740      FOR T = 1 TO 4
750      FOR N = 1 TO 4
760      XCOOR(4 * (T - 1) + N) = N * 2 + 15
770      YCOOR(4 * (T - 1) + N) = T * 2 + 8
780      NEXT N : NEXT T
790      PEN 2
800      PRINT TAB(10) "FIFTEEN PUZZLE"
810      PEN 1
820      LOCATE 4,9 : PRINT "DISPLAY MOVE NUMBER (Y/N) ?"
830      A$ = INKEY$ : IF A$ = "" THEN 830
840      IF A$ = "Y" OR A$ = "y" THEN DISPLAY = 1
850      PRINT : PRINT TAB(4) ; "AUDIO FEEDBACK ON (Y/N) ?"
860      A$ = INKEY$ : IF A$ = "" THEN 860
870      IF A$ = "Y" OR A$ = "y" THEN FEEDBACK = 1
880      PRINT : PRINT TAB (4) "RANDOM SET-UP (Y/N) ?"
890      A$ = INKEY$ : IF A$ = "" THEN GOTO 890 ELSE IF A$ = "Y"
         OR A$ = "y" THEN WIN = 1 ELSE WIN = 0
```

```
895     :
900     MODE 1
910     FOR T = 1 TO 400 STEP 5
920     MOVE 0, 200
930     DRAW 320, T, RND(1) * 2 + 1
940     MOVE 639, 200
950     DRAW 321, T, RND(0) * 2 + 1
960     NEXT
970     LOCATE 16, 7
980     PEN 3
990     PRINT CHR$(214);
1000    FOR T = 1 TO 8
1010    PRINT CHR$(143);
1020    NEXT T
1030    PRINT CHR$(215)
1040    LOCATE 16, 8
1050    PRINT STRING$( 10, CHR$(143))
1060    LOCATE 16, 9
1070    PRINT STRING$( 10,  CHR$(143))
1080    FOR T = 10 TO 17 : LOCATE 16, T : PRINT CHR$(143) + "▲▲
        ▲▲▲▲▲" + CHR$(143) : NEXT T
1090    LOCATE 16, 18 : PRINT CHR$(213);
1100    PRINT STRING$( 8,  CHR$(143)); CHR$(212)
1110    PAPER 3 : PEN 0 : LOCATE 18, 8 : PRINT "PUZZLE" : PAPER
        0 : PEN 1
1120    IF WIN = 0 THEN GOTO 1210
1130    FOR T = 1 TO 30
1140    R1 = CINT( RND(1) * 15 + 1)
1150    R2 = CINT( RND(1) * 15 + 1)
1160    O1 = POSITION(R1)
1170    O2 = POSITION(R2)
1180    POSITION(R1) = O2
1190    POSITION(R2) = O1
1200    NEXT T
1210    FOR T = 1 TO 16 : IF POSITION(T) = 16 THEN SPACE = T EL
        SE NEXT T
1220    DIM COL(16)
1230    FOR T = 1 TO 16 : COL(T) = CINT( RND(1) * 2 + 1) : NEXT
        T
1240    FOR T = 1 TO 16 : Z = POSITION(T) : X = XCOOR(T) : Y =
        YCOOR(T) : GOSUB 1270 : NEXT T
```

```
1250    :
1270    PEN COL(Z)
1280    COUNT = COUNT + 0.5
1290    IF FEEDBACK THEN PRINT CHR$(7) ;
1300    LOCATE X, Y
1310    PRINT LEFT$( CHAR$(Z), 2 )
1320    LOCATE X, Y + 1
1330    PRINT RIGHT$( CHAR$(Z), 2 )
1340    RETURN
```

```
1350  :
1380  LOCATE 1,3 : PRINT "bye.for.now"
1390  END
```

ChexSum Tables

40 =	1075	540 =	3880	970 =	307
50 =	0	550 =	433	980 =	236
80 =	1863	560 =	812	990 =	860
90 =	2175	570 =	875	1000 =	991
100 =	3005	580 =	814	1010 =	789
110 =	15026	590 =	871	1020 =	433
120 =	6268	600 =	863	1030 =	802
130 =	15067	610 =	917	1040 =	308
140 =	6271	620 =	820	1050 =	1268
150 =	12661	630 =	918	1060 =	309
160 =	11742	640 =	864	1070 =	1268
170 =	12593	650 =	917	1080 =	4027
180 =	11745	660 =	812	1090 =	1189
190 =	6737	670 =	923	1100 =	1922
200 =	0	680 =	915	1110 =	2030
230 =	1170	690 =	924	1120 =	1536
240 =	1999	700 =	916	1130 =	1024
250 =	2020	710 =	708	1140 =	1816
260 =	1356	720 =	2476	1150 =	1817
270 =	1624	730 =	2985	1160 =	1631
280 =	202	740 =	987	1170 =	1633
290 =	0	750 =	1013	1180 =	1632
320 =	220	760 =	2914	1190 =	1632
330 =	176	770 =	2903	1200 =	433
340 =	232	780 =	861	1210 =	4445
350 =	266	790 =	235	1220 =	664
360 =	296	800 =	1740	1230 =	3634
370 =	294	810 =	234	1240 =	6087
380 =	304	820 =	2366	1250 =	0
390 =	1610	830 =	1848	1270 =	894
400 =	987	840 =	2953	1280 =	1710
410 =	1630	850 =	2501	1290 =	1856
420 =	1827	860 =	1878	1300 =	704
430 =	1852	870 =	2968	1310 =	1465
440 =	1491	880 =	2229	1320 =	963
450 =	1632	890 =	5757	1330 =	1469
460 =	1185	895 =	0	1340 =	201
470 =	1704	900 =	220	1350 =	0
480 =	2013	910 =	1421	1380 =	1620
490 =	1706	920 =	489	1390 =	152
500 =	2155	930 =	1525		
510 =	718	940 =	630		
520 =	1010	950 =	1525	TOTAL =	257869
530 =	1189	960 =	176		

MIND QUIZ

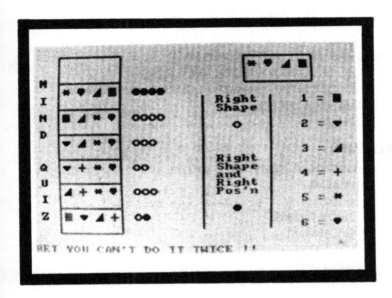

CLASSIFICATION: Memory game

The secret code is a sequence of four shapes chosen from six. Crack the code in less than eight attempts and you have won the game!

A circle means that you have the right shape in the wrong position and a coloured circle indicates the right shape in the right position.

Use the keys numbered '1' to '6' to select a shape. The 'DEL' key can be used to change the shapes entered.

PROGRAMMING SUGGESTIONS

The game could be made more difficult by increasing the number of objects included in the code. Alternatively, if you find this game a little difficult, then try allowing extra guesses, or having different levels of play.

PROGRAM
Variables

CHRVAL(6)   Character values of shapes 1-6
COLS(6)   Colours for shapes
ANSNUM(4)   Answer in digits 1-6
ANSWER(4)   Answer in character values
GUESS(4)   Player's guess
LEVEL, COLUMN   Level (0-6) and column (0-3)
CORSHP   No. of correct shapes in GUESS(4).
CORSHPPOS   No. of correct shapes in correct positions
MES$ Message string
T(6), I, J   Temps

Program Structure

Lines	Function/Activity
10 — 415	Initialise
430 — 400	Editor
1000 — 1040	Check Guess
1060 — 1120	Print Result
5000 — 5020	Print Message
8000 — 8050	Game lost
9000 — 9040	Game won

```
                    ┌─────────────────────────────────────────┐
                    │                                         │
                    │        Initialise game                  │
                    │                                         │
                    └─────────────────────────────────────────┘

10      MODE 1 : INK 0, 13 : INK 1, 1 : INK 2, 0 : INK 3, 3
20      PAPER 0 : BORDER 11 : CLS
30      LOCATE 4, 2 : PEN 1
40      GOTO 100
50      PRINT CHR$( 151 ); STRING$( 7, 154 ); CHR$( 157 ); CHR$
        ( 10 ); STRING$( 9, 8 );
60      PRINT CHR$( 149 ); STRING$( 7, 32 ); CHR$( 149 ); CHR$(
        10 ); STRING$( 9, 8 );
70      PRINT CHR$( 149 ); STRING$( 7, 32 ); CHR$( 149 ); CHR$(
        10 ); STRING$( 9, 8 );
90      RETURN
100     FOR I = 1 TO 7 : GOSUB 50 : NEXT
110     PRINT CHR$( 147 ); STRING$( 7, 154 ); CHR$( 153 )
120     LOCATE 4, 2 : PRINT CHR$( 150 ); STRING$( 7, 154 ); CHR
        $( 156 )
130     PEN 2 : LOCATE 2, 5
140     T$ = CHR$( 10 ) + CHR$( 10 ) + CHR$( 8 ) : PRINT "M"; T
        $; "I"; T$; "N"; T$; "D"; T$; "▲"; T$; "Q"; T$; "U"; T$;
        "I"; T$; "Z"
150     PEN 1 : FOR I = 7 TO 22 : LOCATE 22, I : PRINT CHR$( 14
        9 ); SPACE$( 7 ); CHR$( 149 ) : NEXT
160     LOCATE 27, 2 : PRINT CHR$( 150 ); STRING$( 7, 154 ); CH
        R$( 156 )
170     LOCATE 27, 3 : PRINT CHR$( 149 ); STRING$( 7, 32 ); CHR
        $( 149 )
180     LOCATE 27, 4 : PRINT CHR$( 149 ); STRING$( 7, 32 ); CHR
        $( 149 )
190     LOCATE 27, 5 : PRINT CHR$( 147 ); STRING$( 7, 154 ); CH
        R$( 153 )
200     LOCATE 34, 7 : PRINT "1▲=▲"; CHR$( 143 )
210     LOCATE 34, 10 : PRINT "2▲=▲"; : PEN 2 : PRINT CHR$( 245
        ) : PEN 1
220     LOCATE 34, 13 : PRINT "3▲=▲"; : PEN 3 : PRINT CHR$( 214
        ) : PEN 1
230     LOCATE 34, 16 : PRINT "4▲=▲"; CHR$( 159 )
240     LOCATE 34, 19 : PRINT "5▲=▲"; : PEN 2 : PRINT CHR$( 42
        ) : PEN 1
250     LOCATE 34, 22 : PRINT "6▲=▲"; : PEN 3 : PRINT CHR$( 228
        )
260     PEN 1 : LOCATE 24, 7 : PRINT "Right" : LOCATE 24, 8 : P
        RINT "Shape"
270     LOCATE 24, 14 : PRINT "Right" : LOCATE 24, 15 : PRINT "
        Shape"
280     LOCATE 24, 16 : PRINT "and" : LOCATE 24, 17 : PRINT "Ri
        ght" : LOCATE 24, 18 : PRINT "Pos'n"
290     PEN 2 : LOCATE 26, 10 : PRINT CHR$( 230 )
300     LOCATE 26, 20 : PRINT CHR$( 231 )
305     K = 1
310     I = INT( RND( 1 ) * 6 + 1 )
320     IF T( I ) <> 1 THEN T( I ) = 1 : ANSNUM( K ) = I : ANSW
        ER( K ) = I ELSE 310
330     K = K + 1 : IF K < 5 THEN 310
335     CHRVAL( 1 ) = 143 : CHRVAL( 2 ) = 245 : CHRVAL( 3 ) = 2
        14 : CHRVAL( 4 ) = 159 : CHRVAL( 5 ) = 42 : CHRVAL( 6 )
        = 228
340     FOR I = 1 TO 4
350     ANSWER( I ) = CHRVAL( ANSWER( I ) )
```

129

```
410     NEXT
415     COLS( 1 ) = 1 : COLS( 2 ) = 2 : COLS( 3 ) = 3 : COLS( 4
        ) = 1 : COLS( 5 ) = 2 : COLS( 6 ) = 3
```

```
┌─────────────────────────────────────────────┐
│             Editor                           │
└─────────────────────────────────────────────┘
```

```
420     :
430     IF INKEY( 79 ) = -1 THEN 440 ELSE IF COLUMN = 0 THEN 43
        0
435     COLUMN = COLUMN - 1 : LOCATE 5 + COLUMN * 2, 21 - 3 * L
        EVEL : PRINT "▲" : GOTO 500
440     X$ = INKEY$ : IF X$ < "1" OR X$ > "6" THEN 430
450     PRINT CHR$( 7 ); : GUESS( COLUMN + 1 ) = CHRVAL( VAL( X
        $ ) ) : LOCATE 5 + COLUMN * 2, 21 - 3 * LEVEL : PEN COLS
        ( VAL( X$ ) ) : PRINT CHR$( GUESS( COLUMN + 1 ) ) : COLU
        MN = COLUMN + 1
460     IF COLUMN = 4 THEN MSG$ = "Checking▲your▲answer" : GOSU
        B 5000 : FOR I = 1 TO 1000 : NEXT : GOTO 1000
500     FOR I = 1 TO 100 : NEXT : GOTO 430
```

```
┌─────────────────────────────────────────────┐
│             Check guess                      │
└─────────────────────────────────────────────┘
```

```
990     :
1000    CORSHP = 0 : CORSHPPOS = 0 : FOR I = 1 TO 4
1010    IF GUESS( I ) = ANSWER( I ) THEN CORSHPPOS = CORSHPPOS
        + 1
1020    NEXT : FOR I = 1 TO 4
1030    IF ANSWER( I ) = GUESS( 1 ) OR ANSWER( I ) = GUESS( 2 )
        OR ANSWER( I ) = GUESS( 3 ) OR ANSWER( I ) = GUESS( 4 )
        THEN CORSHP = CORSHP + 1
1040    NEXT : CORSHP = CORSHP - CORSHPPOS
```

```
┌─────────────────────────────────────────────┐
│             Print result                     │
└─────────────────────────────────────────────┘
```

```
1050    :
1060    IF CORSHP = 0 THEN 1080
1070    PEN 2 : FOR I = 1 TO CORSHP : LOCATE 13 + I, 21 - 3 * L
        EVEL : PRINT CHR$( 230 ) : NEXT
1080    IF CORSHPPOS = 0 THEN 1100
1090    PEN 2 : FOR I = 1 TO CORSHPPOS : LOCATE 13 + I + CORSHP
        , 21 - 3 * LEVEL : PRINT CHR$( 231 ) : NEXT
1100    COLUMN = 0 : LEVEL = LEVEL + 1 : MSG$ = SPACE$( 35 ) :
        GOSUB 5000 : IF CORSHPPOS = 4 THEN 9000
1110    IF LEVEL = 7 THEN 8000
1120    MSG$ = "Ready▲when▲you▲are" : GOSUB 5000 : GOTO 430
```

```
┌─────────────────────────────────────────────┐
│             Print message                    │
└─────────────────────────────────────────────┘
```

```
4990    :
5000    LOCATE 1, 25 : PEN 1 : PRINT STRING$( 38, 32 )
5010    LOCATE 1, 25 : PRINT MSG$
5020    RETURN
```

```
7990  :
8000  MSG$ = "No.luck.this.time.!" : GOSUB 5000 : FOR I = 1 [
      O 2000 : NEXT : MSG$ = "Here.is.the.correct.answer" : GO
      SUB 5000
8010  FOR I = 1 TO 4 : SOUND 1, 50 - 10 * I, 15, 15 : PEN COL
      S( ANSNUM( I ) )
8020  LOCATE 26 + 2 * I, 3 : PRINT CHR$( ANSWER( I ) ) : NEXT

8030  FOR I = 1 TO 2500 : NEXT
8040  MSG$ = "Press.a.key.for.another.game" : GOSUB 5000
8050  IF INKEY$ = "" THEN 8050 ELSE RUN
```

```
8990  :
9000  MSG$ = "SUPERB.!!!!!!!!!!!!!!!!!!!!!" : GOSUB 5000
9010  FOR I = 1 TO 4 : SOUND 1, 30 - 5 * I, 45, 15 : PEN COLS
      ( ANSNUM( I ) )
9020  LOCATE 26 + 2 * I, 3 : PRINT CHR$( ANSWER( I ) ) : FOR
      J = 1 TO 400 : NEXT : NEXT
9030  MSG$ = "BET.YOU.CAN'T.DO.IT.TWICE.!!" : GOSUB 5000
9040  IF INKEY$ = "" THEN 9040 ELSE RUN
```

ChexSum Tables

Line	=	Value		Line	=	Value		Line	=	Value
10	=	1322		280	=	3158		1060	=	1439
20	=	570		290	=	1385		1070	=	4606
30	=	514		300	=	1160		1080	=	1701
40	=	322		305	=	470		1090	=	5697
50	=	3339		310	=	1746		1100	=	5487
60	=	3207		320	=	5026		1110	=	1394
70	=	3207		330	=	1984		1120	=	3136
90	=	201		335	=	6745		4990	=	0
100	=	1428		340	=	976		5000	=	1392
110	=	2136		350	=	2709		5010	=	896
120	=	2422		410	=	176		5020	=	201
130	=	516		415	=	4802		7990	=	0
140	=	6752		420	=	0		8000	=	7589
150	=	3741		430	=	3393		8010	=	3904
160	=	2456		435	=	4942		8020	=	2673
170	=	2327		440	=	2950		8030	=	1366
180	=	2328		450	=	11130		8040	=	3647
190	=	2453		460	=	6232		8050	=	1682
200	=	1549		500	=	1658		8990	=	0
210	=	2521		990	=	0		9000	=	2169
220	=	2687		1000	=	2934		9010	=	3930
230	=	1588		1010	=	4648		9020	=	4013
240	=	2394		1020	=	1153		9030	=	2793
250	=	2222		1030	=	10220		9040	=	1652
260	=	2458		1040	=	2715				
270	=	2259		1050	=	0		TOTAL	=	200598

CONCENTRATION

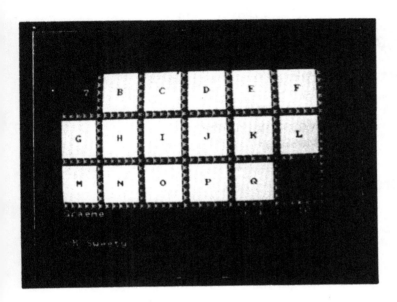

CLASSIFICATION: Memory game

Challenge your opponent to a tough brain battle! You select two cards from 18 and, if they have the same number on their opposite sides you have a match. Otherwise, they are turned face down again and a chance is given to your opponent.

May the best memory win!

Use the corresponding letter of the alphabet to select the card you wish to examine.

PROGRAMMING SUGGESTIONS

For an easier game, use a smaller range of numbers on the backs of the cards.

For a harder game, instead of having two sets of numbers from 1 to 9, have three sets of numbers from 1 to 6 and make each player choose three cards.

The display would look great with some more colouring for the cards!

PROGRAM
Variables

PLAYER$(2)	Player names
SCORE(2)	Player's score
CPLR	Current player number
LASTCARD	Last card examined
CARDX(18), CARDY(18)	Co-ordinates of all cards
FLIPPED(18)	Which cards are facing up
CARD$, BACK$	Strings for printing cards
I, J	Temps
CN	Card number
MN	Message number
MSG$(4)	Messages
NUMBER(18)	The numbers behind each card

Program Structure

Lines	Function/Activity
10 — 270	Initialise Front screen
280 — 480	Editor control
490 — 560	Flip card
570 — 790	Cards matched
800 — 880	Reset card
890 — 930	Update name and score
940 — 990	Print message
1000 — 1070	Game over

```
┌─────────────────────────────────────────────────────────────┐
│                    Initialise game                          │
└─────────────────────────────────────────────────────────────┘
```

```
10      MODE 1 : INK 0, 1 : INK 1, 26 : INK 2, 9 : INK 3, 24
20      DIM CARDX( 18 ), CARDY( 18 ), FLIPPED( 18 ), NUMBERS( 1
        8 )
30      FOR I = 1 TO 9
40      J = INT( RND( 1 ) * 18 ) + 1 : IF NUMBERS( J ) <> 0 THE
        N 40 ELSE NUMBERS( J ) = I
50      K = INT( RND( 1 ) * 18 ) + 1 : IF NUMBERS( K ) <> 0 THE
        N 50 ELSE NUMBERS( K ) = I
60      NEXT
70      FOR I = 1 TO 18 : FLIPPED( I ) = 0 : NEXT
80      FOR I = 1 TO 6 : CARDX( I ) = I * 6 - 5 : CARDY( I ) =
        1 : NEXT
90      FOR I = 7 TO 12 : CARDX( I ) = ( I - 6 ) * 6 - 5 : CARD
        Y( I ) = 7 : NEXT
100     FOR I = 13 TO 18 : CARDX( I ) = ( I - 12 ) * 6 - 5 : CA
        RDY( I ) = 13 : NEXT
110     CARD$ = STRING$( 5, 143 ) : BACK$ = STRING$( 5, 206 )
120     PAPER 0 : CLS : BORDER 1
130     PEN 1 : PRINT TAB( 13 ); "CONCENTRATION"
140     LOCATE 1, 10 : INPUT "Name for player one"; X$ : IF X$
        = "" THEN X$ = "NUTCASE"
150     IF LEN( X$ ) > 23 THEN 140
160     PLAYER$( 1 ) = X$
170     LOCATE 1, 13 : INPUT "Name for player two"; X$ : IF X$
        = "" THEN X$ = "FRUIT CAKE"
180     IF LEN( X$ ) > 23 THEN 170
190     PLAYER$( 2 ) = X$
200     LOCATE 1, 17 : PRINT "OK '"; PLAYER$( 1 ); "' AND '"; P
        LAYER$( 2 ); "'"
210     LOCATE 10, 23 : PRINT "Press a key to begin"
220     IF INKEY$ = "" THEN 220
230     MSG$( 1 ) = "Please select first card" : MSG$( 2 ) = "O
        K Sweety"
240     MSG$( 3 ) = "Now select a second card" : MSG$( 4 ) = "S
        ORRY, THEY ARE NOT A MATCH !"
250     CLS
260     FOR CN = 1 TO 18 : GOSUB 810 : NEXT
270     CPLR = 2
```

```
┌─────────────────────────────────────────────────────────────┐
│                    Editor/Control                           │
└─────────────────────────────────────────────────────────────┘
```

```
280     :
290     IF CPLR = 1 THEN CPLR = 2 : GOSUB 900 ELSE CPLR = 1 : G
        OSUB 900
300     MN = 1 : GOSUB 950
310     X$ = INKEY$ : IF X$ = "" THEN 310
320     IF ( X$ < "A" AND X$ > "R" ) AND ( X$ < "a" AND X$ > "r
        " ) THEN 300
330     IF X$ > "R" THEN LASTCARD = ASC( X$ ) - 96 ELSE LASTCAR
        D = ASC( X$ ) - 64
340     IF FLIPPED( LASTCARD ) = 1 THEN 300 ELSE FLIPPED( LASTC
        ARD ) = 1 : CN = LASTCARD : GOSUB 500
350     MN = 2 : GOSUB 950
360     FOR I = 1 TO 1000 : NEXT
```

135

```
370     MN = 3 : GOSUB 950
380     X$ = INKEY$ : IF X$ = "" THEN 380
390     IF ( X$ < "A" AND X$ > "R" ) AND ( X$ < "a" AND X$ > "r
        " ) THEN 370
400     IF X$ > "R" THEN CN = ASC( X$ ) - 96 ELSE CN = ASC( X$
        ) - 64
410     IF FLIPPED( CN ) = 1 OR LASTCARD = CN THEN 370
420     FLIPPED( CN ) = 1 : GOSUB 500
430     MN = 2 : GOSUB 950
440     FOR I = 1 TO 1000 : NEXT
450     IF NUMBERS( CN ) = NUMBERS( LASTCARD ) THEN GOSUB 580 :
        GOTO 290
460     MN = 4 : GOSUB 950
470     GOSUB 810 : FLIPPED( CN ) = 0 : CN = LASTCARD : GOSUB 8
        10 : FLIPPED( CN ) = 0 : FOR I = 1 TO 1000 : NEXT
480     GOTO 290
```

```
┌─────────────────────────────────────────────┐
│              Flip card                        │
└─────────────────────────────────────────────┘
```

```
490     :
500     PRINT CHR$( 7 ) : PEN 2
510     FOR I = 1 TO 5 : LOCATE CARDX( CN ), CARDY( CN ) + I -
        1
520     PRINT BACK$
530     NEXT
540     PAPER 2 : PEN 3 : LOCATE CARDX( CN ) + 2, CARDY( CN ) +
        2
550     PRINT USING "##"; NUMBERS( CN )
560     PAPER 0 : RETURN
```

```
┌─────────────────────────────────────────────┐
│              Cards matched                    │
└─────────────────────────────────────────────┘
```

```
570     :
580     SCORE( CPLR ) = SCORE( CPLR ) + 10 : GOSUB 900 : FOR I
        = 1 TO 18
590     FOR J = 1 TO 5
600     LOCATE CARDX( I ) + 5, CARDY( I ) + J - 1
610     PEN 3 : PRINT CHR$( 224 )
620     SOUND 1, 4000 - 220 * I + 40 * J, 7, 15
630     NEXT
640     FOR J = 1 TO 6
650     LOCATE CARDX( I ) + J - 1, CARDY( I ) + 5
660     PRINT CHR$( 224 )
670     NEXT : NEXT
680     FOR I = 18 TO 1 STEP -1
690     FOR J = 1 TO 5
700     LOCATE CARDX( I ) + 5, CARDY( I ) + J - 1
710     PRINT "▲"
720     SOUND 1, 220 * I - 40 * J, 7, 15
730     NEXT
740     FOR J = 1 TO 6
750     LOCATE CARDX( I ) + J - 1, CARDY( I ) + 5
760     PRINT "▲"
770     NEXT : NEXT
780     IF SCORE( 1 ) + SCORE( 2 ) = 90 THEN 1010
790     RETURN
```

```
800    :
810    PEN 1
820    FOR I = 1 TO 5
830    LOCATE CARDX( CN ), CARDY( CN ) + I - 1
840    PRINT CARD$
850    NEXT
860    PAPER 1 : PEN 2 : LOCATE CARDX( CN ) + 2, CARDY( CN ) +
       2
870    PRINT CHR$( 64 + CN )
880    PAPER 0 : RETURN
```

Update name and score

```
890    :
900    LOCATE 1, 19 : PEN 3 : PRINT SPACE$( 23 ) : LOCATE 1, 1
       9
910    PRINT PLAYER$( CPLR )
920    LOCATE 25, 19 : PRINT "Score :▲"; SCORE( CPLR )
930    RETURN
```

Print message

```
940    :
950    PEN 3 : LOCATE 1, 23
960    PRINT SPACE$( 35 )
970    LOCATE 1, 23
980    PRINT MSG$( MN )
990    RETURN
```

Game over

```
1000   :
1010   CLS : PRINT SPACE$( 16 ); "GAME▲OVER"
1020   IF SCORE( 1 ) > SCORE( 2 ) THEN X$ = PLAYER$( 1 ) ELSE
       X$ = PLAYER$( 2 )
1030   LOCATE 1, 10 : PRINT "CONGRATULATIONS▲TO▲"; X$
1040   LOCATE 1, 13 : PRINT PLAYER$( 1 ); "▲SCORED▲"; SCORE( 1
       )
1050   LOCATE 1, 16 : PRINT PLAYER$( 2 ); "▲SCORED▲"; SCORE( 2
       )
1060   LOCATE 6, 22 : PRINT "PRESS▲A▲KEY▲FOR▲ANOTHER▲GAME"
1070   IF INKEY$ = "" THEN 1070 ELSE RUN
```

137

ChexSum Tables

10	=	1408	290	=	1864	2190	=	2872
20	=	3168	300	=	4105	2200	=	323
25	=	1013	310	=	4145	2210	=	353
27	=	5199	320	=	3387	2230	=	2430
30	=	5173	330	=	1735	2250	=	201
32	=	176	340	=	928	2990	=	0
35	=	2416	350	=	1428	3000	=	234
40	=	4007	360	=	4141	3010	=	1009
50	=	4382	370	=	930	3020	=	2720
60	=	4439	380	=	6043	3030	=	636
65	=	2739	390	=	432	3040	=	176
70	=	549	990	=	0	3050	=	2992
80	=	1953	1000	=	819	3060	=	1181
90	=	4728	1010	=	3698	3070	=	434
95	=	1467	1020	=	627	3990	=	0
100	=	1146	1030	=	176	4000	=	1476
110	=	4958	1040	=	2994	4010	=	1342
115	=	1487	1050	=	1769	4020	=	2368
120	=	1147	1060	=	434	4030	=	201
130	=	3088	1990	=	0	4990	=	0
140	=	2443	2000	=	4013	5000	=	545
150	=	1301	2010	=	1010	5010	=	641
160	=	4659	2020	=	2840	5020	=	308
165	=	5640	2030	=	1048	5030	=	962
170	=	138	2040	=	2365	5040	=	201
180	=	1667	2050	=	176	8990	=	0
190	=	701	2070	=	979	9000	=	1550
200	=	0	2080	=	2872	9010	=	4442
210	=	3571	2090	=	811	9020	=	2273
220	=	927	2110	=	353	9025	=	2589
230	=	2059	2120	=	1523	9027	=	2594
240	=	4310	2130	=	978	9030	=	2501
245	=	5035	2140	=	2872	9040	=	1652
247	=	6086	2150	=	323			
250	=	960	2160	=	1920			
260	=	1396	2170	=	176	TOTAL	=	202596
270	=	929	2180	=	1011			

CONVOY

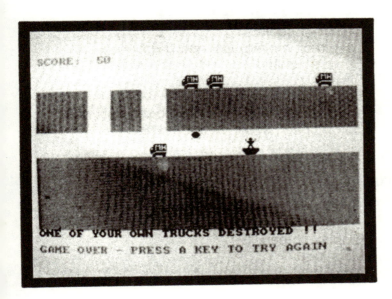

CLASSIFICATION: Time-Limit Game

Use the following keys to move: ',' to move left, '.', to move right, and the space bar to either deposit a bomb or patch up a section of road.

The enemy's trucks are black and yours are red. You are a saboteur and your mission is to stop a convoy of enemy trucks from passing you. The idea is to set the time bombs underneath the road by positioning your boat on the underground river.

The problem: Your own truck must be allowed to pass and you have no control over the fuses on your bombs!

PROGRAMMING SUGGESTIONS

The falling trucks would look great if there was a big splash and noise when they hit the water. The code to achieve this would go in the drop truck routine, lines 2500 — 2550, or a branch to an additional routine.

PROGRAM
Variables

TRUCKX(4)	Truck columns
TRUCK$	String for displaying trucks
BLANK$	Blank string to erase either truck or man
TCOLS(4)	Colour of trucks
LTM, LNT	Last truck moved, last new truck
BOMBC	Bomb's column
PLCOL	Player's column
MAN$	String for displaying man
ROAD(40)	Which portions of road have been destroyed
BCOUNT	Bomb count; seconds to detonation
SCORE	Player's score
I, J, T(16)	Temps

Program Structure

Lines	Function/Activity
10 — 110	Initialise
130 — 200	Display screen
210 — 500	Main loop
1000 — 1020	Move man
2000 — 2090	Move trucks
2500 — 2550	Drop trucks
2800	Man squashed
3000 — 3070	Explode bomb
3500 — 3590	Explode man
4000 — 4050	Patch up road
7000 — 7010	Update score
8000 — 8010	Decrement bomb count
9000 — 9040	Game over

```
┌─────────────────────────────────────────────┐
│                                             │
│            Intialise                        │
│                                             │
└─────────────────────────────────────────────┘

10      MODE 1 : INK 0, 13 : INK 1, 0 : INK 2, 3 : INK 3, 1
20      SYMBOL 240, 0, 0, 0, 0, 15, 25, 26, 123 : SYMBOL 241, 0
        , 0, 0, 255, 45, 173, 161
30      SYMBOL 242, 155, 187, 255, 248, 231, 95, 63, 56 : SYMBO
        L 243, 173, 173, 255, 0, 255, 254, 254, 14
40      SYMBOL 244, 1, 19, 17, 15, 7, 3, 1, 3 : SYMBOL 245, 2,
        6, 255, 255, 255, 127, 63, 31
50      SYMBOL 246, 128, 200, 136, 240, 224, 192, 128, 192 : SY
        MBOL 247, 64, 96, 255, 255, 255, 254, 252, 248
60      TRUCK$ = CHR$( 240 ) + CHR$( 241 ) + CHR$( 10 ) + CHR$(
        8 ) + CHR$( 8 ) + CHR$( 242 ) + CHR$( 243 )
70      BLANK$ = ".." + CHR$( 10 ) + CHR$( 8 ) + CHR$( 8 ) + ".
        "
80      MAN$ = CHR$( 244 ) + CHR$( 246 ) + CHR$( 10 ) + CHR$( 8
        ) + CHR$( 8 ) + CHR$( 245 ) + CHR$( 247 )
90      DIM ROAD( 40 ), T( 16 )
100     FOR I = 1 TO 40 : ROAD( I ) = 1 : NEXT
110     PLCOL = 30

┌─────────────────────────────────────────────┐
│                                             │
│            Screen Display                   │
│                                             │
└─────────────────────────────────────────────┘

130     :
140     PAPER 0 : CLS : BORDER 13
150     PEN 1 : FOR I = 1 TO 40 : FOR J = 5 TO 9 : LOCATE I, J
        : PRINT CHR$( 207 ) : NEXT : NEXT
160     PEN 3 : FOR I = 1 TO 40 : FOR J = 13 TO 21 : LOCATE I,
        J : PRINT CHR$( 143 ) : NEXT : NEXT
170     LOCATE PLCOL, 11 : PEN 2 : PRINT MAN$
180     BCOUNT = 5 : EVERY 50 GOSUB 8000
190     GOSUB 7000
200     LTM = 1 : LNT = 1 : TRUCKX( 1 ) = 38 : TCOLS( 1 ) = 1 :
         PEN 1 : LOCATE 38, 3 : PRINT USING "&"; TRUCK$

┌─────────────────────────────────────────────┐
│                                             │
│            Main program loop                │
│                                             │
└─────────────────────────────────────────────┘

210     :
220     GOSUB 1000
230     IF BCOUNT < 0 THEN GOSUB 3000
240     IF INKEY( 47 ) > -1 THEN IF ROAD( PLCOL ) = 0 THEN GOSU
        B 4000 ELSE IF BOMBC = 0 THEN BOMBC = PLCOL : PEN 1 : LO
        CATE BOMBC, 10 : PRINT CHR$( 231 )
250     GOSUB 2000
260     IF BCOUNT > -1 THEN LOCATE 1, 24 : PEN 3 : PRINT "BOMB.
        FUSE :."; BCOUNT
500     GOTO 220

┌─────────────────────────────────────────────┐
│                                             │
│            Position and move man            │
│                                             │
└─────────────────────────────────────────────┘

990     :
```

```
1000    IF INKEY( 39 ) > -1 AND PLCOL > 1 THEN LOCATE PLCOL, 11
        : PRINT USING "&"; BLANK$ : PLCOL = PLCOL - 1 : LOCATE
        PLCOL, 11 : PEN 2 : PRINT USING "&"; MAN$
1010    IF INKEY( 31 ) > -1 AND PLCOL < 38 THEN LOCATE PLCOL, 1
        1 : PRINT USING "&"; BLANK$ : PLCOL = PLCOL + 1 : LOCATE
        PLCOL, 11 : PEN 2 : PRINT USING "&"; MAN$
1020    RETURN
```

```
                    Position and move trucks
```

```
1990    :
2000    LTM = ( LTM MOD 4 ) + 1
2010    IF TRUCKX( LTM ) = 0 THEN 2060
2020    LOCATE TRUCKX( LTM ), 3 : PRINT USING "&"; BLANK$ : TRU
        CKX( LTM ) = TRUCKX( LTM ) - 1 : PEN TCOLS( LTM ) : LOCA
        TE TRUCKX( LTM ), 3 : PRINT USING "&"; TRUCK$
2030    IF TRUCKX( LTM ) < 2 THEN IF TCOLS( LTM ) = 2 THEN LOCA
        TE TRUCKX( LTM ), 3 : PRINT USING "&"; BLANK$ : TRUCKX(
        LTM ) = 0 ELSE LOCATE 1, 22 : PRINT "YOU_LET_AN_ENEMY_TR
        UCK_ESCAPE_!!" : GOTO 9000
2040    1 = TRUCKX( LTM ) : IF ROAD( I ) = 0 AND ROAD( I + 1 )
        = 0 THEN 2500
2050    RETURN
2060    IF TRUCKX( LNT ) > 35 THEN RETURN
2070    LNT = LTM : TRUCKX( LTM ) = 38 : IF RND( 1 ) < 0.5 THEN
        TCOLS( LTM ) = 1 ELSE TCOLS( LTM ) = 2
2080    PEN TCOLS( LTM ) : LOCATE 38, 3 : PRINT USING "&"; TRUC
        K$
2090    RETURN
```

```
                    Drop truck routine
```

```
2490    :
2500    J = 3 : I = TRUCKX( LTM )
2505    LOCATE I, J : PRINT USING "&"; BLANK$
2510    SOUND 1, 10 * J, 10, 15
2520    J = J + 1 : LOCATE I, J : PEN TCOLS( LTM ) : PRINT USIN
        G "&"; TRUCK$
2530    IF J < 11 THEN 2505 ELSE IF I = PLCOL OR I + 1 = PLCOL
        OR I - 1 = PLCOL THEN 2800
2540    IF TCOLS( LTM ) = 1 THEN SCORE = SCORE + 50 : GOSUB 700
        0 : LOCATE I, J : PRINT USING "&"; BLANK$ : TRUCKX( LTM
        ) = 0 : RETURN
2550    LOCATE 1, 22 : PRINT "ONE_OF_YOUR_OWN_TRUCKS_DESTROYED_
        !!" : GOTO 9000
```

```
                    Squash man!
```

```
2790    :
2800    LOCATE 1, 22 : PRINT "SQUISH_!!!!!" : GOTO 9000
```

```
                    Explode Bomb routine
```

```
2990    :
3000    IF BOMBC = 0 THEN 3500 ELSE LOCATE BOMBC, 10 : PRINT "_
        " :
```

```
3010    IF BOMBC = 1 THEN ST = 1 ELSE ST = BOMBC - 1
3020    FOR I = ST TO BOMBC + 1
3030    FOR J = 5 TO 9 : LOCATE I, J : PRINT "▴" : SOUND 1, 0,
        J, 5, 1, 1, J
3040    NEXT : ROAD( I ) = 0
3050    NEXT
3060    BCOUNT = INT( RND( 1 ) * 10 ) + 2
3070    BOMBC = 0 : RETURN
```

```
┌─────────────────────────────────────────┐
│                                          │
│         Destroy Man                      │
│                                          │
└─────────────────────────────────────────┘
```

```
3490    :
3500    FOR I = 1 TO 10
3510    FOR J = 1 TO 16 : T( J ) = INT( RND( 1 ) * 255 ) : NEXT

3520    SYMBOL 244, T( 1 ), T( 2 ), T( 3 ), T( 4 ), T( 5 ), T(
        6 ), T( 7 ), T( 8 )
3530    SYMBOL 246, T( 9 ), T( 10 ), T( 11 ), T( 12 ), T( 13 ),
        T( 14 ), T( 15 ), T( 16 )
3560    SOUND 1, 0, 25, 15, 1, 1, 3 * I
3570    LOCATE PLCOL, 11 : PEN 2 : PRINT USING "&"; MAN$ : NEXT

3580    SYMBOL 244, 0, 0, 0, 0, 0, 0, 0, 0 : SYMBOL 246, 0, 0,
        0, 0, 0, 0, 0, 0 : LOCATE PLCOL, 11 : PRINT USING "&"; M
        AN$
3590    GOTO 9000
```

```
┌─────────────────────────────────────────┐
│                                          │
│         Mend road routine                │
│                                          │
└─────────────────────────────────────────┘
```

```
3990    :
4000    IF PLCOL = 1 THEN ST = 1 ELSE ST = PLCOL - 1
4010    PEN 1 : FOR I = ST TO PLCOL + 1
4020    ROAD( I ) = 1
4030    FOR J = 5 TO 9 : LOCATE I, J
4040    PRINT CHR$( 207 ) : NEXT : NEXT
4050    RETURN
```

```
┌─────────────────────────────────────────┐
│                                          │
│         Update score                     │
│                                          │
└─────────────────────────────────────────┘
```

```
6990    :
7000    LOCATE 20, 24 : PEN 3 : PRINT "SCORE :▴"; SCORE
7010    RETURN
```

```
┌─────────────────────────────────────────┐
│                                          │
│         Decrement Bomb count             │
│                                          │
└─────────────────────────────────────────┘
```

```
7990    :
8000    BCOUNT = BCOUNT - 1
8010    RETURN
```

```
┌─────────────────────────────────────────┐
│                                          │
│         End of game                      │
│                                          │
└─────────────────────────────────────────┘
```

```
8990    :
9000    DI : SOUND 1, 100, 30, 15 : LOCATE 1, 24 : PRINT SPACE$
        ( 39 ) : LOCATE 1, 24
```

```
9010    PEN 3 : PRINT "GAME OVER - PRESS A KEY TO TRY AGAIN"
9020    LOCATE 1, 1 : PRINT "SCORE : "; SCORE
9030    IF INKEY$ = "" THEN 9040 ELSE 9030
9040    IF INKEY$ = "" THEN 9040 ELSE RUN
```

ChexSum Tables

10 =	1322	2000 =	1668	3510 =	3232		
20 =	2849	2010 =	1908	3520 =	3456		
30 =	4775	2020 =	8953	3530 =	3599		
40 =	3105	2030 =	10597	3560 =	1126		
50 =	5245	2040 =	4801	3570 =	2254		
60 =	5745	2050 =	201	3580 =	3821		
70 =	3066	2060 =	2073	3590 =	297		
80 =	5588	2070 =	6364	3990 =	0		
90 =	1151	2080 =	2748	4000 =	3337		
100 =	2185	2090 =	201	4010 =	2264		
110 =	813	2490 =	0	4020 =	984		
130 =	0	2500 =	2006	4030 =	1693		
140 =	572	2505 =	1887	4040 =	1148		
150 =	4069	2510 =	954	4050 =	201		
160 =	4049	2520 =	4026	6990 =	0		
170 =	1611	2530 =	6247	7000 =	1950		
180 =	1471	2540 =	7065	7010 =	201		
190 =	336	2550 =	3276	7990 =	0		
200 =	4943	2790 =	0	8000 =	1731		
210 =	0	2800 =	1571	8010 =	201		
220 =	456	2990 =	0	8990 =	0		
230 =	1763	3000 =	2741	9000 =	2089		
240 =	8094	3010 =	3291	9010 =	2892		
250 =	436	3020 =	2038	9020 =	1649		
260 =	3836	3030 =	2994	9030 =	1585		
500 =	442	3040 =	1160	9040 =	1652		
990 =	0	3050 =	176				
1000 =	8083	3060 =	2148				
1010 =	8125	3070 =	951	TOTAL =	208731		
1020 =	201	3490 =	0				
1990 =	0	3500 =	993				

144

LASER CROSS

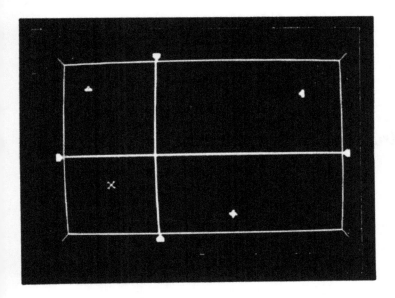

CLASSIFICATION: Shoot-Out Game

Use the following keys to move: 'A' to move laser up, 'Z' to move laser down, ',' to move laser left, '.' to move laser right and the space bar fire.

Waves of guard ships will try to obliterate your planet by striking one of the three energy stores or your laser.

The mother ship adds to the enemy's firepower and is worth more points.

PROGRAMMING SUGGESTIONS

More guard ships could be added, but make sure you update the 'Position Guard Ships', 'Guard Fires' and 'Blow Guard Ship' routines.

PROGRAM
Variables

ENEMX(4), ENEMY(4)	Ships coords
PROW, PCOL	Pointers row and column
EPHASE(4)	Phase of each ship
ETYPE(4)	Types of ships
ENEMY$(2,4)	Strings representing ships
SCORE	Player's score
TM	Time remaining
HIT	Number of ships hit
COLS	Colour of ships
I	Temp

Program Structure

Lines	Function/Activity
10 — 80	Initialise
100 — 500	Screen display and main program loop
1000 — 1070	Move pointers
2000 — 2100	Fire routine
3000 — 3050	Control ships
4000 — 4040	Player hit
8000	Update time
9000 — 9020	Game over

```
┌─────────────────────────────────────────────┐
│          Initialise Game                     │
└─────────────────────────────────────────────┘
```

```
10      MODE 1 : INK 0, 0 : INK 1, 13 : INK 2, 6 : INK 3, 24
20      SYMBOL 240, 255, 255, 255, 255, 126, 60, 24, 24 : SYMBO
        L 241, 24, 24, 60, 126, 255, 255, 255, 255
30      SYMBOL 242, 15, 31, 63, 255, 255, 255, 63, 31, 15 : SYMBOL 2
        43, 240, 248, 252, 255, 255, 252, 248, 240
40      SYMBOL 244, 8, 24, 24, 254, 127, 24, 24, 16 : SYMBOL 24
        5, 131, 194, 36, 24, 24, 36, 67, 193
50      SYMBOL 246, 24, 24, 56, 216, 216, 56, 24, 24 : SYMBOL 2
        47, 24, 24, 36, 255, 255, 0, 0, 0
60      SYMBOL 248, 24, 24, 28, 27, 27, 28, 24, 24 : SYMBOL 249
        , 0, 0, 0, 255, 255, 36, 24, 24
70      FOR I = 1 TO 4 : ENEMY$( 1, I ) = CHR$( 245 + I ) : NEX
        T
80      ENEMY$( 2, 1 ) = CHR$( 244 ) : ENEMY$( 2, 2 ) = CHR$( 2
        45 ) : ENEMY$( 2, 3 ) = CHR$( 244 ) : ENEMY$( 2, 4 ) = C
        HR$( 245 )
```

```
┌─────────────────────────────────────────────┐
│    Screen display and Main Program loop      │
└─────────────────────────────────────────────┘
```

```
90      :
100     BORDER 0 : PAPER 0 : CLS
110     PROW = 12 : PCOL = 20
130     TM = 60 : EVERY 50 GOSUB 8000
140     MOVE 17, 383 : DRAW 17, 17, 1 : DRAW 623, 17, 1 : DRAW
        623, 383, 1 : DRAW 17, 383, 1
150     DRAW 0, 399, 1 : MOVE 0, 0 : DRAW 17, 17, 1 : MOVE 623,
         17 : DRAW 639, 0, 1 : MOVE 623, 383 : DRAW 640, 400, 1
        : PEN 1
160     LOCATE PCOL, 1 : PRINT CHR$( 240 ) : LOCATE PCOL, 25 :
        PRINT CHR$( 241 ) : LOCATE 1, PROW : PRINT CHR$( 243 ) :
         LOCATE 40, PROW : PRINT CHR$( 242 )
200     GOSUB 1000
210     IF INKEY( 47 ) > -1 THEN GOSUB 2000
220     GOSUB 3000
500     GOTO 200
```

```
┌─────────────────────────────────────────────┐
│          Move pointers                       │
└─────────────────────────────────────────────┘
```

```
990     :
1000    IF INKEY( 69 ) = -1 OR PROW < 3 THEN 1020
1010    LOCATE 1, PROW : PRINT "▲" : LOCATE 40, PROW : PRINT "▲
        " : PROW = PROW - 1 : PEN 1 : LOCATE 1, PROW : PRINT CHR
        $( 243 ) : LOCATE 40, PROW : PRINT CHR$( 242 ) : RETURN
1020    IF INKEY( 71 ) = -1 OR PROW > 23 THEN 1040
1030    LOCATE 1, PROW : PRINT "▲" : LOCATE 40, PROW : PRINT "▲
        " : PROW = PROW + 1 : PEN 1 : LOCATE 1, PROW : PRINT CHR
        $( 243 ) : LOCATE 40, PROW : PRINT CHR$( 242 ) : RETURN
1040    IF INKEY( 39 ) = -1 OR PCOL < 3 THEN 1060
1050    LOCATE PCOL, 1 : PRINT "▲" : LOCATE PCOL, 25 : PRINT "▲
        " : PCOL = PCOL - 1 : PEN 1 : LOCATE PCOL, 1 : PRINT CHR
        $( 240 ) : LOCATE PCOL, 25 : PRINT CHR$( 241 ) : RETURN
```

```
1060    IF INKEY( 31 ) = -1 OR PCOL > 38 THEN RETURN
1070    LOCATE PCOL, 1 : PRINT ".." : LOCATE PCOL, 25 : PRINT ".
        " : PCOL = PCOL + 1 : PEN 1 : LOCATE PCOL, 1 : PRINT CHR
        $( 240 ) : LOCATE PCOL, 25 : PRINT CHR$( 241 ) : RETURN
```

```
┌─────────────────────────────────────────────────────┐
│                                                     │
│              Fire laser                             │
│                                                     │
└─────────────────────────────────────────────────────┘
```

```
1990    :
2000    MOVE 16 * PCOL - 8, 18 : DRAW 16 * PCOL - 8, 381, 3 : M
        OVE 18, 407 - 16 * PROW : DRAW 621, 407 - 16 * PROW, 3
2010    SOUND 1, 600, 10, 15
2020    HIT = 0 : FOR I = 1 TO 4 : IF EPHASE( I ) > 0 AND ENEMX
        ( I ) = PCOL AND ENEMY( I ) = PROW THEN HIT = I
2030    NEXT
2040    IF HIT THEN GOSUB 4000 ELSE SCORE = SCORE - 10
2050    MOVE 16 * PCOL - 8, 18 : DRAW 16 * PCOL - 8, 381, 0 : M
        OVE 18, 407 - 16 * PROW : DRAW 621, 407 - 16 * PROW, 0
2100    RETURN
```

```
┌─────────────────────────────────────────────────────┐
│                                                     │
│              Control ships                          │
│                                                     │
└─────────────────────────────────────────────────────┘
```

```
2990    :
3000    IF RND( 1 ) < 0.6 THEN RETURN
3010    FOR I = 1 TO 4 : IF EPHASE( I ) <> 0 THEN EPHASE( I ) =
        ( EPHASE( I ) MOD 4 ) + 1 : GOSUB 3500 : IF RND( 1 ) <
        0.01 THEN COLS( I ) = INT( RND( 1 ) * 2 ) + 2 : GOTO 303
        0 ELSE GOTO 3030
3020    IF RND( 1 ) > 0.05 OR I = HIT THEN 3030 ELSE ENEMX( I )
        = INT( RND( 1 ) * 36 ) + 3 : ENEMY( I ) = INT( RND( 1 )
        * 21 ) + 3 : EPHASE( I ) = 1 : ETYPE( I ) = INT( RND( 1
        ) * 2 ) + 1 : COLS( I ) = INT( RND( 1 ) * 2 ) + 2 : GOT
        O 3040
3030    IF RND( 1 ) < 0.02 AND EPHASE( I ) <> 0 THEN EPHASE( I
        ) = 0 : LOCATE ENEMX( I ), ENEMY( I ) : PRINT ".."
3040    NEXT
3050    RETURN
```

```
┌─────────────────────────────────────────────────────┐
│                                                     │
│              Draw ships                             │
│                                                     │
└─────────────────────────────────────────────────────┘
```

```
3490    :
3500    PEN COLS( I ) : LOCATE ENEMX( I ), ENEMY( I ) : PRINT E
        NEMY$( ETYPE( I ), EPHASE( I ) )
3510    RETURN
```

```
┌─────────────────────────────────────────────────────┐
│                                                     │
│              Hit routine                            │
│                                                     │
└─────────────────────────────────────────────────────┘
```

```
3990    :
4000    LOCATE ENEMX( HIT ), ENEMY( HIT ) : PRINT ".." : SOUND 1
        , 0, 50, 15, 1, 1, 31
4010    IF COLS( HIT ) = 3 THEN LOCATE 10, 10 : PRINT "DESTROYE
        D.YOUR.OWN.SHIP.!" : GOTO 9000
4020    SCORE = SCORE + 10 * ETYPE( HIT )
4030    EPHASE( HIT ) = 0
4040    RETURN
```

```
7990  :
8000  TM = TM - 1 : IF TM > 0 THEN RETURN
```

┌───┐
│ Update time   │
└───┘

```
7990  :
8000  TM = TM - 1 : IF TM > 0 THEN RETURN
```

┌───┐
│ Game over   │
└───┘

```
8990  :
9000  LOCATE 1, 1 : PEN 3 : PRINT "GAME OVER - YOUR SCORE : "
      ; SCORE
9010  IF INKEY$ = "" THEN 9020 ELSE 9010
9020  IF INKEY$ = "" THEN 9020 ELSE RUN
```

ChexSum Tables

Line	=	Value		Line	=	Value		Line	=	Value
10	=	1359		1010	=	7203		3050	=	201
20	=	4622		1020	=	2554		3490	=	0
30	=	4836		1030	=	7202		3500	=	5404
40	=	3317		1040	=	2488		3510	=	201
50	=	3327		1050	=	7013		3990	=	0
60	=	2897		1060	=	2654		4000	=	3247
70	=	3327		1070	=	7012		4010	=	4289
80	=	6075		1990	=	0		4020	=	2789
90	=	0		2000	=	5800		4030	=	1283
100	=	548		2010	=	574		4040	=	201
110	=	1473		2020	=	7695		7990	=	0
130	=	1239		2030	=	176		8000	=	2351
140	=	2336		2040	=	3003		8990	=	0
150	=	3389		2050	=	5826		9000	=	2992
160	=	6270		2100	=	201		9010	=	1545
200	=	456		2990	=	0		9020	=	1632
210	=	1844		3000	=	1998				
220	=	416		3010	=	10643				
500	=	422		3020	=	14557		TOTAL	=	170226
990	=	0		3030	=	6404				
1000	=	2759		3040	=	176				

OBSTACLE

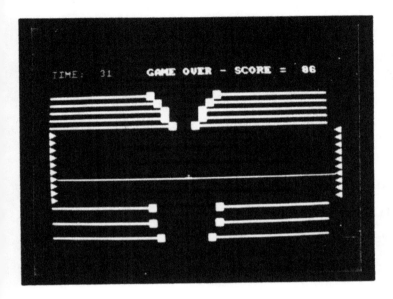

```
TIME:  31    GAME OVER - SCORE =   86
```

CLASSIFICATION: Avoidance Game

Use 'A' and 'Z' to move (up and down respectively) through the obstacle course.

Your goal is to reach the bottom in the best possible time, avoiding the stompers and lasers along the way. At the lower set of stompers, you only need to move one step below the lasers and then you will fall all the way.

PROGRAMMING SUGGESTIONS

To make the game more difficult the number of lasers or the number of stompers could be increased. To make it impossible increase both.

PROGRAM
Variables

TM	Time
PHASE	Phase man has reached (1-3)
MROW	Man's row
LASER(10)	Timer counts for each laser
LASROW(10)	Row of each laser
ASTOMPLXL(5),	Top set stompers
ASTOMPXR(5)	columns (left and right)
BSTOMPXL(3),	Bottom set
BSTOMPXR(3)	stompers columns (left and right)
ASTOMPY(5)	Top stompers rows
BSTOMPY(3)	Bottom stompers rows
ASTOMPDR(5)	Top stompers directions
BSTOMPDR(3)	Bottom stompers directions
I, J, K	Temps

Program Structure

Lines	Function/Activity
10 — 110	Initialise
130 — 500	Program main loop
1000 — 1060	Fire lasers
2000 — 2630	Move stomper
8000	Update time
9000 — 9020	Game over

```
                    ┌──────────────────────────────────────┐
                    │                                      │
                    │         Initialise game              │
                    │                                      │
                    └──────────────────────────────────────┘

10      MODE 1 : INK 0, 0 : INK 1, 6 : INK 2, 11 : INK 3, 24
20      FOR I = 1 TO 10 : LASROW( I ) = 8 + I : NEXT
30      PHASE = 1 : MROW = 2
40      FOR I = 1 TO 5 : ASTOMPY( I ) = 3 + I : ASTOMPXL( I ) =
        15 : ASTOMPXR( I ) = 24 : ASTOMPDR( I ) = 1 : NEXT
50      FOR I = 1 TO 3 : BSTOMPY( I ) = 17 + 2 * I : BSTOMPXL(
        I ) = 15 : BSTOMPXR( I ) = 24 : BSTOMPDR( I ) = 1 : NEXT

60      PAPER 0 : CLS : BORDER 0
70      EVERY 50 GOSUB 8000
80      PEN 2 : FOR I = 1 TO 10 : LOCATE 1, LASROW( I ) : PRINT
         CHR$( 246 ) : LOCATE 40, LASROW( I ) : PRINT CHR$( 247
        ) : NEXT
90      FOR I = 1 TO 5 : FOR J = 1 TO 14 : LOCATE J, ASTOMPY( I
         ) : PRINT CHR$( 154 ) : LOCATE J + 24, ASTOMPY( 1 ) : P
        RINT CHR$( 154 ) : NEXT : NEXT
100     FOR I = 1 TO 3 : FOR J = 1 TO 14 : LOCATE J, BSTOMPY( I
         ) : PRINT CHR$( 154 ) : LOCATE J + 24, BSTOMPY( I ) : P
        RINT CHR$( 154 ) : NEXT : NEXT
110     PEN 1 : LOCATE 20, MROW : PRINT CHR$( 249 )

                    ┌──────────────────────────────────────┐
                    │                                      │
                    │         Main Program loop            │
                    │                                      │
                    └──────────────────────────────────────┘

120     :
130     IF INKEY( 69 ) = -1 OR MROW < 3 THEN 140 ELSE LOCATE 20
        , MROW : PRINT "▪" : MROW = MROW - 1 : IF TEST( 304, 407
         - 16 * MROW ) <> 0 THEN 9000 ELSE PEN 1 : LOCATE 20, MR
        OW : PRINT CHR$( 249 )
140     IF PHASE = 3 THEN 145 ELSE IF INKEY( 71 ) = -1 OR MROW
        > 18 THEN 150
145     LOCATE 20, MROW : PRINT "▪" : MROW = MROW + 1 : IF TEST
        ( 304, 407 - 16 * MROW ) <> 0 THEN 9000 ELSE PEN 1 : LOC
        ATE 20, MROW : PRINT CHR$( 249 ) : IF MROW > 24 THEN 900
        0
150     PHASE = -( MROW > 1 ) - ( MROW > 8 ) -( MROW > 18 )
160     PEN 1 : LOCATE 1, 1 : PRINT "TIME :▪"; TM
170     IF PHASE <> 1 THEN 190 ELSE I = INT( RND( 1 ) * 5 ) + 1
         : GOSUB 2000
180     FOR K = 1 TO 3 : I = INT( RND( 1 ) * 5 ) + 1 : GOSUB 20
        00 : NEXT
190     IF PHASE = 2 THEN GOSUB 1000
200     IF PHASE > 1 THEN FOR K = 1 TO 5 : I = INT( RND( 1 ) *
        3 ) + 1 : GOSUB 2000 : NEXT
500     GOTO 130

                    ┌──────────────────────────────────────┐
                    │                                      │
                    │         Fire lasers                  │
                    │                                      │
                    └──────────────────────────────────────┘

990     :
1000    FOR I = 1 TO 10 : J = INT( RND( 1 ) * 10 ) + 5
1005    IF LASER( I ) < 0 THEN LASER( I ) = 0 : MOVE 17, 407 -
        16 * LASROW( I ) : DRAWR 605, 0, 0
```

153

```
1010    IF LASER( I ) = 0 THEN IF RND( 1 ) < 0.9 THEN 1060 ELSE
        LASER( I ) = J : PEN 3 : LOCATE 1, LASROW( I ) : PRINT
        CHR$( 246 ) : LOCATE 40, LASROW( I ) : PRINT CHR$( 247 )
        : GOTO 1060
1020    LASER( I ) = LASER( I ) - 1 : IF LASER( I ) > 0 THEN 10
        60
1030    PEN 2 : LOCATE 1, LASROW( I ) : PRINT CHR$( 246 ) : LOC
        ATE 40, LASROW( I ) : PRINT CHR$( 247 ) : MOVE 17, 407 -
        16 * LASROW( I )
1040    SOUND 1, 400, 10, 15 : DRAWR 605, 0, 3
1050    LASER( 1 ) = -1 : IF LASROW( I ) = MROW THEN 9000
1060    NEXT : RETURN
```

```
┌──────────────────────────────────────────────────────────────┐
│                                                              │
│            Move stomper                                      │
│                                                              │
└──────────────────────────────────────────────────────────────┘
```

```
1990    :
2000    IF PHASE = 1 THEN 2500
2010    PEN 2 : LOCATE BSTOMPXL( I ), BSTOMPY( I ) : IF BSTOMPD
        R( I ) = 1 THEN PRINT CHR$( 154 ) ELSE PRINT "▲"
2020    LOCATE BSTOMPXR( I ), BSTOMPY( I ) : IF BSTOMPDR( I ) =
        1 THEN PRINT CHR$( 154 ) ELSE PRINT "▲"
2030    IF BSTOMPDR( I ) = -1 THEN 2100 ELSE IF BSTOMPXL( I ) =
        19 THEN IF BSTOMPY( I ) = MROW THEN 9000 ELSE BSTOMPDR(
        I ) = -1 : GOTO 2050
2040    BSTOMPXL( I ) = BSTOMPXL( I ) + BSTOMPDR( I ) : BSTOMPX
        R( I ) = BSTOMPXR( I ) - BSTOMPDR( I )
2050    LOCATE BSTOMPXL( I ), BSTOMPY( I ) : PRINT CHR$( 143 )
        : LOCATE BSTOMPXR( I ), BSTOMPY( I ) : PRINT CHR$( 143 )

2060    RETURN
2100    IF BSTOMPXL( I ) = 15 THEN BSTOMPDR( I ) = 1 : GOTO 212
        0
2110    BSTOMPXL( I ) = BSTOMPXL( I ) + BSTOMPDR( I ) : BSTOMPX
        R( I ) = BSTOMPXR( I ) - BSTOMPDR( I )
2120    LOCATE BSTOMPXL( I ), BSTOMPY( I ) : PRINT CHR$( 143 )
        : LOCATE BSTOMPXR( I ), BSTOMPY( I ) : PRINT CHR$( 143 )

2130    RETURN
2500    PEN 2 : LOCATE ASTOMPXL( I ), ASTOMPY( I ) : IF ASTOMPD
        R( I ) = 1 THEN PRINT CHR$( 154 ) ELSE PRINT "▲"
2510    LOCATE ASTOMPXR( I ), ASTOMPY( I ) : IF ASTOMPDR( I ) =
        1 THEN PRINT CHR$( 154 ) ELSE PRINT "▲"
2520    IF ASTOMPDR( I ) = -1 THEN 2600 ELSE IF ASTOMPXL( I ) =
        19 THEN IF ASTOMPY( I ) = MROW THEN 9000 ELSE ASTOMPDR(
        I ) = -1 : GOTO 2540
2530    ASTOMPXL( I ) = ASTOMPXL( I ) + ASTOMPDR( I ) : ASTOMPX
        R( I ) = ASTOMPXR( I ) - ASTOMPDR( I )
2540    LOCATE ASTOMPXL( I ), ASTOMPY( I ) : PRINT CHR$( 143 )
        : LOCATE ASTOMPXR( I ), ASTOMPY( I ) : PRINT CHR$( 143 )

2550    RETURN
2600    IF ASTOMPXL( I ) = 15 THEN ASTOMPDR( I ) = 1 : GOTO 262
        0
2610    ASTOMPXL( I ) = ASTOMPXL( I ) + ASTOMPDR( I ) : ASTOMPX
        R( I ) = ASTOMPXR( I ) - ASTOMPDR( I )
2620    LOCATE ASTOMPXL( I ), ASTOMPY( I ) : PRINT CHR$( 143 )
        : LOCATE ASTOMPXR( I ), ASTOMPY( I ) : PRINT CHR$( 143 )

2630    RETURN
```

```
7990 :
8000 TM = TM + 1 : RETURN
```

┌───┐
│   │
│   Game over   │
│   │
└───┘

```
8990 :
9000 LOCATE 15, 1 : PRINT "GAME▲OVER▲-▲SCORE▲=▲"; MROW * 10
     - TM * 2 - 100 * ( MROW > 23 )
9005 FOR I = 1 TO 1500 : NEXT
9007 IF MROW > 23 THEN LOCATE 1, 2 : PEN 3 : PRINT "CONGRATU
     LATIONS!!▲-▲YOU▲HAVE▲WON!!"
9010 IF INKEY$ = "" THEN 9020 ELSE 9010
9020 IF INKEY$ = "" THEN 9020 ELSE RUN
```

ChexSum Tables

10 =	1357	990 =	0	2510 =	5393
20 =	2798	1000 =	2760	2520 =	8684
30 =	1486	1005 =	4952	2530 =	7392
40 =	6882	1010 =	9352	2540 =	6113
50 =	7171	1020 =	3747	2550 =	201
60 =	548	1030 =	6203	2600 =	3472
70 =	612	1040 =	1051	2610 =	7392
80 =	5463	1050 =	3521	2620 =	6113
90 =	7015	1060 =	378	2630 =	201
100 =	7047	1990 =	0	7990 =	0
110 =	1860	2000 =	1491	8000 =	1304
120 =	0	2010 =	5594	8990 =	0
130 =	9990	2020 =	5396	9000 =	4932
140 =	4293	2030 =	8431	9005 =	1386
145 =	8515	2040 =	7366	9007 =	4292
150 =	3951	2050 =	6085	9010 =	1545
160 =	1588	2060 =	201	9020 =	1632
170 =	3845	2100 =	5452		
180 =	3337	2110 =	7398		
190 =	1713	2120 =	6117	TOTAL =	233818
200 =	4624	2130 =	201		
500 =	352	2500 =	5623		

155

ALLIGATOR

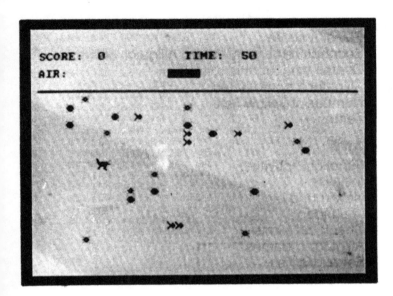

CLASSIFICATION: Time-Limit Game

Help the starving alligator to find food by guiding it to plants, exotic fish and the delicious yellow fish. All of the yellow fish must be eaten and the Alligator must reach the right hand side of the screen within the given time-limit.

If you forget that Alligators can't stay under water forever then the poor thing will drown! Keep an eye on the air gauge at the top of the screen and don't eat the mines.

Use 'A' to move up, 'Z' to move down, '.' to move right.

PROGRAMMING SUGGESTIONS

What if the Alligator had bigger lungs? Increase the value of GAUGE. The game could be made significantly more complex by randomly swapping mines for fish or making mines invisible for a short period.

PROGRAM
Variables

NR	Number of rounds
PHASE	Alligator's phase (1 or 2)
ALLIG$(2)	Strings to display Alligator
BLANK$	String to erase Alligator
SCORE	Player's score
GAUGE	Seconds remaining before Alligator drowns
OTIME	Overall time left this round
ALLIGX, ALLIGY	Alligator's coordinates
NYFISH	Number of yellow fish
I, J, T1	Temps

Program Structure

Lines	Function/Activity
10 — 110	Initialise
120 — 290	New round
300 — 590	Main loop
600 — 990	Check collisions
1000 — 1990	Alligator breathes
2000 — 2490	Eat exotic fish
2500 — 2990	Eat yellow fish
3000 — 3990	Eat mine
4000 — 4490	Alligator drowns
4500 — 4990	Time up
5000 — 5990	Update Gauge and Time
6000 — 6990	Update score
7000 — 7990	Decrement Gauge and Time
8000 — 8990	Animate Alligator
9000 — 9040	Game over

```
                    ┌─────────────────────────────────────┐
                    │                                     │
                    │         Initialise game             │
                    │                                     │
                    └─────────────────────────────────────┘

10      MODE 1 : INK 0, 14 : INK 1, 0 : INK 2, 12 : INK 3, 1 :
        SYMBOL AFTER 231
20      SYMBOL 240, 0, 0, 0, 0, 192, 96, 96, 119 : SYMBOL 241,
        63, 63, 31, 15, 24, 48, 48, 0
30      SYMBOL 242, 0, 0, 0, 0, 0, 1, 2, 180 : SYMBOL 243, 248,
        255, 240, 224, 96, 192, 96, 48
40      SYMBOL 244, 0, 0, 0, 128, 192, 192, 96, 119 : SYMBOL 24
        5, 63, 63, 31, 15, 24, 48, 97, 97
50      SYMBOL 246, 0, 0, 0, 0, 0, 0, 16, 184 : SYMBOL 247, 255
        , 255, 240, 224, 96, 192, 128, 128
60      SYMBOL 249, 129, 90, 60, 231, 60, 90, 129, 0
70      SYMBOL 248, 128, 196, 110, 63, 63, 110, 196, 128
75      SYMBOL 231, 129, 60, 126, 255, 255, 126, 60, 129
80      ALLIG$( 1 ) = CHR$( 240 ) + CHR$( 242 ) + CHR$( 10 ) +
        STRING$( 2, 8 ) + CHR$( 241 ) + CHR$( 243 )
90      ALLIG$( 2 ) = CHR$( 244 ) + CHR$( 246 ) + CHR$( 10 ) +
        STRING$( 2, 8 ) + CHR$( 245 ) + CHR$( 247 )
100     BLANK$ = CHR$( 32 ) + CHR$( 32 ) + CHR$( 10 ) + STRING$
        ( 2, 8 ) + CHR$( 32 ) + CHR$( 32 )

                    ┌─────────────────────────────────────┐
                    │                                     │
                    │         New round of game           │
                    │                                     │
                    └─────────────────────────────────────┘

110     :
120     PAPER 0 : CLS : BORDER 14
125     NYFISH = 0 : NR = NR + 1
130     FOR I = 3 TO 38 : FOR J = 6 TO 24
140     K = RND( 1 ) : IF K < 0.015 THEN PEN 1 : LOCATE I, J :
        PRINT CHR$( 231 ) : GOTO 200
150     IF K < 0.035 THEN PEN 3 : LOCATE I, J : PRINT CHR$( 249
        ) : GOTO 200
160     IF K < 0.045 AND NYFISH < 7 THEN PEN 2 : LOCATE I, J :
        PRINT CHR$( 248 ) : NYFISH = NYFISH + 1
200     NEXT : NEXT
210     PEN 3 : FOR I = 1 TO 40 : LOCATE I, 5 : PRINT CHR$( 154
        ) : NEXT
220     LOCATE 1, 1 : PRINT "SCORE :."; SCORE : LOCATE 20, 1 :
        PRINT "TIME :.60"
230     LOCATE 1, 3 : PRINT "AIR :." : PEN 1
240     FOR I = 7 TO 22 - NR : LOCATE I, 3 : PRINT CHR$( 143 )
        : NEXT
250     GUAGE = 15 - NR : OTIME = 60
260     ALLIGX = 1 : ALLIGY = 15 : PEN 1 : LOCATE ALLIGX, ALLIG
        Y : PRINT USING "&"; ALLIG$( 1 ) : PHASE = 1
270     EVERY 30, 1 GOSUB 8000 : EVERY 50, 2 GOSUB 7000

                    ┌─────────────────────────────────────┐
                    │                                     │
                    │         Main program loop           │
                    │                                     │
                    └─────────────────────────────────────┘

290     :
300     LOCATE ALLIGX, ALLIGY : PEN 1 : PRINT USING "&"; ALLIG$
        ( PHASE )
310     IF INKEY( 69 ) = -1 OR ALLIGY < 6 THEN 350
```

```
320     LOCATE ALLIGX, ALLIGY : PRINT USING "&"; BLANK$ : ALLIG
        Y = ALLIGY - 1 : GOSUB 600
330     IF ALLIGY < 6 THEN GOSUB 1000
350     IF INKEY( 71 ) = -1 OR ALLIGY > 23 THEN 380
360     LOCATE ALLIGX, ALLIGY : PRINT USING "&"; BLANK$ : ALLIG
        Y = ALLIGY + 1 : GOSUB 600
380     IF INKEY( 31 ) = -1 THEN 410
390     LOCATE ALLIGX, ALLIGY : PRINT USING "&"; BLANK$ : ALLIG
        X = ALLIGX + 1 : GOSUB 600
400     IF ALLIGX > 38 THEN CLS : IF NYFISH > 0 THEN LOCATE 1,
        3 : PRINT "YOU MISSED SOME YELLOW FISH !!!" : GOSUB 6000
        : GOTO 9000 ELSE SCORE = SCORE + 100 : GOTO 120
410     IF GUAGE < 1 THEN 4000 ELSE IF OTIME < 1 THEN 4500
420     GOSUB 5000
500     GOTO 300
```

┌──┐
│   Check collisions   │
└──┘

```
590     :
600     T1 = TEST( ALLIGX * 16 - 16, 415 - 16 * ALLIGY )
610     IF T1 = 1 THEN 3000 ELSE IF T1 = 2 THEN GOSUB 2500 ELSE
        IF T1 = 3 THEN GOSUB 2000
620     T1 = TEST( ALLIGX * 16, 415 - 16 * ALLIGY )
630     IF T1 = 1 THEN 3000 ELSE IF T1 = 2 THEN GOSUB 2500 ELSE
        IF T1 = 3 THEN GOSUB 2000
640     T1 = TEST( ALLIGX * 16, 399 - 16 * ALLIGY )
650     IF T1 = 1 THEN 3000 ELSE IF T1 = 2 THEN GOSUB 2500 ELSE
        IF T1 = 3 THEN GOSUB 2000
660     T1 = TEST( ALLIGX * 16 - 16, 399 - 16 * ALLIGY )
670     IF T1 = 1 THEN 3000 ELSE IF T1 = 2 THEN GOSUB 2500 ELSE
        IF T1 = 3 THEN GOSUB 2000
680     PEN 1 : LOCATE ALLIGX, ALLIGY : PRINT USING "&"; ALLIG$
        ( PHASE )
690     RETURN
```

┌──┐
│   Alligator Breathes   │
└──┘

```
990     :
1000    LOCATE ALLIGX, 5 : PEN 3 : PRINT CHR$( 154 ); CHR$( 154
        )
1010    ALLIGY = ALLIGY + 1 : GUAGE = 15 - NR
1020    PEN 1 : FOR I = 8 TO 22 - NR : LOCATE I, 3 : PRINT CHR$
        ( 143 ) : NEXT
1030    RETURN
```

┌──┐
│   Player eats exotic fish   │
└──┘

```
1990    :
2000    SCORE = SCORE + 10 : GOSUB 6000
2010    SOUND 1, 50, 15, 15 : SOUND 1, 40, 15, 15 : SOUND 1, 60
        , 25, 15
2020    RETURN
```

┌──┐
│   Player eats yellow fish   │
└──┘

```
2490    :
```

```
2500    SCORE = SCORE + 50 : GOSUB 6000
2510    FOR I = 100 TO 30 STEP -8 : SOUND 1, I, 5, 15 : NEXT
2520    NYFISH = NYFISH - 1 : GUAGE = GUAGE + 1
2530    RETURN
```

```
┌─────────────────────────────────────────┐
│                                          │
│          Player eats mine                │
│                                          │
└─────────────────────────────────────────┘
```

```
2990    :
3000    FOR I = 1 TO 25 : BORDER I
3010    SOUND 1, 0, 10, 15, 1, 1, 1
3015    INK 0, INT( RND( 1 ) * 26 )
3020    FOR J = 1 TO 70 : NEXT : NEXT
3030    GOTO 9000
```

```
┌─────────────────────────────────────────┐
│                                          │
│       Alligator Drowns (no air left)     │
│                                          │
└─────────────────────────────────────────┘
```

```
3990    :
4000    GOSUB 5000
4010    PEN 3 : LOCATE 1, 2 : PRINT "POOR ALLIGATOR HAS DROWNED
        !!!!"
4020    GOTO 9000
```

```
┌─────────────────────────────────────────┐
│                                          │
│          Time has run out                │
│                                          │
└─────────────────────────────────────────┘
```

```
4490    :
4500    PEN 1 : LOCATE 1, 2 : PRINT "YOU ARE TOO SLOW - TIME UP
        !!"
4510    PRINT CHR$( 7 )
4520    GOTO 9000
```

```
┌─────────────────────────────────────────┐
│                                          │
│         Displays remaining air           │
│                                          │
└─────────────────────────────────────────┘
```

```
4990    :
5000    LOCATE 22 - NR - GUAGE, 3 : PRINT " "
5010    LOCATE 20, 1 : PEN 3 : PRINT "TIME : "; OTIME
5020    RETURN
```

```
┌─────────────────────────────────────────┐
│                                          │
│             Update score                 │
│                                          │
└─────────────────────────────────────────┘
```

```
5990    :
6000    PEN 3 : LOCATE 1, 1 : PRINT "SCORE : "; SCORE
6010    RETURN
```

```
┌─────────────────────────────────────────┐
│                                          │
│   Decrement Air Gauge and time elapsed   │
│                                          │
└─────────────────────────────────────────┘
```

```
6990    :
7000    GUAGE = GUAGE - 1 : OTIME = OTIME - 1
7010    RETURN
```

```
7990  :
8000  PHASE = ( PHASE MOD 2 ) + 1
8010  RETURN
```

Animate Alligator

End of Game

```
8990  :
9000  SOUND 1, 1000, 50, 15
9010  FOR I = 10 TO 30 : FOR J = 10 TO 15 : LOCATE I, J : PRI
      NT "▲" : NEXT : NEXT
9020  PEN 1 : LOCATE 13, 12 : PRINT "G▲A▲M▲E▲▲O▲V▲E▲R"
9025  SOUND 1, 1000, 50, 15
9030  IF INKEY$ = "" THEN 9040 ELSE 9030
9040  IF INKEY$ = "" THEN 9040 ELSE RUN
```

ChexSum Tables

10 =	1999	390 =	4630	3020 =	1408
20 =	2854	400 =	8320	3030 =	297
30 =	3623	410 =	3105	3990 =	0
40 =	3254	420 =	376	4000 =	376
50 =	3778	500 =	267	4010 =	2807
60 =	1843	590 =	0	4020 =	297
70 =	2058	600 =	3521	4490 =	0
75 =	2187	610 =	4518	4500 =	2642
80 =	5384	620 =	3235	4510 =	583
90 =	5433	630 =	4550	4520 =	297
100 =	4481	640 =	3219	4990 =	0
110 =	0	650 =	4550	5000 =	1926
120 =	573	660 =	3505	5010 =	1841
125 =	1960	670 =	4550	5020 =	201
130 =	2037	680 =	3434	5990 =	0
140 =	4675	690 =	201	6000 =	1886
150 =	3668	990 =	0	6010 =	201
160 =	6248	1000 =	2442	6990 =	0
200 =	353	1010 =	3008	7000 =	3049
210 =	2658	1020 =	3178	7010 =	201
220 =	2742	1030 =	201	7990 =	0
230 =	1114	1990 =	0	8000 =	1930
240 =	2942	2000 =	1917	8010 =	201
250 =	2175	2010 =	1626	8990 =	0
260 =	5420	2020 =	201	9000 =	759
270 =	1344	2490 =	0	9010 =	3406
290 =	0	2500 =	1957	9020 =	1701
300 =	3434	2510 =	2486	9025 =	791
310 =	2724	2520 =	3214	9030 =	1585
320 =	4601	2530 =	201	9040 =	1652
330 =	1800	2990 =	0		
350 =	2781	3000 =	1585		
360 =	4632	3010 =	848	TOTAL =	202352
380 =	1578	3015 =	1317		

162

DRAUGHTS

CLASSIFICATION: Simulation Game

A two player game of draughts for all ages, suited for the novice and experienced alike. The game is played using a mock board and the player moves his player to the appropriate position.

The play is controlled with the following keys:

'A' to move the cursor up
'Z' to move the cursor down
',' to move the cursor left
'.' to move the cursor right

Use the 'SPACE' bar to deposit or pick up the player and the 'C' to change a move. Press 'SHIFT' and 'Q' to replay or quit.

PROGRAMMING SUGGESTIONS

The game could of course be changed in many ways. As it stands it plays a reasonable game. It could be altered to play against the computer, have different levels of play and have time differing time limits for moving in each level of play.

PROGRAM
Variables

A, B	Cursor coordinates
C	Colour
REPLAY	Flag for replay
FLAG	Has 'C' been pressed?
X(8,8), Y(8,)	Coordinates of each square
COL (8,8)	Paper colours for each square
CONTENTS(8,8)	Contents of each square
MX(3000), MY(3000)	Moves coordinates
COUNT	Moves count
BPIECES	Number of black pieces
RPIECES	Number of red pieces taken
N	Temp
PIECE$	String for draughts piece
SP$	Space string
T	Temp
FROMX, FROMY	Coordinates of location to move piece from
DESX, DESY	Coordinates to move piece to
BLOCK$	String to draw

Program Structure

Lines	Function/Activity
30 — 70	Call initialise
100 — 490	Main loop
520 — 660	Cursor control
690 — 770	Replay
800 — 900	Draw board
930 — 980	Block routine
1010 — 1130	Initial initialisation
1160 — 1440	Replay initialisation
1470 — 1520	Menu

```
                    ┌─────────────────────────────────────────────┐
                    │                                             │
                    │   Call initialise Game                      │
                    │                                             │
                    └─────────────────────────────────────────────┘

40      GOSUB 1010
50      A = 1 : B = 1
60      COUNT = 1

                    ┌─────────────────────────────────────────────┐
                    │                                             │
                    │   Main program loop                         │
                    │                                             │
                    └─────────────────────────────────────────────┘

70      :
100     GOSUB 120
110     GOTO 100
120     C = 4
130     LOCATE 1, 23
140     PEN C : PAPER 0 : PRINT "RED'S.MOVE.."
150     IF REPLAY <> 1 THEN GOSUB 520 : PRINT CHR$(7) ELSE GOTO
        180
160     IF FLAG = 1 THEN GOTO 120
170     IF CONTENTS(A, B) <> C THEN GOTO 150 ELSE FROMX = A : F
        ROMY = B
180     IF REPLAY <> 1 THEN GOSUB 520 : PRINT CHR$(7) ELSE GOSU
        B 690
190     IF FLAG = 1 THEN GOTO 120
200     IF COL(A, B) = 3 OR CONTENTS(A, B) <> 0  OR A > FROMX +
        2 OR A < FROMX - 2 OR A = FROMX THEN GOTO 180
210     DESX = A : DESY = B
220     IF FROMX < 8 THEN IF (A = FROMX + 2 AND CONTENTS(FROMX
        + 1, FROMY + ((DESY  - FROMY) / 2)) <> 5) THEN GOTO 180
230     IF FROMX > 1 THEN IF (A = FROMX - 2 AND CONTENTS(FROMX
        - 1, FROMY + ((DESY - FROMY) / 2)) <> 5) THEN GOTO 180
240     PEN C : CONTENTS(A, B) = C : PAPER COL(A, B) : BLOCK$ =
        PIECE$ : GOSUB 930
250     CONTENTS(FROMX, FROMY) = 0 : A = FROMX : B = FROMY : PA
        PER COL(A, B) : BLOCK$ = SP$ : GOSUB 930
260     IF REPLAY <> 1 THEN MX(COUNT) = FROMX : MY(COUNT) = FRO
        MY : COUNT = COUNT + 1 : MX(COUNT) = DESX : MY(COUNT) =
        DESY : COUNT = COUNT + 1
270     IF ABS(FROMY - DESY) = 2 THEN CONTENTS(FROMX + ((DESX -
        FROMX) / 2), (FROMY + ((DESY - FROMY) / 2))) = 0 : BPIE
        CES = BPIECES + 1 : LOCATE BPIECES, 21 : PEN 5 : PAPER 0
        : PRINT CHR$(231) ELSE 290
280     A = FROMX + (( DESX - FROMX) / 2)  : B = FROMY + ((DESY
        - FROMY) / 2) : PAPER COL(A, B) : BLOCK$ = SP$ : GOSUB
        930
290     IF BPIECES = 12 THEN LOCATE 1, 23 : PAPER 0 : PRINT "RE
        D.WINS!!!....." : FOR N = 1 TO 10 : FOR T = 1 TO 1000 STE
        P 50 : SOUND 129, T, 10, 15 : NEXT T : NEXT N : FOR T =
        1 TO 3000 : NEXT T : GOTO 1470
300     C = 5
310     LOCATE 1, 23
320     PEN C : PAPER 0 : PRINT "BLUE'S.MOVE.."
330     IF REPLAY <> 1 THEN GOSUB 520 : PRINT CHR$(7) ELSE 360
340     IF FLAG = 1 THEN GOTO 300
350     IF CONTENTS(A, B) <> C THEN GOTO 330 ELSE FROMX = A : F
        ROMY = B
360     IF REPLAY <> 1 THEN GOSUB 520 : PRINT CHR$(7) ELSE GOSU
        B 690
```

165

```
370    IF FLAG = 1 THEN GOTO 300
380    IF COL(A, B) = 3 OR CONTENTS(A, B) <> 0 OR A > FROMX +
       2 OR A < FROMX - 2 OR A = FROMX THEN GOTO 360
390    DESX = A : DESY = B
400    IF FROMX < 8 THEN IF (A = FROMX + 2 AND CONTENTS(FROMX
       + 1, FROMY + ((DESY  - FROMY) / 2)) <> 4) THEN GOTO 360
410    IF FROMX > 1 THEN IF (A = FROMX - 2 AND CONTENTS(FROMX
       - 1, FROMY + ((DESY - FROMY) / 2)) <> 4) THEN GOTO 360
420    PEN C : CONTENTS(A, B) = C : PAPER COL(DESX, DESY) : A
       = DESX : B = DESY : BLOCK$ = PIECE$ : GOSUB 930
430    IF REPLAY <> 1 THEN MX(COUNT) = FROMX : MY(COUNT) = FRO
       MY : COUNT = COUNT + 1 : MX(COUNT) = DESX : MY(COUNT) =
       DESY : COUNT = COUNT + 1
440    CONTENTS(FROMX, FROMY) = 0 : A = FROMX : B = FROMY : PA
       PER COL(A, B) : BLOCK$ = SP$ : GOSUB 930
450    IF ABS(FROMY - DESY) = 2 THEN CONTENTS(FROMX + ((DESX -
       FROMX) / 2), (FROMY + ((DESY - FROMY) / 2))) = 0 : RPIE
       CES = RPIECES + 1 : LOCATE 20, RPIECES : PEN 4 : PAPER 0
       : PRINT CHR$(231) ELSE 470
460    A = FROMX + (( DESX - FROMX) / 2)   : B = FROMY + ((DESY
       - FROMY) / 2) : PAPER COL(A, B) : BLOCK$ = SP$ : GOSUB
       930
470    IF RPIECES = 12 THEN LOCATE 1, 23 : PAPER 0 : PRINT "BL
       UE.WINS!!...." : FOR N = 1 TO 10 : FOR T = 1 TO 1000 STE
       P 50 : SOUND 129, T, 10, 15 : NEXT T : NEXT N : FOR T =
       1 TO 3000 : NEXT T : GOTO 1470
480    RETURN
```

```
┌─────────────────────────────────────┐
│                                     │
│          Cursor control             │
│                                     │
└─────────────────────────────────────┘
```

```
490    :
520    IF INKEY(67) = 32 THEN GOTO 1470
530    IF INKEY(62) = -1 THEN FLAG = 0 :  PAPER 10 ELSE FLAG =
       1 : RETURN
540    PEN CONTENTS(A, B)
550    IF CONTENTS(A, B) > 0 THEN BLOCK$ = PIECE$ ELSE BLOCK$
       = SP$
560    GOSUB 930
570    PAPER COL(A, B)
580    GOSUB 930
590    IF INKEY(47) > -1 THEN RETURN
600    A = A + (INKEY(39) > -1) - (INKEY(31) > -1) : B = B + (
       INKEY(69) > -1) - (INKEY(71) > -1)
610    IF A > 8 THEN A = 1
620    IF A < 1 THEN A = 8
630    IF B > 8 THEN B = 1
640    IF B < 1 THEN B = 8
650    GOTO 520
```

```
┌─────────────────────────────────────┐
│                                     │
│          Replay game                │
│                                     │
└─────────────────────────────────────┘
```

```
660    :
690    FROMX = MX(COUNT) : FROMY = MY(COUNT)
700    COUNT = COUNT + 1
710    A = MX(COUNT)
720    B = MY(COUNT)
730    COUNT = COUNT + 1
740    IF MX(COUNT) = 0 THEN GOTO 1470
750    IF INKEY(67) > -1 THEN REPLAY = 0
760    RETURN
```

```
770     :
800     FOR T = 1 TO 8
810     FOR N = 1 TO 8
820     PAPER COL(N, T)
830     IF CONTENTS(N, T) = 0 THEN BLOCK$ = SP$
840     A = N : B = T
850     IF CONTENTS(N, T) > 0 THEN BLOCK$ = PIECE$
860     PEN CONTENTS(N, T)
870     GOSUB 930
880     NEXT N : NEXT T
890     RETURN
```

```
900     :
930     LOCATE X(A, B), Y(A, B)
940     PRINT LEFT$(BLOCK$, 2)
950     LOCATE X(A, B), Y(A, B) + 1
960     PRINT RIGHT$(BLOCK$, 2)
970     RETURN
```

```
980     :
1010    MODE 0
1020    PEN 1 : INK 1, 18
1030    PAPER 0
1040    BORDER 1
1050    INK 0, 1 : CLS
1060    INK 2, 26
1070    INK 3, 0
1080    INK 4, 6
1090    REPLAY = 0
1100    INK 5, 20
1110    INK 7, 8
1120    DIM X(8, 8), Y(8, 8), COL(8, 8), CONTENTS(8, 8), MX(300
        0), MY(3000)
```

```
1130    :
1160    CLS : COUNT = 1 : BPIECES = 0 : RPIECES = 0
1170    FOR T = 1 TO 8 : FOR N = 1 TO 8 : CONTENTS(N, T) = 0 :
        NEXT N : NEXT T
1180    FOR N = 1 TO 8 STEP 2
1190    CONTENTS(N, 1) = 4 : CONTENTS(N + 1, 2) = 4 : CONTENTS(
        N, 3) = 4
1200    CONTENTS(N + 1, 8) = 5 : CONTENTS(N, 7) = 5 : CONTENTS(
        N + 1, 6) = 5
1210    NEXT N
1220    SYMBOL 240, 0, 3, 15, 31, 63 , 63 , 127, 127
```

```
1230   SYMBOL 241, 0  , 192, 240, 248, 252, 252, 254, 254
1240   SYMBOL 242, 127, 127, 63, 63, 31, 15, 3, 0
1250   SYMBOL 243, 254, 254, 252, 252, 248, 240, 192, 0
1260   PIECE$ = CHR$(240) + CHR$(241) + CHR$(242) + CHR$(243)
1270   SP$ = "▲▲▲▲"
1280   FOR T = 1 TO 8 STEP 2 : FOR N = 1 TO 8 STEP 2
1290   COL(N, T) = 2 : COL(N+ 1, T) = 3
1300   NEXT N : NEXT T
1310   FOR T = 2 TO 8 STEP 2 : FOR N = 1 TO 8 STEP 2
1320   COL(N, T) = 3 : COL(N + 1, T) = 2
1330   NEXT N : NEXT T
1340   FOR T = 1 TO 8
1350   FOR N = 1 TO 8
1360   X(N, T) = N * 2 : Y(N, T) = T * 2
1370   NEXT N : NEXT T
1380   GOSUB 800
1390   LOCATE 1, 1 : PAPER 0 : PEN 1 : PRINT STRING$(18, CHR$(
       143))
1400   LOCATE 1, 18 : PAPER 0 : PEN 1 : PRINT STRING$(18, CHR$
       (143))
1410   FOR T = 2 TO 17 : LOCATE 1, T : PRINT CHR$(143) : LOCAT
       E 18, T : PRINT CHR$(143) : NEXT T
1420   LOCATE 6, 1 : PEN 7 : PRINT "DRAUGHTS"
1430   PEN 1 : RETURN
```

```
┌─────────────────────────────────────────────┐
│                                             │
│         Menu                                │
│                                             │
└─────────────────────────────────────────────┘
```

```
1440   :
1470   LOCATE 1, 25
1480   PRINT "REPLAY▲[Y/N]"
1490   A$ = INKEY$ : IF A$ = "" THEN GOTO 1490
1500   IF A$ = "Y" OR A$ = "y" THEN REPLAY = 1 : GOSUB 1160 :
       GOTO 60
1510   IF A$ = "N" OR A$ = "n" THEN RUN
1520   GOTO 1490
```

ChexSum Tables

40	=	466	530	=	3417	1060	=	305
50	=	922	540	=	1520	1070	=	269
60	=	788	550	=	4510	1080	=	276
70	=	0	560	=	386	1090	=	855
100	=	341	570	=	1119	1100	=	302
110	=	322	580	=	386	1110	=	281
120	=	465	590	=	1609	1120	=	3877
130	=	308	600	=	6293	1130	=	0
140	=	1700	610	=	1418	1160	=	2747
150	=	2752	620	=	1421	1170	=	4425
160	=	1511	630	=	1420	1180	=	1295
170	=	4766	640	=	1423	1190	=	4401
180	=	2751	650	=	232	1200	=	4678
190	=	1511	660	=	0	1210	=	427
200	=	8340	690	=	3397	1220	=	1559
210	=	1791	700	=	1566	1230	=	2802
220	=	8240	710	=	1366	1240	=	1497
230	=	8200	720	=	1368	1250	=	2740
240	=	4906	730	=	1566	1260	=	3882
250	=	6719	740	=	2083	1270	=	729
260	=	11104	750	=	2283	1280	=	2597
270	=	12690	760	=	201	1290	=	2635
280	=	8336	770	=	0	1300	=	861
290	=	9375	800	=	991	1310	=	2598
300	=	466	810	=	985	1320	=	2635
310	=	308	820	=	1150	1330	=	861
320	=	1777	830	=	3104	1340	=	991
330	=	2485	840	=	1336	1350	=	1017
340	=	1436	850	=	3298	1360	=	3044
350	=	4691	860	=	1551	1370	=	861
360	=	2751	870	=	386	1380	=	256
370	=	1436	880	=	861	1390	=	2020
380	=	8265	890	=	201	1400	=	2048
390	=	1791	900	=	0	1410	=	3908
400	=	8164	930	=	1780	1420	=	1423
410	=	8124	940	=	1230	1430	=	436
420	=	7184	950	=	2039	1440	=	0
430	=	11104	960	=	1234	1470	=	310
440	=	6719	970	=	201	1480	=	1182
450	=	12916	980	=	0	1490	=	2190
460	=	8336	1010	=	219	1500	=	3525
470	=	9435	1020	=	531	1510	=	2204
480	=	201	1030	=	232	1520	=	437
490	=	0	1040	=	177			
520	=	1611	1050	=	406	TOTAL	=	333786

BRICK BUSTER

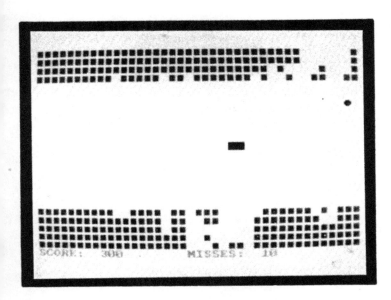

CLASSIFICATION: Bat Game

You have fifteen balls with which to bat your way through the brick walls. Try your friends out on this one and see who can get the best score.

PROGRAMMING SUGGESTIONS

This game can be altered very easily by reducing the number of bricks (NBRICKS) to make it easier or by allowing more by altering the number of balls allowed.

PROGRAM
Variables

NBRICKS	Number of bricks remaining
DECX(3,3,3),	Three decision
DECY(3,3,3)	tables giving X and Y speeds respectively
XSPD, YSPD	Current X-speed and Y-speed
BATCOL	Bat's column
BALLX, BALLY	Ball's coordinates
NMISSES	Number of misses
HIT	Ball hits something
DCT	Decision table number (1-3)

171

Program Structure

Lines		Function/Activity
10	— 90	Initialise
100	— 190	New round
200	— 990	Control
1000	— 1990	Move ball
2000	— 2990	Collision
3000	— 3990	Screen finished
4000	— 4990	Update score
9000	— 9990	Game over
10000	— 10050	Decision Table Data

```
┌─────────────────────────────────────────┐
│                                         │
│         Initialise                      │
│                                         │
└─────────────────────────────────────────┘
```

```
10      MODE 1 : INK 0, 13 : INK 1, 3 : INK 2, 0 : INK 3, 1
20      FOR I = 1 TO 3 : FOR J = 1 TO 3 : FOR K = 1 TO 3
30      READ Q : DECX( I, J, K ) = Q
40      NEXT : NEXT : NEXT
50      FOR I = 1 TO 3 : FOR J = 1 TO 3 : FOR K = 1 TO 3
60      READ Q : DECY( I, J, K ) = Q
70      NEXT : NEXT : NEXT
```

```
┌─────────────────────────────────────────┐
│                                         │
│         New round                       │
│                                         │
└─────────────────────────────────────────┘
```

```
80      :
90      REM
100     BALLX = 1 : BALLY = 10 : BATCOL = 19 : NBRICKS = 360 :
        NMISSES = 0
110     PAPER 0 : CLS : BORDER 13
120     PEN 1 : FOR I = 1 TO 40 : FOR J = 1 TO 4 : LOCATE I, J
        : PRINT CHR$( 233 ) : NEXT : NEXT
130     FOR I = 1 TO 40 : FOR J = 20 TO 24 : LOCATE I, J : PRIN
        T CHR$( 233 ) : NEXT : NEXT
140     GOSUB 4000
150     PEN 2 : LOCATE BATCOL, 12 : PRINT CHR$( 143 ); CHR$( 14
        3 )
160     XSPD = 1 : YSPD = 1
```

```
┌─────────────────────────────────────────┐
│                                         │
│         Control                         │
│                                         │
└─────────────────────────────────────────┘
```

```
190     :
200     PEN 2 : LOCATE BATCOL, 12 : PRINT CHR$( 143 ); CHR$( 14
        3 )
210     GOSUB 1000
220     IF INKEY( 39 ) = -1 OR BATCOL < 3 THEN 240
230     LOCATE BATCOL, 12 : PRINT "▲▲" : BATCOL = BATCOL - 2
240     IF INKEY( 31 ) = -1 OR BATCOL > 37 THEN 260
250     LOCATE BATCOL, 12 : PRINT "▲▲" : BATCOL = BATCOL + 2
260     REM
500     GOTO 200
```

```
┌─────────────────────────────────────────┐
│                                         │
│         Move ball                       │
│                                         │
└─────────────────────────────────────────┘
```

```
990     :
1000    LOCATE BALLX, BALLY : PRINT "▲"
1005    IF BALLY = 12 AND YSPD <> 0 THEN NMISSES = NMISSES + 1
        : PEN 3 : LOCATE 20, 25 : PRINT "MISSES :▲"; NMISSES : I
        F NMISSES > 14 THEN 9000
1010    BALLX = BALLX + XSPD : BALLY = BALLY + YSPD
1020    BALLX = ( BALLX > 40 ) - ( BALLX < 1 ) + BALLX : BALLY
        = ( BALLY > 24 ) - ( BALLY < 1 ) + BALLY : IF BALLX = 1
        OR BALLX = 40 THEN HIT = 4 : GOTO 2000
```

```
1040   IF BALLY = 1 OR BALLY = 24 THEN HIT = 4 : GOTO 2000
1060   HIT = TEST( 16 * BALLX - 8, 407 - 16 * BALLY ) : IF HIT
       <> 0 THEN GOTO 2000
1070   PEN 2 : LOCATE BALLX, BALLY : PRINT CHR$( 231 )
1080   RETURN
```

```
┌─────────────────────────────────────────┐
│           Collision                       │
└─────────────────────────────────────────┘
```

```
1990   :
2000   IF HIT = 2 THEN NMISSES = NMISSES - 1 : IF RND( 1 ) < 0
       .5 THEN DCT = 3 : GOTO 2020 ELSE DCT = 1 : GOTO 2020
2005   IF RND(1) < 0.5 THEN DCT = 2 ELSE DCT = 3
2010   IF HIT <> 4 THEN SOUND 1, 0, 5, 15, 1, 1, 31 : SCORE =
       SCORE + 5 : NBRICKS = NBRICKS - 1 : IF NBRICKS < 1 THEN
       3000 ELSE GOSUB 4000
2020   XT = DECX( DCT, YSPD + 2, XSPD + 2 ) : YSPD = DECY( DCT
       , YSPD + 2, XSPD + 2 ) : XSPD = XT
2030   PEN 3 : LOCATE BALLX, BALLY : PRINT CHR$( 231 )
2040   RETURN
```

```
┌─────────────────────────────────────────┐
│           Screen finished                 │
└─────────────────────────────────────────┘
```

```
2990   :
3000   SCORE = SCORE + 100 : PAPER 1 : CLS : PEN 2 : PRINT "NE
       W ROUND - YOUR SCORE SO FAR : "; SCORE
3010   FOR I = 1 TO 3000 : NEXT
3020   GOTO 100
```

```
┌─────────────────────────────────────────┐
│           Update score                    │
└─────────────────────────────────────────┘
```

```
3990   :
4000   PEN 3 : LOCATE 1, 25 : PRINT "SCORE : "; SCORE
4010   RETURN
```

```
┌─────────────────────────────────────────┐
│           Game over                       │
└─────────────────────────────────────────┘
```

```
4990   :
9000   LOCATE 15, 1 : PEN 2 : PRINT "GAME OVER"
9010   IF INKEY$ = "" THEN 9020 ELSE 9010
9020   IF INKEY$ = "" THEN 9020 ELSE RUN
```

```
┌─────────────────────────────────────────┐
│           Decision data table             │
└─────────────────────────────────────────┘
```

```
9990   :
10000 DATA -1, 0, 1, 1, 0, -1, -1, 0, 1
10010 DATA -1, 0, 0, 1, 0, -1, 0, 0, 0
10020 DATA 0, 1, 1, 1, 0, -1, -1, -1, 1
10030 DATA 1, 1, 1, 0, 0, 0, -1, -1, -1
10040 DATA 1, 1, 1, 0, 0, 0, -1, -1, -1
10050 DATA 1, 1, 1, 0, 0, 0, -1, -1, -1
```

ChexSum Tables

10 =	1322	240 =	2622	3000 =	5210
20 =	2930	250 =	2872	3010 =	1356
30 =	2158	260 =	0	3020 =	322
40 =	530	500 =	422	3990 =	0
50 =	2962	990 =	0	4000 =	1921
60 =	2159	1000 =	1594	4010 =	201
70 =	562	1005 =	7952	4990 =	0
80 =	0	1010 =	3938	9000 =	1458
90 =	0	1020 =	10407	9010 =	1545
100 =	4393	1040 =	3441	9020 =	1632
110 =	572	1060 =	4990	9990 =	0
120 =	4086	1070 =	2325	10000 =	1097
130 =	3912	1080 =	201	10010 =	1049
140 =	396	1990 =	0	10020 =	1098
150 =	2425	2000 =	6633	10030 =	1097
160 =	1430	2005 =	2759	10040 =	1097
190 =	0	2010 =	7390	10050 =	1097
200 =	2425	2020 =	7073		
210 =	456	2030 =	2326		
220 =	2823	2040 =	201	TOTAL =	125740
230 =	2873	2990 =	0		

THIRTY-ONE

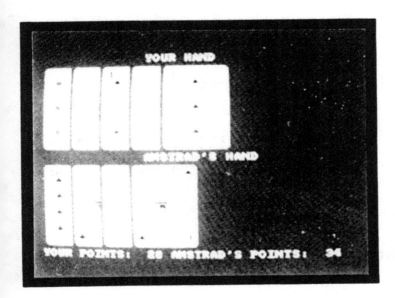

CLASSIFICATION: Parlor Game

Inflation comes even to Blackjack in this game where the Amstrad challenges you to a game of cards! Add the value of your cards and if you are closer to 31 than the Amstrad then you win! Of course, a hand over 31 costs you (or the Amstrad) the game.

Answer the questions asked of you by pressing the required numbers and then <RETURN>.

PROGRAMMING SUGGESTIONS

The game could be made more complex by getting the Amstrad to remember what cards have already been used and calculating the probabilities for the next card.

PROGRAM
Variables

CARD$	String for card face
CARD$(52)	Each string to be printed on the card face
DECK(52)	Deck of cards
CC(52)	Colours of cards
CHAND(16)	Computer's hand
NEXTCD	Number of the next card on the deck
ACCOUNT	Account balance
MBET	Money bet on this hand
PPTS	Player's points
CPTS	Computer's points
NPCDS	Number of player's cards
NCCDS	Number of computer's cards
COL, ROW	Column and row for drawing cards
CDRAW	Card to draw
BLANK$	Initialise card strings
PSTOP	Player stopped flag
I, J, K, T$	Temps

Program Structure

Lines	Function/Activity
5 — 420	Initialise variables
430 — 480	Initialise Screen and Player's hand
490 — 990	Main loop
1077 — 1990	Draw card
2077 — 2490	Hand finished
2507 — 2990	Next round or finish
3077 — 3017	Player loses

```
┌─────────────────────────────────────┐
│                                     │
│         Initialise variables        │
│                                     │
└─────────────────────────────────────┘
```

```
5     DEF FNPTS( C ) = ( C MOD 13 ) - 13 * ( ( C / 13 ) = INT
      ( C / 13 ) )
10    MODE 1 : INK 0, 1 : INK 1, 26 : INK 2, 6 : INK 3, 0
15    DEF FNSUIT( C ) = - 228 * ( C < 14 ) - 229 * ( C > 39 )
      - 227 * ( ( C >= 14 ) AND ( C <= 26 ) ) - 226 * ( ( C >
      = 27 ) AND ( C <= 39 ) )
20    SYMBOL AFTER 236 : SYMBOL 236, 255, 127, 42, 31, 19, 29
      , 9, 16 : SYMBOL 237, 32, 56, 16, 28, 16, 16, 17, 14
30    SYMBOL 238, 255, 254, 172, 248, 248, 248, 188, 136 : SY
      MBOL 239, 116, 92, 84, 108, 106, 218, 151, 7
40    SYMBOL 240, 0, 0, 0, 0, 3, 7, 15, 15 : SYMBOL 241, 0, 0
      , 0, 0, 255, 255, 255, 255
50    SYMBOL 242, 0, 0, 0, 0, 192, 224, 240, 240 : SYMBOL 243
      , 15, 15, 15, 15, 15, 15, 15, 15
60    SYMBOL 244, 240, 240, 240, 240, 240, 240, 240, 240 : SY
      MBOL 245, 15, 15, 7, 3, 0, 0, 0, 0
70    SYMBOL 246, 255, 255, 255, 255, 0, 0, 0, 0 : SYMBOL 247
      , 240, 240, 224, 192, 0, 0, 0, 0
80    SYMBOL 248, 4, 10, 15, 5, 7, 5, 10, 10 : SYMBOL 249, 10
      , 10, 21, 21, 26, 54, 73, 48
90    SYMBOL 250, 68, 170, 254, 84, 252, 72, 136, 152 : SYMBO
      L 251, 132, 130, 28, 8, 24, 8, 8, 240
100   SYMBOL 252, 0, 5, 11, 15, 31, 62, 60, 121 : SYMBOL 253,
      120, 120, 120, 124, 124, 124, 62, 31
110   SYMBOL 254, 128, 80, 232, 248, 28, 12, 14, 39 : SYMBOL
      255, 7, 7, 199, 15, 207, 15, 30, 252
120   CARD$ = CHR$( 240 ) + STRING$( 7, 241 ) + CHR$( 242 ) +
      CHR$( 10 ) + STRING$( 9, 8 ) : T$ = CHR$( 243 ) + STRIN
      G$( 7, 143 ) + CHR$( 244 )
130   FOR I = 1 TO 9 : CARD$ = CARD$ + T$ + CHR$( 10 ) + STRI
      NG$( 9, 8 ) : NEXT
140   CARD$ = CARD$ + CHR$( 245 ) + STRING$( 7, 246 ) + CHR$(
      247 )
150   DIM CC( 52 ), CARDS$( 52 ), DECK( 52 ), CHAND( 16 )
160   FOR I = 1 TO 26 : CC( I ) = 2 : NEXT
170   FOR I = 27 TO 52 : CC( I ) = 3 : NEXT
180   T$ = STRING$( 9, 9 ) : FOR I = 1 TO 10 : BLANK$ = BLANK
      $ + T$ + CHR$( 10 ) + STRING$( 9, 8 ) : NEXT
190   FOR I = 1 TO 52 : CARDS$( I ) = BLANK$ : DECK( I ) = I
      : NEXT
200   MID$( CARDS$( 1 ), 21, 1 ) = "A" : MID$( CARDS$( 1 ), 1
      79, 1 ) = "A" : FOR I = 2 TO 9 : MID$( CARDS$( I ), 21,
      1 ) = CHR$( 48 + I ) : MID$( CARDS$( I ), 179, 1 ) = CHR
      $( 48 + I ) : NEXT
210   MID$( CARDS$( 14 ), 21, 1 ) = "A" : MID$( CARDS$( 14 ),
      179, 1 ) = "A" : FOR I = 2 TO 9 : MID$( CARDS$( I + 13
      ), 21, 1 ) = CHR$( 48 + I ) : MID$( CARDS$( I + 13 ), 17
      9, 1 ) = CHR$( 48 + I ) : NEXT
220   MID$( CARDS$( 27 ), 21, 1 ) = "A" : MID$( CARDS$( 27 ),
      179, 1 ) = "A" : FOR I = 2 TO 9 : MID$( CARDS$( I + 26
      ), 21, 1 ) = CHR$( 48 + I ) : MID$( CARDS$( I + 26 ), 17
      9, 1 ) = CHR$( 48 + I ) : NEXT
230   MID$( CARDS$( 40 ), 21, 1 ) = "A" : MID$( CARDS$( 40 ),
      179, 1 ) = "A" : FOR I = 2 TO 9 : MID$( CARDS$( I + 39
      ), 21, 1 ) = CHR$( 48 + I ) : MID$( CARDS$( I + 39 ), 17
      9, 1 ) = CHR$( 48 + I ) : NEXT
```

```
240    FOR I = 10 TO 49 STEP 13 : MID$( CARDS$( I ), 21, 1 ) =
       "1" : MID$( CARDS$( I ), 22, 1 ) = "0" : MID$( CARDS$(
       I ), 178, 1 ) = "1" : MID$( CARDS$( I ), 179, 1 ) = "0"
       : NEXT
250    FOR I = 11 TO 50 STEP 13 : MID$( CARDS$( I ), 21, 1 ) =
       "J" : MID$( CARDS$( I ), 179, 1 ) = "J" : NEXT
260    FOR I = 12 TO 51 STEP 13 : MID$( CARDS$( I ), 21, 1 ) =
       "Q" : MID$( CARDS$( I ), 179, 1 ) = "Q" : NEXT
270    FOR I = 13 TO 52 STEP 13 : MID$( CARDS$( I ), 21, 1 ) =
       "K" : MID$( CARDS$( I ), 179, 1 ) = "K" : NEXT
280    FOR I = 1 TO 40 STEP 13 : MID$( CARDS$( I ), 100, 1 ) =
       CHR$( FNSUIT( I ) ) : NEXT
290    FOR I = 2 TO 41 STEP 13 : MID$( CARDS$( I ), 43, 1 ) =
       CHR$( FNSUIT( I ) ) : MID$( CARDS$( I ), 157, 1 ) = CHR$
       ( FNSUIT( I ) ) : NEXT
300    FOR I = 3 TO 42 STEP 13 : MID$( CARDS$( I ), 43, 1 ) =
       CHR$( FNSUIT( I ) ) : MID$( CARDS$( I ), 157, 1 ) = CHR$
       ( FNSUIT( I ) ) : MID$( CARDS$( I ), 100, 1 ) = CHR$( FN
       SUIT( I ) ) : NEXT
310    FOR I = 4 TO 43 STEP 13 : T$ = CHR$( FNSUIT( I ) ) : MI
       D$( CARDS$( I ), 41, 1 ) = T$ : MID$( CARDS$( I ), 45, 1
       ) = T$ : MID$( CARDS$( I ), 155, 1 ) = T$ : MID$( CARDS
       $( I ), 159, 1 ) = T$ : NEXT
320    FOR I = 5 TO 44 STEP 13 : T$ = CHR$( FNSUIT( I ) ) : MI
       D$( CARDS$( I ), 41, 1 ) = T$ : MID$( CARDS$( I ), 45, 1
       ) = T$ : MID$( CARDS$( I ), 155, 1 ) = T$ : MID$( CARDS
       $( I ), 159, 1 ) = T$ : MID$( CARDS$( I ), 100, 1 ) = T$
       : NEXT
330    FOR I = 6 TO 45 STEP 13 : T$ = CHR$( FNSUIT( I ) ) : MI
       D$( CARDS$( I ), 41, 1 ) = T$ : MID$( CARDS$( I ), 45, 1
       ) = T$ : MID$( CARDS$( I ), 155, 1 ) = T$ : MID$( CARDS
       $( I ), 159, 1 ) = T$ : MID$( CARDS$( I ), 102, 1 ) = T$
335    MID$( CARDS$( I ), 98, 1 ) = T$ : NEXT
340    FOR I = 7 TO 46 STEP 13 : T$ = CHR$( FNSUIT( I ) ) : MI
       D$( CARDS$( I ), 41, 1 ) = T$ : MID$( CARDS$( I ), 45, 1
       ) = T$ : MID$( CARDS$( I ), 155, 1 ) = T$ : MID$( CARDS
       $( I ), 159, 1 ) = T$ : MID$( CARDS$( I ), 102, 1 ) = T$
345    MID$( CARDS$( I ), 62, 1 ) = T$ : MID$( CARDS$( I ), 98
       , 1 ) = T$ : NEXT
350    FOR I = 8 TO 47 STEP 13 : T$ = CHR$( FNSUIT( I ) ) : MI
       D$( CARDS$( I ), 41, 1 ) = T$ : MID$( CARDS$( I ), 45, 1
       ) = T$ : MID$( CARDS$( I ), 155, 1 ) = T$ : MID$( CARDS
       $( I ), 159, 1 ) = T$ : MID$( CARDS$( I ), 102, 1 ) = T$
355    MID$( CARDS$( I ), 62, 1 ) = T$ : MID$( CARDS$( I ), 98
       , 1 ) = T$ : MID$( CARDS$( I ), 138, 1 ) = T$ : NEXT
360    FOR I = 9 TO 48 STEP 13 : T$ = CHR$( FNSUIT( I ) ) : MI
       D$( CARDS$( I ), 41, 1 ) = T$ : MID$( CARDS$( I ), 45, 1
       ) = T$ : MID$( CARDS$( I ), 79, 1 ) = T$ : MID$( CARDS$
       ( I ), 83, 1 ) = T$ : MID$( CARDS$( I ), 117, 1 ) = T$
365    MID$( CARDS$( I ), 121, 1 ) = T$ : MID$( CARDS$( I ), 1
       55, 1 ) = T$ : MID$( CARDS$( I ), 159, 1 ) = T$ : MID$(
       CARDS$( I ), 100, 1 ) = T$ : NEXT
370    FOR I = 10 TO 49 STEP 13 : T$ = CHR$( FNSUIT( I ) ) : M
       ID$( CARDS$( I ), 41, 1 ) = T$ : MID$( CARDS$( I ), 45,
       1 ) = T$ : MID$( CARDS$( I ), 79, 1 ) = T$ : MID$( CARDS
       $( I ), 83, 1 ) = T$ : MID$( CARDS$( I ), 117, 1 ) = T$
375    MID$( CARDS$( I ), 121, 1 ) = T$ : MID$( CARDS$( I ), 1
       55, 1 ) = T$ : MID$( CARDS$( I ), 159, 1 ) = T$ : MID$(
       CARDS$( I ), 62, 1 ) = T$ : MID$( CARDS$( I ), 138, 1 )
       = T$ : NEXT
```

```
380    FOR I = 11 TO 50 STEP 13 : T$ = CHR$( FNSUIT( I ) ) : M
       ID$( CARDS$( I ), 27, 1 ) = T$ : MID$( CARDS$( I ), 173,
       1 ) = T$ : MID$( CARDS$( I ), 99, 1 ) = CHR$( 236 ) : M
       ID$( CARDS$( I ), 100, 1 ) = CHR$( 238 ) : MID$( CARDS$(
       I ), 118, 1 ) = CHR$(237)
385    MID$( CARDS$( I ), 119, 1 ) = CHR$(239) : NEXT
390    FOR I = 12 TO 51 STEP 13 : T$ = CHR$( FNSUIT( I ) ) : M
       ID$( CARDS$( I ), 27, 1 ) = T$ : MID$( CARDS$( I ), 173,
       1 ) = T$ : MID$( CARDS$( I ), 99, 1 ) = CHR$( 252 ) : M
       ID$( CARDS$( I ), 100, 1 ) = CHR$( 254 ) : MID$( CARDS$(
       I ), 118, 1 ) = CHR$(253)
395    MID$( CARDS$( I ), 119, 1 ) = CHR$(255) : NEXT
400    FOR I = 13 TO 52 STEP 13 : T$ = CHR$( FNSUIT( I ) ) : M
       ID$( CARDS$( I ), 27, 1 ) = T$ : MID$( CARDS$( I ), 173,
       1 ) = T$ : MID$( CARDS$( I ), 99, 1 ) = CHR$( 248 ) : M
       ID$( CARDS$( I ), 100, 1 ) = CHR$( 250 ) : MID$( CARDS$(
       I ), 118, 1 ) = CHR$(249)
405    MID$( CARDS$( I ), 119, 1 ) = CHR$(251) : NEXT
410    ACCOUNT = 100 : FOR I = 1 TO 100 : J = INT( RND( 1 ) *
       52 ) + 1 : K = INT( RND( 1 ) * 52 ) + 1 : T = DECK( J )
       : DECK( J ) = DECK( K ) : DECK( K ) = T : NEXT
```

```
┌─────────────────────────────────────────────────┐
│        Initialise screen and player's hand        │
└─────────────────────────────────────────────────┘
```

```
420    :
430    PAPER 0 : CLS : BORDER 1
440    PEN 1 : LOCATE 15, 1 : PRINT "YOUR_HAND" : LOCATE 15, 2
       5 : PRINT "ACCOUNT :_"; : PRINT USING "$$######.##"; ACC
       OUNT
450    NEXTCD = 2 : CDRAW = DECK( 1 ) : COL = 1 : ROW = 2 : GO
       SUB 1000 : NPCDS = 1
460    PPTS = FNPTS( CDRAW ) : LOCATE 15, 15 : PEN 1 : PRINT "
       POINTS :_"; PPTS
470    LOCATE 1, 20 : INPUT "Initial_bet_"; X$ : MBET = VAL( X
       $ )
```

```
┌─────────────────────────────────────────────────┐
│              Main program loop                    │
└─────────────────────────────────────────────────┘
```

```
480    :
490    NCCDS = NCCDS + 1 : CPTS = CPTS + FNPTS( DECK( NEXTCD )
       ) : CHAND( NCCDS ) = DECK( NEXTCD ) : NEXTCD = NEXTCD +
       1 : IF CPTS > 25 AND PSTOP = 1 THEN 2000
500    IF PSTOP = 1 THEN 490 ELSE CDRAW = DECK( NEXTCD ) : COL
       = 1 + 4 * NPCDS : ROW = 2 : GOSUB 1000 : NEXTCD = NEXTC
       D + 1 : NPCDS = NPCDS + 1
505    PPTS = PPTS + FNPTS( CDRAW ) : LOCATE 15, 15 : PEN 1 :
       PRINT "POINTS :_"; PPTS : IF PPTS > 31 THEN 3000
510    LOCATE 1, 22 : PEN 1 : INPUT "WANT_TO_STOP_(Y/N)"; X$ :
       IF X$ <> "Y" AND X$ <> "y" THEN 520 ELSE PSTOP = 1 : IF
       CPTS > 25 THEN 2000 ELSE 490
520    LOCATE 1, 20 : INPUT "HOW_MUCH_TO_ADD_TO_YOUR_BET"; X$
       : MBET = MBET + VAL( X$ )
530    LOCATE 1, 20 : PRINT SPACE$( 39 ) : LOCATE 1, 22 : PRIN
       T SPACE$( 39 ) : IF CPTS > 25 THEN 500 ELSE GOTO 490
```

```
┌─────────────────────────────────────────────────┐
│                  Draw card                        │
└─────────────────────────────────────────────────┘
```

```
990    :
```

```
1000   PEN 1 : LOCATE COL, ROW
1010   PRINT USING "&"; CARD$ : PAPER 1
1020   PEN CC( CDRAW ) : LOCATE COL, ROW : PRINT USING "&"; CA
       RDS$( CDRAW )
1030   PAPER 0
1040   RETURN
```

```
                        ┌─────────────────────────────────────┐
                        │  Hand finished                      │
                        └─────────────────────────────────────┘
```

```
1990   :
2000   LOCATE 15, 15 : PRINT SPACE$( 20 ) : LOCATE 15, 13 : PE
       N 1 : PRINT "AMSTRAD'S_HAND___" : FOR I = 1 TO NCCDS : C
       OL = 4 * I - 3 : ROW = 14 : CDRAW = CHAND( I ) : GOSUB 1
       000 : NEXT
2010   PEN 1 : LOCATE 1, 25 : PRINT "YOUR_POINTS :_"; PPTS; "A
       MSTRAD'S_POINTS :_"; CPTS
2020   FOR I = 1 TO 6000 : NEXT
2030   LOCATE 1, 25 : PRINT SPACE$( 39 ) : IF CPTS > 31 THEN 2
       050
2040   IF CPTS > PPTS THEN 3000 ELSE IF PPTS = CPTS THEN CLS :
       PRINT "IT_IS_A_DRAW_!!" : GOTO 2500
2050   CLS : PRINT "YOUR_WIN_!!" : ACCOUNT = ACCOUNT + MBET :
       GOTO 2500
```

```
                        ┌─────────────────────────────────────┐
                        │  Next round or finish               │
                        └─────────────────────────────────────┘
```

```
2490   :
2500   FOR I = 1 TO 4000 : NEXT
2510   FOR I = 1 TO 100 : J = INT( RND( 1 ) * 52 ) + 1 : K = I
       NT( RND( 1 ) * 52 ) + 1 : T = DECK( J ) : DECK( J ) = DE
       CK( K ) : DECK( K ) = T : NEXT
2520   CPTS = 0 : NCCDS = 0 : PSTOP = 0 : MBET = 0
2530   PRINT : INPUT "ANOTHER_HAND"; X$ : IF X$ = "Y" OR X$ =
       "y" THEN 430
2540   PRINT : PRINT "YOUR_ACCOUNT :_"; : PRINT USING "$$######
       #.##"; ACCOUNT
2550   IF ACCOUNT < 0 THEN PRINT "EXPECT_A_VISIT_BY_THE_BOYS_!
       !!" ELSE PRINT "ENJOY_YOUR_WINNINGS_!!!"
2560   END
```

```
                        ┌─────────────────────────────────────┐
                        │  Player loses                       │
                        └─────────────────────────────────────┘
```

```
2990   :
3000   FOR I = 1 TO 2000 : NEXT : CLS : PRINT "AMSTRAD_WINS_!!
       " : ACCOUNT = ACCOUNT - MBET
3010   GOTO 2500
```

ChexSum Tables

5	=	4223	290	=	7246	505	=	6085
10	=	1338	300	=	10056	510	=	7340
15	=	8647	310	=	10261	520	=	4633
20	=	3511	320	=	11958	530	=	4057
30	=	4730	330	=	11817	990	=	0
40	=	3064	335	=	1901	1000	=	1232
50	=	3090	340	=	11819	1010	=	1336
60	=	4016	345	=	3590	1020	=	3860
70	=	3954	350	=	11821	1030	=	232
80	=	2415	355	=	5355	1040	=	201
90	=	3867	360	=	11686	1990	=	0
100	=	3246	365	=	7251	2000	=	8504
110	=	3633	370	=	11699	2010	=	4280
120	=	7400	375	=	8978	2020	=	1296
130	=	4093	380	=	12979	2030	=	2238
140	=	3812	385	=	2342	2040	=	5448
150	=	2589	390	=	13029	2050	=	3814
160	=	2012	395	=	2326	2490	=	0
170	=	2076	400	=	13019	2500	=	1336
180	=	5297	405	=	2354	2510	=	8939
190	=	3903	410	=	9938	2520	=	2990
200	=	8815	420	=	0	2530	=	3885
210	=	9459	430	=	581	2540	=	3240
220	=	9511	440	=	4495	2550	=	5628
230	=	9563	450	=	4608	2560	=	152
240	=	8075	460	=	3893	2990	=	0
250	=	4903	470	=	3233	3000	=	5036
260	=	4919	480	=	0	3010	=	427
270	=	4909	490	=	11390			
280	=	4340	500	=	9554			

TOTAL = 450778

THE CHEAP DETECTIVE

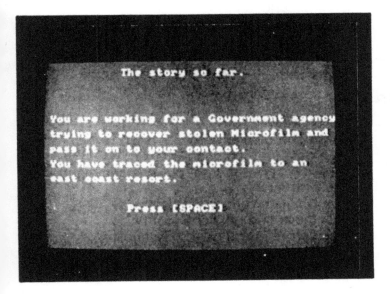

The story so far.

You are working for a Government agency
trying to recover stolen Microfilm and
pass it on to your contact.
You have traced the microfilm to an
east coast resort.

Press [SPACE]

CLASSIFICATION: Adventure Game

This is a standard text adventure. The object of the game is to find the hidden microfilm and pass it on to your contact. Along the way you will find some unfriendly characters. If they decide to attack you, you can defend yourself with one of the weapons scattered around, you may sometimes need to look to yourself!

The commands are the usual verb, object and the vocabulary is fairly standard, but if a word does not work then try a different one.

PROGRAMMING SUGGESTIONS

To make it harder simply reduce the Hit Points (HP) or make the attacks more frequent. It would be nice to add some graphics and a sizeable sound routine. The game could be made more complex by the addition of a few mazes and a thief.

PROGRAM
Variables

A$	Verb
B$	Object
D$(X)	Room description
D$ & E$	Codeword
L(X)	Room number
O$ & W$	Tokens
O$(X)	Objects

Program Structure

Lines	Function/Activity
10 — 40	Initialise and display intro
60 — 280	Set up data for rooms, objects
307 — 380	Set input window and get player's command
407 — 480	Display inventory
507 — 730	Set verb/check verb and object
750 — 880	Check move and describe room
900 — 930	Check verb and call object description
950 — 1430	Messages
1450 — 1620	Intro and Instructions
1640	Calculate hit points
1660 — 1670	Sound routine
1690 — 2510	Messages
2530 — 2590	Phone routine
2610 — 2660	Code word and completed mission
2910 — 2970	Messages
2990 — 3067	Wait for keypress
3080 — 3130	End game

THE CHEAP DETECTIVE

```
                    ┌─────────────────────────────────────────────┐
                    │                                             │
                    │    Initialise variables and Introduction    │
                    │                                             │
                    └─────────────────────────────────────────────┘

10      RANDOMIZE TIME
20      MODE 1
30      CLEAR : WINDOW #0, 1, 40, 1, 20
40      DIM L(38) ,O$(45) ,H(11) ,P(17,6) ,D$(17) : PQ=38

                    ┌─────────────────────────────────────────────┐
                    │                                             │
                    │       Set up data for rooms and objects     │
                    │                                             │
                    └─────────────────────────────────────────────┘

50      :
60      FOR X=1 TO 8 : D$=D$+CHR$(INT(RND(4)*26)+65) : E$=E$+CH
        R$(INT(RND(1)*26)+65) : NEXT X
70      FOR X=1 TO 30 : READ L(X) : NEXT X : FOR X=1 TO 30 : IF
        L(X)=0 THEN L(X)=INT(RND(1)*18)+1 : IF L(X)=18 THEN L(X
        )=25
80      NEXT X
90      DATA 13 ,5 ,14 ,2 ,16 ,0 ,0 ,11 ,3 ,10 ,20 ,2 ,9 ,11 ,6
        ,4 ,12 ,14 ,1 ,8 ,8 ,0 ,25 ,0 ,25 ,0 ,7 ,25 ,0 ,25
100     FOR X=31 TO 38 : L(X)=INT(RND(1)*17)+1 : NEXT X : FOR X
        =1 TO 11 : READ H(X) : NEXT X : FOR X=1 TO 44 : READ O$(
        X) : NEXT X
110     FOR X=12 TO 38 : IF L(X)=5 AND X<>27 THEN L(X)=25
120     NEXT X
130     DATA 20 ,40 ,100, 20 ,400 ,75 ,175 ,100 ,75 ,100 ,100
140     DATA German sheperd, Shark, Tall man in stocking mask,
        Two teens necking, Cycle gang
150     DATA Wino, Lenny the loan-shark , Teddy the torch, Casi
        no guard, Hostess, Contact, Railing
160     DATA Slot machine, Car, Ferris wheel, Life guard stand,
        Closed doors, Locked hatch, Rubbish bin
170     DATA Cabinet, Gas can, Knife, Stick, Telephone, $25000
        in metal box, Bullets
180     DATA Fishing rod, Lighter, Keys, Gun, Newspaper, $10 Do
        llar tokens, Shells, Metal detector, Message
190     DATA Suitcase, Flashlight, Microfilm, North, South, Eas
        t, West, Up*, Down
200     FOR Y=1 TO 16 : FOR X=1 TO 6 : READ P(Y,X) : NEXT X,Y :
        FOR X=1 TO 17 : READ D$(X) : NEXT X
210     DATA 1, 2,, 3,, 4, 1, 2, 6, 8,,, 10, 9, 1,, 12, 14, 7,
        4, 5, 16, 1,, 5, 5, 5, 4,, 5,,,, 2,, 5,, 4, 5,,, 5,,, 2,
        ,, 11
220     DATA 3,,,,,,,, 3,,,,, 14,,, 11, 8,, 15, 12, 12, 12,, 3,
        13, 11, 14,,,,, 11, 16, 13, 3,,, 12,,,,,,, 16, 4, 14,,
230     O$="GERSHATALTWOCYCWINLENTEDCASHOSCONRAISLOCARFERLIFCLO
        LOCTRACABGASKNISTI"
240     O$=O$+"TEL$25BULFISLIGKEYGUNNEWCHISHEMETMESSUIFLAMICNOR
        SOUEASWESUP*DOW"
250     W$="GOTADILOREATOPLIDRCA" : CLS : BORDER 0 : PAPER 0 :
        GOTO 1450
260     DATA SIDEWALK IN FRONT OF CASINO, SIDEWALK IN FRONT OF
        BATHOUSE, ENTRY TO CASINO, BEACH
270     DATA WATER, AMUSEMENT PIER, JETTY, BATHOUSE, CASINO IN
        HOTEL, THEATRE IN HOTEL, STREET
280     DATA HALLWAY IN HOTEL, BACK ALLEY, CAR PARK, YOUR HOTEL
        ROOM, UNDER THE SIDEWALK, CAR
```

```
290     :
300     WINDOW #1, 1,40,23,25 : CLS #1 : INPUT #1, A$ : a$=UPPE
        R$(a$) : FB=0 : FOR KY=1 TO LEN (A$) : IF MID$ (A$,KY,1)
        ="▴" AND LEN (A$)>KY+1 THEN B$=MID$ (A$,KY + 1,3)
310     IF MID$ (A$,KY,1)="▴" THEN DP=1
320     NEXT KY : IF LEN (A$)>1 THEN A$=LEFT$  (A$,2)
330     IF DP<>1 THEN B$="" : DP=0
340     IF B$<>"" AND LEN (B$)<>3 THEN 300
350     IF LEN (A$)<>2 THEN 300
360     IF RIGHT$ (B$,1)="▴" THEN 300
370     CLS
380     RETURN
```

```
390     :
400     WINDOW 1,40,1,21 : CLS : PRINT "You▴are▴carrying : " :
        FOR CRY=1 TO 38 : IF L(CRY)<>0 THEN GOTO 470
410     INK 1,24
420     Q$=O$(CRY)
430     PRINT LEFT$(Q$,1);
440     Q$=RIGHT$(Q$,LEN(Q$)-1)
450     PRINT LOWER$(Q$)
460     Y=1
470     NEXT CRY : IF Y=0 THEN PRINT "Nothing" : RETURN
480     RETURN
```

```
490     :
500     IF A$="GE" THEN A$="TA"
510     IF B$="TEE" THEN B$="TWO"
520     IF B$="ROD" THEN B$="FIS"
530     IF B$="MAS" THEN B$="TAL"
540     IF A$="HI" THEN A$="AT"
550     IF A$="FI" THEN A$="AT"
560     IF B$="TOR" THEN B$="TED"
570     IF B$="LOA" THEN B$="LEN"
580     IF B$="BOX" THEN B$="$25"
590     IF A$="IN" THEN Y=0 : GOSUB 400 : GOTO 1080
600     IF B$="MAC" THEN B$="SLO"
610     IF B$="DOO" THEN B$="CLO"
620     IF A$="KI" THEN A$="AT"
630     IF B$="PHO" THEN B$="TEL"
640     IF A$="GI" THEN A$="DR"
650     IF B$="GANG" THEN B$="CYC"
660     IF B$="MAN" THEN B$="TAL"
670     IF B$="DET" THEN B$="MET"
680     IF B$="GUA" THEN B$="CAS"
690     IF B$="STA" THEN B$="LIF"
700     IF B$="DOG" THEN B$="GER"
710     IF A$="SH" THEN A$="AT"
720     IF B$="HAT" THEN B$="LOC"
730     IF B$="$10" THEN B$="CHI"
```

```
740    :
750    FOR Y=1 TO LEN (W$) : IF MID$ (W$,Y,2)=A$ THEN F=(Y+1)/
       2 : GOTO 770
760    NEXT Y : F=0
770    FOR X=1 TO LEN (O$) STEP 3 : IF MID$ (O$,X,3)=B$ THEN S
       =INT((X+2)/3) : GOTO 790
780    NEXT X : IF (S>45 OR S<1) AND B$<>"" THEN F=-1
790    IF F<1 OR F>10 THEN PRINT "What.the.hell.Mac!" : GOTO 1
       080
800    ON F-1 GOTO 1810, 1110, 900, 1020, 1930, 1180, 1290, 13
       40, 2530
810    MM=MM+1 : IF MM/5=INT(MM/5) THEN GOSUB 1760
820    IF PJ<>0 THEN S=1
830    IF S<39 THEN GOSUB 2920 : GOTO 1080
840    IF S>38 THEN S=S-38
850    IF P(L,S) THEN L=P(L,S) : L2=L
860    IF IT=0 THEN GOSUB 2750 : PRINT "You.are.in." : PRINT L
       OWER$(D$(L)) : Y=0 : IF L=5 AND C>4 THEN 1890 ELSE 880
870    IF IT<>0 THEN GOSUB 2770 : PRINT "You.are.in." : PRINT
       LOWER$(D$(L)) : Y=0 : IF L=5 AND C>4 THEN 1890
880    GOSUB 1690 : GOSUB 1140 : GOTO 1080
```

```
890    :
900    IF B$="" THEN 860
910    DD=1 : IF S<39 AND S>0 THEN 950
920    S=S-38 : L2=P(L,S) : IF L2=0 THEN L2=L
930    GOSUB 1690 : PRINT "in";LOWER$(D$(L2)) : L2=L : GOTO 10
       80
```

```
940    :
950    IF L(S)<>L AND L(S)<>0 THEN PRINT "That.isn't.here!" :
       GOTO 1080
960    IF S=31 AND RND(TIME / 300)>0.3 THEN PRINT "Code.word.i
       s.";D$ : GOTO 1080
970    IF S=31 THEN PRINT "Code.word.is.";E$ : GOTO 1080
980    IF S=35 AND L(38)<>0 THEN GOSUB 2640 : PRINT "Microfilm
       .in" : PRINT LOWER$(D$(X)) : L(38)=X : PQ=37 : GOTO 1080
990    IF S=20 OR S=26 THEN PRINT "locked" : GOTO 1080
1000   PRINT "ordinary.";LOWER$(O$(S)) : GOTO 1080
```

```
1010   :
1020   IF S<>31 AND S<>35 THEN PRINT "Nothing.there.to.read" :
        GOTO 1080
1030   IF L(S)<>0 THEN PRINT "You.don't.have.it!" : GOTO 1080
1040   GOTO 960
```

Locks all exits

```
1050  :
1060  L=15 : L2=L : FOR I=1 TO ZC : FOR DN=0 TO  2 : PRINT :
      NEXT DN : GOSUB 2990 : NEXT I
1070  PRINT : PRINT "You▲are▲in▲" : PRINT LOWER$(D$(L)) : GOS
      UB 1690 : GOSUB 1140
1080  A$="" : B$="" : S=0 : F=0 : H=0
1090  GOSUB 2250 : GOSUB 300 : GOTO 500
```

Messages for digging, exits blocked and legal exits

```
1100  :
1110  IF L=4 AND L(33)=0 THEN GOSUB 2800 : GOTO 1080
1120  IF L=4 THEN PRINT "You▲don't▲have▲any▲tools!" : GOTO 10
      80
1130  PRINT "You▲can't▲dig▲here!" : GOTO 1080
1140  IF PJ=1 THEN PRINT"All▲visible▲exits▲blocked" : RETURN
1150  PRINT "Visible▲exits▲are▲:▲" : FOR X=1 TO 6 : IF P(L,X)
      >0 AND P(L,X)<>L THEN PRINT LOWER$(O$(X+38));"▲";
1160  NEXT : PRINT : RETURN
```

Messages for open

```
1170  :
1180  IF L(S)<>L THEN PRINT "Not▲here!" : PRINT : GOTO 1080
1190  IF S=14 AND L(29)=0 AND L(21)=0 THEN L(29)=-1 : PRINT "
      Car▲unlocked!" : GOTO 1080
1200  IF S=14 AND L(30)=0 AND L(26)=0 THEN PRINT "Shot▲throug
      h▲window▲to▲unlock" : L (29)=-1 : GOTO 1080
1210  IF S=20 AND L(29)=0 THEN GOSUB 2370 : GOSUB 2440 : GOSU
      B 1690 : GOTO 1080
1220  IF S=36 AND L(29)<>0 THEN PRINT "locked!" : PRINT : GOT
      O 1080
1230  IF S=36 AND L(29)=0 THEN GOSUB 2370 : GOSUB 1690 : GOSU
      B 2610 : GOTO 1080
1240  IF S=17 THEN PRINT "Fell▲down▲utility▲chute" : GOSUB 28
      80 : L2=L : PJ=0 : GOTO 860
1250  IF S=18 AND L(29)=0 THEN GOSUB 2440 : O$(18)="OPEN▲HATC
      H" : GOTO 1080
1260  IF (S=18 OR S=20) AND L(29)<>0 THEN PRINT"It's▲locked!!
      " : PRINT : GOTO 1080
1270  GOTO 1080
```

Can explodes

```
1280  :
1290  IF S<>37 AND S<>28 THEN PRINT "Can't!" : PRINT : GOTO 1
      080
1300  IF L(S)<>0 THEN PRINT "Don't▲have▲it!" : PRINT : GOTO 1
      080
1310  IF S=28 AND (L(21)=0 OR L(21)=L) THEN GOSUB 2680 : PRIN
      T : PRINT "Leaky▲gas▲can▲explode" : PRINT : GOTO 1080
1320  FL=1 : GOTO 1080
```

```
1330   :
1340   IF L(S)<>0 THEN PRINT "Don't have it!" : PRINT : GOTO 1
       080
1350   IF S=25 OR S=36 THEN C=C-1
1360   IF S=21 AND L(8)=L THEN PRINT O$(8); " took gas and" :
       L(S)=30 : C=C-1 : S=8 : GOSUB 2360 : GOTO 1080
1370   C=C-1 : L(S)=L
1380   IF S=25 AND L(5)=L THEN PRINT O$(5); " took money and"
       : L(S)=30 : S=5 : GOSUB 2360 : GOTO 1080
1390   IF S=38 AND L(11)=L THEN 2620
1400   IF S=25 AND L(7)=L THEN PRINT O$(7) : PRINT "paid off!"
       : L(S)=30 : C=C-1 : S=7 : GOSUB 2360 : GOTO 1080
1410   IF S=32 AND L(7)=L THEN PRINT O$(7) : PRINT "paid off!"
       : L(S)=30 : C=C-1 : S=7 : GOSUB 2360 : GOTO 1080
1420   IF S=38 AND L(10)=L THEN PRINT O$(10); " enemy agent an
       d disables you anyway" : PRINT : GOTO 2190
1430   GOTO 1080
```

```
1440   :
1450   CLS : LOCATE 15,2 : PRINT "Welcome to " : LOCATE 10,4 :
       PRINT "THE CHEAP DETECTIVE"
1460   PRINT : PRINT "     Stumble your way around this one" :
       LOCATE 10,8 : PRINT "AND PLAY IT AGAIN!!"
1470   LOCATE 1,20 :   PRINT "Do you wish to view the plot (Y/N
       ) ?";
1480   PRK$ = UPPER$(INKEY$) : IF PRK$ = "" THEN GOTO 1480 ELS
       E IF PRK$ = "Y" OR PRK$ = "N"THEN 1490 ELSE PRINT CHR$(7
       );CHR$(7) : GOTO 1480
1490   IF PRK$="N" THEN GOSUB 1640 : ZC=1 : GOTO 1060
```

```
1500   :
1510   CLS : LOCATE 12,2 : PRINT"The story so far."
1520   LOCATE 1,8 : PRINT " You are working for a Government a
       gency"
1530   PRINT " trying to recover stolen Microfilm and"
1540   PRINT : PRINT " pass it on to your contact."
1550   PRINT : PRINT " You have traced the microfilm to an" :
       PRINT : PRINT " east coast resort."
1560   GOSUB 2990
1570   GOSUB 1640 : PRINT : PRINT " You are Hospitalised if yo
       ur hit points"
1580   PRINT " go to zero."
1590   GOSUB 2990
1600   PRINT : PRINT " Use TWO word commands, of the form : "
       : PRINT : PRINT " VERB OBJECT" : PRINT
1610   PRINT : PRINT " You may use 2 letters of verb and" : PR
       INT : PRINT " 3 of object."
1620   PRINT : PRINT " Use UP* for up" : GOSUB 2990 : LOCATE 1
       ,1 : CLS : GOTO 1060
```

191

```
1630    :
1640    HP=INT(RND(2)*25)+25 : CLS : LOCATE 8,5 : PRINT "You▲ha
        ve▲";hp;"▲hit▲points" : LOCATE 1,8 : RETURN
```

```
1650    :
1660    FOR J=3 TO 15 : ENV J,100,2,20 : SOUND 1,50,50,J,4,1 :
        NEXT J
1670    FOR J=15 TO 1 STEP-1 : ENV J,100,2,20 : SOUND 1,50,50,J
        ,4,1 : NEXT J : RETURN
```

```
1680    :
1690    IF L2 = 10 OR L2 = 16 OR L2 = 14 THEN GOSUB 2390
1700    IF FL = 2 THEN FL = 0 : GOTO 1740
1710    Y = 0 : YY = 0 : GOSUB 2490 : PRINT : PRINT "You▲see :
        " : FOR X = 1 TO 38
1720    IF L(X) = L2 THEN PRINT O$(X); "."; : Y = Y + 1 : IF X
        < 11 AND PJ = 0 THEN GOSUB 2260
1730    NEXT X : PRINT : IF Y = 0 THEN PRINT "▲Nothing"
1740    PRINT : DD = 0 : RETURN
```

```
1750    :
1760    FOR X = 33 TO PQ
1770    IF L(X) <> 0 THEN L(X) = INT(RND (1) * 18) + 1 : IF L(X
        ) = 18 THEN L(X) = 25
1780    IF (X = 34 OR X = 38) AND L(X) = 5 THEN 1770
1790    NEXT X : GOSUB 2830 : RETURN
```

```
1800    :
1810    IF S > 38 THEN PRINT "You▲can't▲take▲a▲▲▲▲▲▲direction"
        : GOTO 1080
1820    IF S < 21 THEN PRINT "You▲can't▲take▲that!!" : GOTO 108
        0
1830    IF S = 24 THEN PRINT "It's▲wired▲to▲the▲wall" : GOTO 10
        80
1840    IF L(S) <> L THEN PRINT "That's▲not▲here!!" : GOTO 1080
1850    IF C > 6 THEN PRINT "You▲can't▲carry▲that▲much!" : GOTO
        1080
1860    IF S = 38 THEN HP = HP + 10
1870    IF S=25 OR S=36 THEN C=C+1
1880    L(S) = 0 : C = C + 1 : GOTO 1080
1890    GOSUB 1910 : PRINT "You▲are▲carrying▲too▲much▲to▲swim"
        : GOSUB 1910 : PRINT "You▲drowned" : GOSUB 1910
```

```
1900    GOSUB 2700 : PRINT "But▲you▲are▲revived▲by▲paramedics."
        : GOTO 2190
1910    RETURN
```

```
                        ┌─────────────────────────────────────────┐
                        │                                         │
                        │       Drowned routine                   │
                        │                                         │
                        └─────────────────────────────────────────┘
```

```
1920    :
1930    IF S > 11 THEN PRINT "There▲is▲nothing▲to▲attack" : GOT
        O 1080
1940    IF L(S) <> L THEN PRINT "Not▲here!" : GOTO 1080
1950    INPUT "With▲what"; X$ : B$ = LEFT$(X$, 3) : B$=UPPER$(B
        $)
1960    IF B$ = "FOO" THEN PRINT "▲Good▲move!▲▲Black▲belt!" : H
        = 0 : DP = 4 : GOTO 2020
1970    IF B$ = "HAN" THEN H = 0 : DP = 2 : GOTO 2020
1980    FOR X = 1 TO LEN(O$) STEP 3 : IF MID$(O$, X, 3) = B$ TH
        EN H = INT((X + 2) / 3) : GOTO 1080
1990    NEXT X
2000    IF L(H) <> 0 THEN PRINT "You▲don't▲have▲that" : GOTO 10
        80
2010    IF H <> 22 AND H <> 23 AND H <> 30 AND H <> 27 AND H <>
        28 AND H <> 34 AND H <> 37 THEN PRINT "That's▲not▲a▲wea
        pon!" : GOTO 1080
2020    IF H = 30 AND L(26) <> 0 THEN PRINT "Not▲loaded-use▲as▲
        a▲club▲only" : DP = 5
2030    IF S = 1 OR S = 4 THEN DD = 1
2040    IF S = 2 THEN DD = 2
2050    IF H = 23 OR H = 27 THEN DP = 3
2060    IF S = 3 OR S = 8 OR S = 10 OR S = 11 THEN DD = 4
2070    IF S = 5 THEN DD = 10
2080    IF S = 6 OR  S = 9 THEN DD = 5
2090    IF H = 28 OR H = 37 OR H = 22 THEN DP = 5
2100    IF S = 7 THEN DD = 6
2110    IF H = 30 THEN DP = 12
2120    PRINT "You▲have"; HP; "hit▲points" : PRINT O$(S) : PRIN
        T "has"; H(S); "hit▲points"
2130    YO = INT(RND(1) * DP * 3) + DP : OP = INT(RND(4) * DD *
        3) : PRINT "YOU▲ATTACK▲AND▲INFLICT"; YO; "HIT▲POINTS"
2140    PRINT : PRINT O$(S) : PRINT "ATTACKS▲AND▲INFLICTS" : PR
        INT OP; "HIT▲POINTS" : H(S) = H(S) - YO
2150    IF H(S) < 1 THEN PRINT : PRINT "YOU▲OVERCAME▲OPPONENT!"
        : L(S) = 30 : PJ = 0 : HP = HP + 3 * DD : L(H) = 25 : C
        = C - 1 : GOTO 1080
2160    IF RND(1) > 0.85 THEN GOSUB 2360
2170    HP = HP - OP : IF HP < 1 THEN GOTO 2190
2180    GOTO 1080
2190    PRINT CHR$(7) : PRINT "YOU▲ARE▲IN▲HOSPITAL." : PRINT :
        PRINT"WITHOUT▲THE▲MICROFILM!"
2200    PRINT : PRINT "DO▲YOU▲WANT▲TO▲RETURN▲TO▲YOUR▲HOTEL▲ROOM
        ▲AND▲TRY▲AGAIN"
2210    INPUT REP$ : REP$=UPPER$(REP$) : IF LEFT$(REP$, 1) = "Y
        " THEN GOTO 2190
2220    IF LEFT$(REP$, 1) = "N" THEN 3080
2230    PRINT CHR$(7);CHR$(7);CHR$(7) : GOTO 2210
2240    END
2250    PRINT : PRINT "What▲do▲you▲want▲to▲do" : RETURN
2260    IF (X = 4 OR X = 6) AND RND(1) > 0.25 THEN RETURN
2270    IF X > 8 AND RND(1) > 0.4 THEN RETURN
2280    IF F = 4 THEN RETURN
2290    IF RND(6) < 0.35 THEN RETURN
```

```
2300    IF X = 4 THEN O$(X) = "TWO▲TEENS"
2310    OP = INT(RND(5) * 10) : PRINT CHR$(7) : PRINT O$(X) : P
        RINT "ATTACKS▲AND▲INFLICTS" : PRINT OP; "HIT▲POINTS▲DAMA
        GE!"
2320    HP = HP - OP : IF HP < 1 THEN GOTO 2190
2330    PJ = 1 : RETURN
2340    PRINT CHR$(7)
2350    RETURN
2360    PJ = 0 : L(S) = 25 : IT = 100 : PRINT CHR$(7) : PRINT "
        THEN▲RAN▲AWAY!" : RETURN
2370    FOR X = 12 TO 30 : IF L(X) = 25 AND RND(1) > 0.5 THEN L
        (X)=L
2380    NEXT X : RETURN
2390    IF L(28) <> 0 AND L(37) <> 0 THEN PRINT "DARK,▲CAN'T▲SE
        E" : FL = 2 : RETURN
2400    IF L(37) = 0 AND FL = 1 THEN RETURN
2410    IF L(28) = 0 AND FL = 1 THEN RETURN
2420    IF L(37) <> 0 OR FL <> 1 THEN PRINT "DARK,▲CAN'T▲SEE" :
        FL = 2 : RETURN
2430    IF L(28) <> 0 OR FL <> 1 THEN PRINT "DARK,▲CAN'T▲SEE" :
        FL = 2 : RETURN
2440    T = 0 : FOR X = 1 TO 6 : IF P(L, X) = 0 THEN T = X
2450    NEXT X : X = RND(-TIME / 300)
2460    IF T <> 0 THEN P(L, T) = INT(RND(1) * 17 ) + 1 : IF P(L
        , T) = L THEN GOTO 2460
2470    IF T <> 0 THEN PRINT "SECRET▲PASSAGE!" : T = 0 : RETURN

2480    RETURN
2490    T = 0 : FOR X = 1 TO 6 : IF AX(X) <> 0 THEN T = 1
2500    NEXT X : IF T <> 0 THEN YY = 3
2510    RETURN
```

+---+
| |
| Attack routine |
| |
+---+

```
2520    :
2530    IF S > 11 THEN PRINT "CAN'T▲CALL▲AN▲OBJECT!" : GOTO 108
        0
2540    IF L(24) <> L THEN PRINT "NO▲PHONE!" : GOTO 1080
2550    IF S <> 11 THEN PRINT "LINE▲IS▲BUSY" : GOTO 1080
2560    GOSUB 2720 : PRINT "CALL▲ESTABLISHED : ▲GIVE"
2570    INPUT "CODE▲PHRASE", C$ : C$=UPPER$(C$)
2580    IF C$ <> D$ THEN PRINT "INCORRECT" : GOTO 1080
2590    IF C$ = D$ THEN L(11) = INT(RND(1) * 16) + 1 : PRINT "C
        ORRECT▲CODE" : GOTO 1080
```

+---+
| |
| Phone routine |
| |
+---+

```
2600    :
2610    PRINT "PAPER▲WITH▲CODE▲WORD" : PRINT "CODE▲WORD▲IS▲"; D
        $ : RETURN
2620    CLS : FOR ERE = 1 TO 10 : FOR ER = 300 TO 1000 STEP 50
        : SOUND 129, T, 10, 15 : NEXT ER : NEXT ERE
2630    GOSUB 2340 : PRINT "YOU▲COMPLETED▲YOUR▲MISSION!!!!!" : F
        OR ER = 1 TO 12 : LOCATE 1, 1 : PRINT CHR$(11) : NEXT ER

2640    X = INT(RND(1) * 17) + 1 : IF L(20) = 30 AND X = 17 THE
        N GOTO 2640
2650    IF X = 5 THEN 2640
2660    RETURN
```

```
2670    :
2680    PRINT CHR$(7)
2690    RETURN
2700    PRINT CHR$(7)
2710    RETURN
2720    PRINT CHR$(7)
2730    RETURN
```

Short beep

```
2740    :
2750    IF F = 4 THEN RETURN
2760    IT = ( INT(RND(2) * 3 ) + 1) * 100
2770    PRINT CHR$(7)
2780    RETURN
```

Check flag

```
2790    :
2800    IF L(26) = 0 THEN PRINT "STRUCK.WATER" : RETURN
2810    L(26) = 4   : PRINT "BULLETS" : RETURN
```

Water and bullets routine

```
2820    :
2830    FOR X = 1 TO 10
2840    IF L(X) = 25 THEN L(X) = INT(RND(4) * 17 ) + 1
2850    IF L(X) = 5 AND X <> 2 THEN L(X) = 25 : GOTO 2840
2860    NEXT X : RETURN
```

Randomise routine

```
2870    :
2880    L = INT(RND(1) * 16) + 1 : IF L = 12 THEN 2880
2890    IT = 25 : RETURN
```

Check random number

```
2900    :
2910    PRINT "LOST"; Y; "HIT.POINTS" : HP = HP - Y : RETURN
2920    IF S <> 14 AND S <> 15 AND S <> 16 THEN PRINT "CAN'T.GO
        .THERE!" : RETURN
2930    IF (S = 15 OR S = 16) AND L(S) <> L THEN PRINT "NOT.HER
        E" : RETURN
2940    IF S = 15 OR S = 16 THEN PRINT "FELL.OFF" : Y = -(S = 1
        5) * 25 + 10 * ( -(S = 16)) : GOSUB 2910 : RETURN
2950    IF S = 14 AND L(29) <> -1 THEN PRINT "LOCKED" : RETURN
2960    IF S = 14 AND L(29) = -1 THEN P(17, 1) = L2 : L2 = L :
        PRINT "IN.CAR : .LOOK!" : L(29) = 0 : RETURN
```

195

```
2970    RETURN
```

```
2980    :
2990    PRINT CHR$(7)
3000    LOCATE 13,20 : PRINT"Press▴[SPACE]" : ZZ=0
3010    IF INKEY$="▴" THEN 3060
3020    ZZ=ZZ+1 : IF ZZ<100 THEN 3010
3030    LOCATE 13,20 : PRINT STRING$(13,32)
3040    IF INKEY$="▴" THEN 3060
3050    ZZ=ZZ+1 : IF ZZ<150 THEN 3040 ELSE 3000
3060    CLS : RETURN
```

```
3070    :
3080    CLS
3090    FOR T=1 TO 40
3100    PRINT TAB(T)"BYE"CHR$(7)
3110    NEXT T
3120    PRINT
3130    END
```

ChexSum Tables

10	=	551	620	=	1795	1230	=	3178
20	=	220	630	=	1960	1240	=	5424
30	=	748	640	=	1792	1250	=	3906
40	=	2902	650	=	2008	1260	=	4626
50	=	0	660	=	1945	1270	=	282
60	=	6678	670	=	1951	1280	=	0
70	=	8723	680	=	1936	1290	=	3081
80	=	437	690	=	1951	1300	=	3218
90	=	4554	700	=	1940	1310	=	6398
100	=	8025	710	=	1802	1320	=	824
110	=	3989	720	=	1943	1330	=	0
120	=	437	730	=	1845	1340	=	3218
130	=	2297	740	=	0	1350	=	2760
140	=	7181	750	=	4850	1360	=	6738
150	=	7566	760	=	903	1370	=	1894
160	=	7985	770	=	5527	1380	=	6086
170	=	5871	780	=	3870	1390	=	2222
180	=	8151	790	=	3913	1400	=	6503
190	=	5834	800	=	2652	1410	=	6510
200	=	5945	810	=	3741	1420	=	6847
210	=	4039	820	=	1521	1430	=	282
220	=	4053	830	=	1640	1440	=	0
230	=	5682	840	=	2012	1450	=	3641
240	=	5660	850	=	3246	1460	=	5501
250	=	2957	860	=	6464	1470	=	3679
260	=	5599	870	=	6190	1480	=	7192
270	=	5480	880	=	1006	1490	=	2392
280	=	5322	890	=	0	1500	=	0
290	=	0	900	=	1121	1510	=	2244
300	=	9579	910	=	2558	1520	=	4344
310	=	2263	920	=	4025	1530	=	4035
320	=	3013	930	=	2854	1540	=	3040
330	=	2085	940	=	0	1550	=	6084
340	=	2226	950	=	4542	1560	=	406
350	=	1403	960	=	5225	1570	=	4589
360	=	1651	970	=	2983	1580	=	1354
370	=	138	980	=	6529	1590	=	406
380	=	201	990	=	3030	1600	=	5106
390	=	0	1000	=	2405	1610	=	5009
400	=	5616	1010	=	0	1620	=	2760
410	=	334	1020	=	4426	1630	=	0
420	=	1121	1030	=	3407	1640	=	5528
430	=	974	1040	=	417	1650	=	0
440	=	1986	1050	=	0	1660	=	3047
450	=	756	1060	=	5042	1670	=	3737
460	=	484	1070	=	3221	1680	=	0
470	=	2783	1080	=	2418	1690	=	3073
480	=	201	1090	=	1166	1700	=	2007
490	=	0	1100	=	0	1710	=	3718
500	=	1787	1110	=	2643	1720	=	5793
510	=	1972	1120	=	3803	1730	=	2655
520	=	1955	1130	=	2209	1740	=	924
530	=	1950	1140	=	3910	1750	=	0
540	=	1792	1150	=	7749	1760	=	1318
550	=	1790	1160	=	570	1770	=	5475
560	=	1966	1170	=	0	1780	=	3444
570	=	1943	1180	=	3029	1790	=	886
580	=	1872	1190	=	5446	1800	=	0
590	=	2279	1200	=	7142	1810	=	4136
600	=	1947	1210	=	3247	1820	=	3371
610	=	1948	1220	=	3363	1830	=	3568

1840 =	3489	2290 =	1721	2730 =	201
1850 =	3878	2300 =	2470	2740 =	0
1860 =	2122	2310 =	6515	2750 =	1161
1870 =	2759	2320 =	2784	2760 =	2280
1880 =	1973	2330 =	751	2770 =	583
1890 =	5854	2340 =	583	2780 =	201
1900 =	4227	2350 =	201	2790 =	0
1910 =	201	2360 =	4000	2800 =	2482
1920 =	0	2370 =	4473	2810 =	1671
1930 =	4034	2380 =	639	2820 =	0
1940 =	2837	2390 =	4017	2830 =	1008
1950 =	3621	2400 =	2161	2840 =	3392
1960 =	4945	2410 =	2152	2850 =	3152
1970 =	2680	2420 =	3956	2860 =	639
1980 =	5487	2430 =	3947	2870 =	0
1990 =	437	2440 =	3703	2880 =	2861
2000 =	3575	2450 =	2199	2890 =	789
2010 =	8407	2460 =	5439	2900 =	0
2020 =	5398	2470 =	2980	2910 =	3334
2030 =	2298	2480 =	201	2920 =	4087
2040 =	1503	2490 =	3304	2930 =	4249
2050 =	2357	2500 =	1986	2940 =	6208
2060 =	3936	2510 =	201	2950 =	3089
2070 =	1525	2520 =	0	2960 =	5721
2080 =	2312	2530 =	2892	2970 =	201
2090 =	3189	2540 =	2472	2980 =	0
2100 =	1512	2550 =	2407	2990 =	583
2110 =	1564	2560 =	2196	3000 =	2268
2120 =	5770	2570 =	2318	3010 =	1438
2130 =	7854	2580 =	2386	3020 =	2555
2140 =	5875	2590 =	4435	3030 =	1086
2150 =	8296	2600 =	0	3040 =	1438
2160 =	2144	2610 =	3313	3050 =	3044
2170 =	2784	2620 =	4864	3060 =	340
2180 =	282	2630 =	5039	3070 =	0
2190 =	4261	2640 =	4049	3080 =	138
2200 =	4205	2650 =	1099	3090 =	1034
2210 =	4020	2660 =	201	3100 =	1415
2220 =	1801	2670 =	0	3110 =	433
2230 =	1814	2680 =	583	3120 =	191
2240 =	152	2690 =	201	3130 =	152
2250 =	2689	2700 =	583		
2260 =	3194	2710 =	201		
2270 =	3001	2720 =	583	TOTAL =	853295
2280 =	1161				

BOMB BOUNCER

CLASSIFICATION: Shoot-up Game

Try and trap as many of the bombs as possible use ',' to move left and '.' to move right.

PROGRAMMING SUGGESTIONS

There could well be some sound effects designed to put the player off and levels, so that each level could have different elements in. For instance obstacles to distract, or a faster mode of play.

PROGRAM
Variables

POSITION	Shield's position
SHIELD$	String for displaying shield
SCORE	Number of bombs bounced
T	Temp
FLAG	The second bomb has been sent
N	Temp

Program Structure

Lines	Function/Activity
40 — 110	Initialise
140 — 307	Main loop
330 — 440	Deflect bomb
470 — 580	Game over

```
                    ┌─────────────────────────────────────┐
                    │         Initialise game             │
                    │                                     │
                    └─────────────────────────────────────┘

50      PEN 1 : MODE 1 : INK 0, 0 : PAPER 0 : BORDER 0 : INK 1,
        18 : INK 2, 24 : INK 3, 7
60      POSITION = 20
70      SYMBOL 240, 0, 0, 0, 0, 3, 15, 63, 255 : SYMBOL 241, 3,
        15, 63, 255, 255, 255, 255, 255
80      SHIELD$ = CHR$(240) + CHR$(241)
90      SCORE = 0
100     GOTO 250

                    ┌─────────────────────────────────────┐
                    │         Main loop                   │
                    │                                     │
                    └─────────────────────────────────────┘

110     :
140     FOR T = 1 TO 20
150     LOCATE POSITION, 25
160     PRINT SHIELD$
170     POSITION = POSITION + ( INKEY(39) > -1 ) - ( INKEY(31)
        > -1 )
180     IF POSITION < 4 THEN POSITION = 35
190     IF POSITION > 35 THEN POSITION = 4
200     LOCATE 1, 1 : PRINT CHR$(11)
210     IF ( TEST( POSITION * 16 - 8, 8 ) = 2  OR TEST( POSITIO
        N * 16 + 8, 8 ) = 2 AND T = 4 )THEN GOSUB 330 : GOTO 230

220     IF T = 4 AND FLAG THEN 470
230     NEXT T
240     FLAG = 1
250     LOCATE RND(1) * 30 + 5, 1
260     PEN 2
270     PRINT CHR$(252)
280     PEN 1
290     GOTO 140

                    ┌─────────────────────────────────────┐
                    │         Deflect bomb                │
                    │                                     │
                    └─────────────────────────────────────┘

300     :
330     LOCATE POSITION, 25
340     PRINT SHIELD$
350     PEN 2
360     FOR N = POSITION - 2 TO 1 STEP - 1
370     LOCATE N, 25
380     CALL &BD19
390     PRINT CHR$(252); CHR$(32)
400     NEXT N
410     PEN 1
420     SCORE = SCORE + 1
430     RETURN

                    ┌─────────────────────────────────────┐
                    │         Game over                   │
                    │                                     │
                    └─────────────────────────────────────┘

440     :
```

```
470    FOR T = 8 TO 15
480    SOUND 1, 200, 15, T
490    NEXT T
500    SOUND 1, 300, 100, 15
510    FOR T = 1 TO 26
520    LOCATE 1, 25
530    PRINT CHR$(10)
540    NEXT T
550    LOCATE 10, 10
560    PRINT "YOU BOUNCED";SCORE ; "BOMBS"
570    FOR T = 1 TO 2000 : NEXT T
580    RUN
```

ChexSum Tables

50	=	2010	240	=	677	430	=	201
60	=	1054	250	=	1244	440	=	0
70	=	3740	260	=	235	470	=	1016
80	=	2264	270	=	839	480	=	873
90	=	774	280	=	234	490	=	433
100	=	472	290	=	362	500	=	619
110	=	0	300	=	0	510	=	1020
140	=	1014	330	=	1065	520	=	310
150	=	1097	340	=	795	530	=	597
160	=	795	350	=	235	540	=	433
170	=	4238	360	=	2516	550	=	315
180	=	2590	370	=	514	560	=	2230
190	=	2587	380	=	405	570	=	1644
200	=	874	390	=	1294	580	=	202
210	=	6611	400	=	427			
220	=	1956	410	=	234			
230	=	433	420	=	1540	TOTAL	=	55018

SPRITE EDITOR

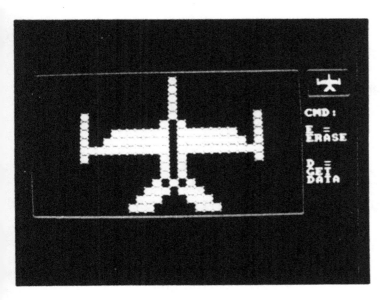

CLASSIFICATION: Utility

This program allows you to create sprites on your Amstrad a facility that has been left out of this otherwise fine machine!

You can select a sprite which is a maximum of 4 characters across and 3 characters down. If you already have the raw data for a sprite that you wish to modify, then you can key them in at the start.

To edit a sprite, move the cursor using the cursor keys, and press <ENTER> to either plot a point or erase one, depending what is under the cursor. Press 'C' to enter command mode: then press 'E' to erase the sprite, or 'D' to obtain the Data representing the sprite.

Note that the sprite is made up of several characters, numbered across and then down.

The small box in the top-right corner of the screen is the actual sprite that you are working on.

PROGRAM
Variables

ROW, COL	Row and column of cursor on main grid
MCROW, MCCOL	Maximum number of rows and columns in characters
GRID(MCROW,MCCOL 8)	Numbers stored for grid
GC, GR	Grid's starting column and row
I, J	Temps for row, column
L, K	Temps for numbers in the grid
NM, NUM, X$, POWER	Temps
CU	Character under cursor
C, Q	Editor temps
CH	Cursor character

Program Structure

Lines	Function/Activity
10 — 180	Front Screen and Initialise
200 — 340	Set up screen
350 — 990	Main loop
1000 — 1999	Draw grid
2000 — 2990	Draw sprite
3000 — 3990	Toggle point on grid
4000 — 4490	Commands
4500 — 4990	Print out data
5000 — 5050	Set CU (character under cursor)

```
                    ┌─────────────────────────────────────────┐
                    │                                         │
                    │        Front screen and initialise      │
                    │                                         │
                    └─────────────────────────────────────────┘

10      MODE 1 : INK 0, 0 : INK 1, 20 : INK 2, 6 : INK 3, 25
20      PAPER 0 : CLS : BORDER 4
30      PEN 1 : LOCATE 15, 1 : PRINT "SPRITE▲EDITOR"
40      LOCATE 1, 8 : INPUT "HOW▲MANY▲CHARACTERS▲ACROSS▲(1▲-▲4)
        "; X$
50      IF VAL( X$ ) > 4 OR VAL( X$ ) < 1 THEN 40
60      MCCOL = VAL( X$ )
70      LOCATE 1, 11 : INPUT "HOW▲MANY▲CHARACTERS▲DOWN▲(1▲-▲3)"
        ; X$
80      IF VAL( X$ ) > 3 OR VAL( X$ ) < 1 THEN 70
90      MCROW = VAL( X$ )
100     LOCATE 1, 14 : INPUT "KEY▲IN▲NUMBERS(▲K▲)▲OR▲BUILD▲▲▲▲▲
        ▲▲▲▲▲▲NEW▲SPRITE(▲N▲)"; X$
110     IF X$ = "N" OR X$ = "n" THEN 200
120     FOR I = 1 TO MCROW
130     FOR J = 1 TO MCCOL : FOR K = 1 TO 8
140     PRINT "CHARACTER▲NO.▲"; MCCOL * ( I - 1 ) + J; "▲NUMBER
        ▲"; K;
150     INPUT X$ : IF VAL( X$ ) < 0 OR VAL( X$ ) > 255 THEN 140

160     GRID( I, J, K ) = VAL( X$ )
170     NEXT : NEXT : NEXT
                    ┌─────────────────────────────────────────┐
                    │                                         │
                    │            Set up screen                │
                    │                                         │
                    └─────────────────────────────────────────┘

180     :
200     BORDER 0 : GC = 2 : GR = 2 : CLS
210     IF X$ = "N" OR X$ = "n" THEN 250 ELSE GOSUB 1000
220     FOR I = 1 TO MCROW : FOR J = 1 TO MCCOL
230     GOSUB 2000
240     NEXT : NEXT
250     PEN 2 : LOCATE 1, 1 : PRINT CHR$( 150 ) : FOR I = 2 TO
        GR + MCROW * 8 - 1 : LOCATE GC - 1, I : PRINT CHR$( 149
        ) : LOCATE GC + MCCOL * 8, I : PRINT CHR$( 149 ) : NEXT
260     FOR I = 2 TO GC + MCCOL * 8 - 1 : LOCATE I, GR - 1 : PR
        INT CHR$( 154 ) : NEXT
270     LOCATE GC + MCCOL * 8, 1 : PRINT CHR$(156)
280     FOR I = 36 TO 35 + MCCOL : LOCATE I, 1 : PRINT CHR$( 15
        4 ) : LOCATE I, MCROW + 2 : PRINT CHR$( 154 ) : NEXT
290     FOR I = 2 TO 1 + MCROW : LOCATE 35, I : PRINT CHR$( 149
        ) : LOCATE 36 + MCCOL, I : PRINT CHR$( 149 ) : NEXT
300     LOCATE 35, 1 : PRINT CHR$( 150 ) : LOCATE 36 + MCCOL, 1
        : PRINT CHR$( 156 )
310     LOCATE 35, 2 + MCROW : PRINT CHR$( 147 ) : LOCATE 36 +
        MCCOL, 2 + MCROW : PRINT CHR$( 153 )
320     IF MCROW = 3 THEN 340
330     FOR I = GC TO MCCOL * 8 + 1 : LOCATE I, GR + MCROW * 8
        : PRINT CHR$( 154 ) : NEXT : LOCATE 1, GR + MCROW * 8 :
        PRINT CHR$( 147 ) : LOCATE MCCOL * 8 + 2, GR + MCROW * 8
        : PRINT CHR$( 153 )
```

```
340    :
350    COL = 2 : ROW = 2 : GOSUB 5000 : C = 0 : Q = 1 : CH = 1
       43
360    X$ = INKEY$ : C = C + 1
370    IF C = 7 THEN C = 0 : Q = 1 - Q
380    IF Q <> 0 THEN 410
390    IF CH = 143 THEN CH = 0 : LOCATE COL, ROW : PEN 1 : PRI
       NT CHR$( CU ) : Q = 1 : GOTO 410
400    LOCATE COL, ROW : PEN 1 : PRINT CHR$( 143 ) : Q = 1 : C
       H = 143
410    IF X$ = "" THEN 360
420    IF INKEY( 2 ) > -1 THEN LOCATE COL, ROW : PRINT CHR$( C
       U ) : IF ROW > GR - 2 + ( MCROW ) * 8 THEN 360 ELSE ROW
       = ROW + 1 : GOSUB 5000 : GOTO 360
430    IF INKEY( 1 ) > -1 THEN LOCATE COL, ROW : PRINT CHR$( C
       U ) : IF COL > GC - 2 + MCCOL * 8 THEN 360 ELSE COL = CO
       L + 1 : GOSUB 5000 : GOTO 360
440    IF INKEY( 0 ) > -1 THEN LOCATE COL, ROW : PRINT CHR$( C
       U ) : IF ROW < GR + 1 THEN 360 ELSE ROW = ROW - 1 : GOSU
       B 5000 : GOTO 360
450    IF INKEY( 8 ) > -1 THEN LOCATE COL, ROW : PRINT CHR$( C
       U ) : IF COL < GC + 1 THEN 360 ELSE COL = COL - 1 : GOSU
       B 5000 : GOTO 360
460    IF INKEY( 18 ) > -1 THEN GOSUB 3000
470    IF INKEY( 62 ) > -1 THEN GOTO 4000
500    GOTO 360
```

```
990    :
1000   PEN 1 : FOR I = 1 TO MCROW : FOR J = 1 TO MCCOL : FOR K
       = 1 TO 8
1010   LOCATE GC + 8 * ( J - 1 ), GR + 8 * ( I - 1 ) + K - 1
1020   FOR L = 1 TO 8
1025   NUM = GRID( I, J, K )
1030   NM = NUM AND ( 2 ^ ( 8 - L ) )
1040   IF NM = 0 THEN PRINT "."; ELSE PRINT CHR$( 231 );
1050   NEXT : NEXT : NEXT : NEXT
1060   RETURN
```

```
1990   :
2000   SYMBOL 240 + MCCOL * ( I - 1 ) + J, GRID( I, J, 1 ), GR
       ID( I, J, 2 ), GRID( I, J, 3 ), GRID( I, J, 4 ), GRID( I
       , J, 5 ), GRID( I, J, 6 ), GRID( I, J, 7 ), GRID( I, J,
       8 )
2010   PEN 1 : LOCATE 35 + J, 1 + I : PRINT CHR$( 240 + MCCOL
       * ( I - 1 ) + J )
2020   RETURN
```

```
2990    :
3000    GOSUB 5000
3010    NUM = NUM AND ( 255 - POWER )
3020    NM = NM XOR POWER : NUM = NUM OR NM
3030    GRID( I, J, K ) = NUM
3040    GOSUB 5000
3050    GOSUB 2000
3060    RETURN
```

```
3990    :
4000    PEN 3 : LOCATE 35, 6 : PRINT "CMD : "
4010    LOCATE 35, 8 : PRINT "E.=" : LOCATE 35, 9 : PRINT "ERAS
        E"
4020    LOCATE 35, 12 : PRINT "D.=" : LOCATE 35, 13 : PRINT "GE
        T" : LOCATE 35, 14 : PRINT "DATA"
4030    X$ = INKEY$ : IF X$ = "" THEN 4030
4040    IF X$ <> "E" AND X$ <> "e" THEN 4060
4050    FOR I = 1 TO MCROW : FOR J = 1 TO MCCOL : FOR K = 1 TO
        8 : GRID( I, J, K ) = 0 : NEXT : NEXT : NEXT : FOR I = 3
        5 TO 40 : FOR J = 6 TO 23 : LOCATE I, J : PRINT "." : NE
        XT : NEXT : GOSUB 1000 : GOTO 220
4060    IF X$ = "D" OR X$ = "d" THEN 4500
4070    FOR I = 35 TO 40 : FOR J = 6 TO 23 : LOCATE I, J : PRIN
        T "." : NEXT : NEXT
4100    GOTO 360
```

```
4490    :
4500    CLS
4510    LOCATE 12, 1 : PRINT "DATA.PRINTOUT"
4520    LOCATE 1, 5 : PRINT "CHARACTERS.ARE.NUMBERED.LEFT.TO.RI
        GHT." : LOCATE 1, 6 : PRINT "AND.THEN.TOP.TO.BOTTOM"
4530    LOCATE 1, 8 : PRINT "FOR.EXAMPLE :..1..2..3" : LOCATE 1
        5, 10 : PRINT "4..5..6"
4535    PRINT
4540    FOR I = 1 TO MCROW
4550    FOR J = 1 TO MCCOL : PRINT "CHARACTER.NO..."; MCCOL * (
        I - 1 ) + J; "DATA :."
4560    FOR K = 1 TO 8 : PRINT USING "###"; GRID( I, J, K ); :
        PRINT ",."; : NEXT : PRINT
4565    TP = ( MCCOL * ( I - 1 ) + J ) : IF TP = 4 OR TP = 11 T
        HEN LOCATE 1, 25 : PRINT "PRESS.SPACE.TO.CONTINUE" : X$
        = INKEY$ : IF X$ <> "." THEN 4565
4570    NEXT : NEXT
4580    LOCATE 1, 25 : PRINT CHR$( 10 ); CHR$( 10 ) : LOCATE 1,
        24 : PRINT "RETAIN.THIS.SHAPE.(R)," : LOCATE 1, 25 : PR
        INT "START.FROM.SCRATCH.(S),.OR.QUIT.(Q).?";
4590    X$ = INKEY$ : IF X$ = "" THEN 4590
4600    IF X$ = "R" OR X$ = "r" THEN 200
4610    IF X$ = "S" OR X$ = "s" THEN RUN
4620    IF X$ = "Q" OR X$ = "q" THEN END ELSE 4580
```

207

```
4990   :
5000   I = INT( ( ROW - GR ) / 8 ) + 1
5010   J = INT( ( COL - GC ) / 8 ) + 1
5020   K = ROW - ( GR + 8 * ( I - 1 ) ) + 1
5030   POWER = 2 ^ ( 7 - COL + GC + 8 * ( J - 1 ) ) : NUM = GR
       [D( I, J, K ) : NM = NUM AND POWER
5040   IF NM = 0 THEN CU = 32 ELSE CU = 231
5050   RETURN
```

ChexSum Tables

10 =	1367	370 =	2365	4010 =	1770
20 =	552	380 =	1155	4020 =	2574
30 =	1785	390 =	4656	4030 =	2034
40 =	3017	400 =	3128	4040 =	2299
50 =	2558	410 =	1153	4050 =	10342
60 =	1330	420 =	8306	4060 =	2223
70 =	2883	430 =	8105	4070 =	3434
80 =	2587	440 =	7180	4100 =	327
90 =	1356	450 =	7095	4490 =	0
100 =	4018	460 =	1795	4500 =	138
110 =	2278	470 =	1820	4510 =	1548
120 =	1491	500 =	327	4520 =	5243
130 =	2449	990 =	0	4530 =	2661
140 =	4115	1000 =	4176	4535 =	223
150 =	3334	1010 =	3673	4540 =	1491
160 =	2072	1020 =	983	4550 =	5067
170 =	530	1025 =	1869	4560 =	3843
180 =	0	1030 =	2140	4565 =	8673
200 =	1400	1040 =	2484	4570 =	385
210 =	2968	1050 =	707	4580 =	6439
220 =	2958	1060 =	201	4590 =	2084
230 =	436	1990 =	0	4600 =	2286
240 =	353	2000 =	11279	4610 =	2292
250 =	8216	2010 =	4311	4620 =	2665
260 =	4450	2020 =	201	4990 =	0
270 =	2302	2990 =	0	5000 =	2338
280 =	5204	3000 =	376	5010 =	2298
290 =	5194	3010 =	2459	5020 =	2790
300 =	2875	3020 =	3300	5030 =	6981
310 =	4425	3030 =	1869	5040 =	2602
320 =	1396	3040 =	376	5050 =	201
330 =	10670	3050 =	436		
340 =	0	3060 =	201		
350 =	3267	3990 =	0	TOTAL =	272032
360 =	1695	4000 =	1124		

APPENDIX A

Joystick Routine

Below is a short general purpose joystick routine. It is included as an example of using joysticks with the Amstrad and as a routine to include with your own games or with the games from this book.

```
                    ┌─────────────────────────────────────────┐
                    │ Define all variables as Integers for speed │
                    └─────────────────────────────────────────┘

10      DEFINT a-z
                    ┌─────────────────────────────────────────┐
                    │ Select and set screen mode               │
                    └─────────────────────────────────────────┘

20      :
30      type=1
40      MODE type
                    ┌─────────────────────────────────────────┐
                    │ Set vertical and horizontal dimensions   │
                    └─────────────────────────────────────────┘

50      :
60      ymax=24
70      xmax=20 : IF type=1 THEN xmax=40 ELSE IF type=2 THEN xm
        ax=80
                    ┌─────────────────────────────────────────┐
                    │ Set starting position                    │
                    └─────────────────────────────────────────┘

80      :
90      x=20 : y=10
100     xold=x : yold=y
                    ┌─────────────────────────────────────────┐
                    │ Read Joystick                            │
                    └─────────────────────────────────────────┘

110     :
120     a=JOY(0)
                    ┌─────────────────────────────────────────┐
                    │ Adjust Horizontal and vertical position  │
                    └─────────────────────────────────────────┘

130     :
140     IF a AND 1 THEN y=y-1 ELSE IF a AND 2 THEN y=y+1
150     IF a AND 4 THEN x=x-1 ELSE IF a AND 8 THEN x=x+1
                    ┌─────────────────────────────────────────┐
                    │ Select face and alternate when fire button pressed │
                    └─────────────────────────────────────────┘

160     :
170      IF a AND 16 THEN a$=CHR$(225) ELSE a$=CHR$(224)
```

209

```
180    :
190    IF y<1 THEN y=y+23 ELSE IF y>23 THEN y=y-23
200    IF x<1 THEN x=x+xmax ELSE IF x>xmax THEN x=x-xmax
```

Erase old position

```
210    :
220    LOCATE xold,yold
230    PRINT".";
```

Display character (face)

```
240    :
250    LOCATE x,y
260    PRINT a$;
```

Update old position and loop

```
270    :
280    xold=x : yold=y
290    GOTO 120
```

ChexSum Tables

10 = 438	120 = 838	230 = 350	
20 = 0	130 = 0	240 = 0	
30 = 843	140 = 4336	250 = 764	
40 = 796	150 = 4341	260 = 510	
50 = 0	160 = 0	270 = 0	
60 = 874	170 = 3378	280 = 2155	
70 = 5543	180 = 0	290 = 342	
80 = 0	190 = 4333		
90 = 1078	200 = 5906		
100 = 2155	210 = 0	TOTAL = 40382	
110 = 0	220 = 1402		

NOTES

You may also enjoy...

ATARI 130XE GAMES BOOK

RICHARD WOOLCOCK
& GRAEME STRETTON

www.ingramcontent.com/pod-product-compliance
Lightning Source LLC
LaVergne TN
LVHW092011050326
832904LV00001B/10